Overcentralization in Economic Administration

Overcentralization in Economic Administration

A Critical Analysis Based on Experience in Hungarian Light Industry

BY

JÁNOS KORNAI

TRANSLATED BY

JOHN KNAPP

Lecturer in Economics University of Manchester

Great Clarendon Street, Oxford, OX2 6DP,
United Kingdom

Oxford University Press is a department of the University of Oxford.
It furthers the University's objective of excellence in research, scholarship,
and education by publishing worldwide. Oxford is a registered trade mark of
Oxford University Press in the UK and in certain other countries

Published in the United States of America by Oxford University Press
198 Madison Avenue, New York, NY 10016, United States of America

British Library Cataloguing in Publication Data
Data available

Library of Congress Control Number: 2023930300

ISBN 978–0–19–289442–7

DOI: 10.1093/oso/9780192894427.001.0001

Printed and bound by
CPI Group (UK) Ltd, Croydon, CR0 4YY

PREFACE TO THE ENGLISH EDITION

I FEEL honoured by the fact that my book is to be made available in English to Western readers. This is an event I did not reckon with when I wrote the book. I consequently feel a need to make certain preliminary statements for the benefit of readers of this edition.

This book was not intended to pose and discuss the problems of socialist economic planning in general. My aim in writing it was a good deal narrower, and more modest than that. My discussion is confined to an account of Hungarian experience. Moreover, my attempt at analysing the problem of economic administration is limited to the consideration of examples drawn from a single field, namely, that of light industry.[1]

In order to obtain a full picture of the way in which the Hungarian economy has been administered, readers abroad would naturally need a realistic view of the advantages and successes, as well as of the disadvantages and shortcomings, of our economic practices. But it was not my purpose to give a summary account and evaluation of these things. It is true that my book does mention some of the many significant achievements which stand to the credit of our performance in light industry. I will only mention one of them here: production in light industry was doubled in five years. And this was done while investment in this branch of industry was on an extremely small scale, mainly by securing full employment of the labour force, by full utilization of capacity, and by skilful organization of the production process. Achievements of this kind deserve a detailed appraisal, but my own work was not devoted to this. My study was intended as a contribution to a debate which was already in full swing when I wrote. It had the explicit object of calling the attention of Hungarian economists participating in this debate to a number of shortcomings in our methods, which were insufficiently recognized.[2] By concentrating on our shortcomings, and laying the resulting faults bare in a merciless fashion, I hoped to assist the process of remedial action.

---

[1] In Hungary, the difficulties associated with excessive centralization presented themselves with particular force in light industry. I refer to this fact in the book. Excessive centralization was carried to its greatest lengths in this field.

[2] I could take it for granted that my economist colleagues were fully aware of the great advantages inherent in our having a planned economy.

We are, by now, in a position to say that the efforts which went into our debates have been fruitful. At the time when it was written, my book gave a 'snapshot' of the contemporary situation in 1955–6. Since then, a great deal of change has taken place as a result of the measures affecting methods of economic administration which were put into effect in 1957. In 1955–6 the initiative of enterprises was severely hampered by the long list of obligatory plan index numbers prescribed for them by higher authorities. By now, the number of indices which have binding force has been reduced to 4–6 in light industry. In 1955–6 the exact amount of every article to be produced by each enterprise was prescribed for them centrally in the greatest possible detail. At present, product-mixes and detailed production programmes are, very largely, the outcome of direct contacts between industrial enterprises and the distributive trades. This has made industry far more sensitive to the real requirements of its customers. Again, in 1955–6 profits were ignored by both the top managements and the other employees of enterprises. At present the financial incentives offered to top managements are, to a large extent, made to depend on profits realized, and the general body of employees receive a part of these profits. The fields in which changes in economic administration have been most substantial are precisely those which have been most subject to criticism on the part of several Hungarian economists, one of whom was myself. The changes which have been made are in line with the proposals briefly sketched in this book.

Judging from the initial experience we have gained it appears that the effects of the reforms are, generally speaking, beneficial.[3] I regard the fact that these changes have been made as one among a number of proofs of the proposition that the mistakes and harmful tendencies shown up in my book are not inherent in the nature of socialist economic planning. They can be eliminated within that framework.

To sum up. My readers should not expect to find a rounded picture of economic planning in this book. Nor should they look for a sensational 'exposure' of some sort in what I have written. My own hope is that Western readers will regard my book as evidence of the considerable efforts made by Hungarian economists to obtain an objective picture of the realities of economic life in the course of their attempts to help overcome the difficulties which stand in the way of a more perfect functioning of the socialist economy of the country.

[3] Since publishing the present volume I have been engaged in research designed to assess the results of the changes referred to in the text.

I would like to take this opportunity to express my thanks to those who have helped me in my researches and in making the publication of this book possible. I am indebted to the Institute of Economics of the Hungarian Academy of Sciences where my work was carried out, and to those in charge of the Institute and to my colleagues, who helped me in my researches. Without their support and encouragement my work would never have reached the stage of publication first in its Hungarian, and now in an English edition.

I am very grateful to the Clarendon Press, Oxford, for offering to publish my work, thus making it accessible to readers in the English-speaking world. I also wish to express my thanks to Mr. John Knapp, who, besides performing the difficult task of translating my book, has also given me much assistance in the matter of explaining concepts and expressions which are unfamiliar to readers in the English-speaking world.

J. K.
Budapest, January 1958

PREFACE TO THE ORIGINAL EDITION

I WISH, first of all, to acquaint the reader with the circumstances in which this study came to be written.[4]

The present volume is one of the products of a larger scale inquiry started by several members of the Institute of Economics in the spring of 1955.[5] What was the original objective of this research? Since 1953–4 it was becoming increasingly clear that our methods of planning and administering our economy were faulty. The independent initiative of managements and workers of individual enterprises and of local bodies was being stifled by overcentralization of direction and by the bureaucracy that goes with it.

The idea from which this research started was that it was necessary to produce proposals for a large reduction in the number of compulsorily determined plan index numbers laid down for individual enterprises, thus giving them much more freedom of action. It was therefore necessary to start with an examination of the present system of compulsory plan index numbers, to discover what the economic meaning of each of them is, and what effects they have on the way enterprises function.

It soon became clear, however, that this question cannot be singled out for study in isolation from other problems of our economic mechanism. So the scope of the research broadened. It came to include such matters, for example, as the bonus system, other economic incentives, the system of producers' prices, relations with distribution, and so on. We had to proceed in this way if we were to examine our present economic mechanism as a coherent whole.

The first necessary step is a description of the situation as it is. This, it may be thought, should already be available in dozens of books. Unfortunately this is not the case. There are, of course, dozens of textbooks and collections of

---

[4] A number of changes of emphasis have been made by the author in this preface and also in the text of the book since its original publication in Hungary in 1957. —Translator.

[5] The research was carried out under the auspices of the Institute. However, the present study reflects the conclusions of the author alone. It cannot be regarded as containing, in some sense, the 'official' view of the Institute of Economics.

notes for use at universities which describe our methods of economic admin-istration and planning, our pricing and wage systems, &c. However, all these have a serious fault in common: instead of telling us how our economic mecha-nism really works, they merely describe how it would work if it worked as their authors would wish. These textbooks and notes have the effect of suggesting to their readers that a fully harmonious state of affairs prevails everywhere in our planned economy. For this reason a coherent description of how the mech-anism of our economy really does work represents a new task, not hitherto performed in the economic literature of our country.

It is true that, since 1953–4, a number of articles have been published which are free of this idealizing outlook, and contain pointed and courageous dis-cussions of real problems. These writings have helped and stimulated our researches greatly. But some of these articles dealt with a narrow field, being concerned only with the analysis of particular problems; while the discussions on a general plane have not gone into a detailed consideration of the present mechanism of the economy—they have merely indicated the problems. Thus, research designed to provide a connected as well as detailed description and analysis of our present-day methods of running our economy has not been made superfluous by these articles. On the contrary, they have made it very timely.

This very situation, the novelty of the task, has also affected the meth-ods of research employed. It was not enough to study figures and statistics (although, of course, they had to be made use of, and will have to be uti-lized even more in the course of further research). Nor was it enough to become acquainted with the orders and directives which regulate the conduct of economic administration. What needed investigation was the way in which annual and quarterly plans are prepared in practice (irrespectively of what the relevant decrees enjoin), the manner in which negotiations between manu-facturing industry and distribution are carried on in real life, and so on. For this reason, particularly important roles were accorded in the present inquiry to direct observation, to a manifold process of discussion with experts and persons in leading positions in the practical conduct of economic life, and to the summing up of their experience.[6] It unavoidably follows from this that the study includes several statements which are not really strictly 'proven' (and are perhaps hardly capable of proof). Their proof lies merely in this, that they

---

[6] I would like here to repeat my thanks for valuable assistance to all those experts and persons in leading economic positions in ministries and in enterprises who, by providing me with information, made it easier to reveal the facts of the situation.

are based on the unanimous opinion of experts, often men working in different fields, so that particular questions will tend to be evaluated by them from different, and possibly conflicting, points of view.

The present study is restricted to the consideration of a single field, that of light industry. Moreover, within this it is primarily concerned with four branches of State-owned and Ministry-controlled industry: the shoe, leather, woollen, and cotton trades. Naturally, this must limit its significance. I think, however, that many of the phenomena described in this study are also to be encountered in other fields and can be regarded as more or less general.

In any case, there is much evidence for the view that light industry has provided an extreme example of overcentralization. For this reason its experience is singularly striking. There are few other industrial sectors in our national economy in which the full quarterly production programme of enterprises is centrally laid down to the extent of its 'full breakdown', i.e. detailing every single concrete product—as was the case in light industry in 1955 and in previous years. And this in a branch of industry where the bulk of production consists of consumer goods, so that quick and sensitive adjustment is required to a demand which is often unpredictable and subject to changes of fashion. It is a branch of industry which does a very large export trade, directed, to a significant extent, towards capitalist markets, a circumstance which, again, calls for much flexibility in day-to-day management.

In general, the study treats of the experiences of light industry. However, in some chapters it has been necessary to take a wider view, especially where I try to throw light on certain interrelations of a theoretical kind[7] or where I describe phenomena of a sociopolitical character.[8] In these places I have attempted broader discussions of some questions. I know these to be the least finished parts of the study. Nevertheless, I have felt compelled to write them down, even in their present sketchy form, because doing so helps to complete the picture of overcentralization, of bureaucratic methods of administering the economy.

In general, the study describes the position in 1955. In a few places, where this is specially indicated, I also deal with the position in the first half of 1956. In the eighteen-month period under examination in this study, the economic machinery of overcentralization could still be studied more or less in its entirety. It is true that efforts to suppress the bureaucratic characteristics of administration had already been made by that time. But—as the study will

---

[7] As in the third and fourth parts of Chapter IV.
[8] As in Chapter V.

try to show—these efforts had achieved very little. Already, by the second half of 1956, the effect of the critical atmosphere which developed in the wake of the XXth Congress of the Communist Party of the Soviet Union was increasingly to be felt. The preparation of more far-reaching and fundamental reforms had—if slowly and haltingly—begun. Work having this as its object was set in train in the field of my investigations, in light industry, as well.

I cannot extend the analysis of my study to this last period. I had to finish collecting material at the end of the first half of 1956. At a public debate held in September, numerous economists and people in leading positions in economic life discussed the study; their comments helped considerably in improving the work.[9]

Finally, two short further remarks about what the reader should not expect to find in the present work.

He should not expect practical, detailed proposals, a set of recipes for remedying what is amiss. It has not been my object to recommend a detailed programme of action in this study. I have merely tried to depict reality and to analyse actual practice. This is an aim more modest than the elaboration of a general scheme of reforms—but it is easier to accomplish with some precision. Given a desire to make use of it, a description and analysis of this kind can, I think, serve as a useful point of departure for the formulation of economic policy. The second thing I wish to say is this: the reader must not expect this study to strike a just balance of some sort as between the achievements and the defects, or the advantages and disadvantages of the methods which have been employed in running our economy. This study deliberately eschews any claim to provide an evaluation. As everyone, including the author of the present study, knows, we have scored some considerable successes in our light industry: production has risen a great deal; in the last few years quality has improved, and the variety of goods available has increased. And this has been attained by light industry amidst serious difficulties, for it has received a very meagre share of investments made, and it has had, for years, to contend with difficulties in the matter of raw material supplies. It is clear that these successes were attained while the methods of running the economy which have been in use hitherto were being employed. They were achieved within the old system of planning.

---

[9] The present study also constituted the author's dissertation for the title of candidate. Following his public viva voce defence of it, held on 24 Sept. 1956, the author was awarded the title of 'candidate of economic sciences' by the Science Degree Committee of the Hungarian Academy (Hungarian Publisher).

Yet, at the same time, these methods were increasingly beginning to show the disadvantages attached to them. The task set for the present study lies in just this sphere. It is to reveal these faults, the contradictions within the economic mechanism we have used. Hence, this study necessarily concentrates attention on defects; on the harmful consequences of excessive centralization. In any case, my own view is that the criterion of the constructive character of criticism is not to be found in the proportions in which it doles out 'positive' and 'negative' assessments. That turns, rather, on whether the critique is motivated by a wish to put faults right, and on the degree to which it contributes to remedying defects in practice.

J. K.
Budapest, January 1957

PREFACE TO THE SECOND
HUNGARIAN EDITION

THIRTY THREE years ago, in the autumn of 1956, I submitted the manuscript of this book to the Economic and Legal Publishing House. Now, the preface to a new edition offers me a choice as to what to discuss from a variety of issues that come to mind. Personal reminiscences might be in order, invoking the tempestuous times of first publication. Another possibility might be to take inspiration from Frigyes Karinthy's classic short story 'Meeting a Young Man' and to ask to what extent I fulfilled the plans of my youth. But no matter how attractive these approaches are, I propose to discuss a different question: to what extent do I still consider the message of this small book valid and in what respects has my opinion changed since.

Given my choice for the subject of the new preface, I would like to implement this task as objectively as I can. False modesty will not prompt me to gloss over points that I still consider timely and instructive, but I shall also discuss the weaknesses and problematic features of the work. This does not, however, pre-empt criticism of the second edition. Critics will certainly find in this work things to which they take exception, and perhaps also merits.

Let me quote from the preface of the first edition:

> The first necessary step is a description of the situation as it is. This, it may be thought, should already be available in dozens of books. Unfortunately this is not the case. There are, of course, dozens of textbooks and collections of notes for use at universities which describe our methods of economic administration and planning, our pricing and wage systems, etc. However, all these have a serious fault in common: instead of telling us how our economic mechanism really works, they merely describe how it would work if it worked as their authors would wish ... For this reason a coherent description of how the mechanism of our economy really does work represents a new task, not hitherto performed in the economic literature of our country.

Or: These methods of running the economy were increasingly beginning to show the disadvantages attached to them. The task set for the present study lies in just this sphere. It is to reveal these faults, the contradictions within the economic mechanism we have used.'

This is still my aim. I have considered it the principal objective of my research activity ever since. This is not a self-evident pledge. Frequently the committed partisans of some system, political current or party feel that they must primarily and above all emphasize in all their written and oral presentations, whatever serves the interests of the system, current, or party supported by them, keeping silent as far as possible about what could damage those interests. The conviction to play a different role ripened in my mind in the 1954–5 period: I would no longer be the propagandist of the socialist or any other system, but become a researcher. Before I committed pen to paper, I would ask first of all whether what I wanted to say was true, and not to which cause it did harm or benefit. To use an almost forgotten but again timely expression, I have no wish to practise partisan science. To avoid any misunderstanding, I have no desire to eliminate from the public sphere and the sphere of ideas, the desire by political actors to be in the company of their fellows, to serve a common cause, and to identify themselves with a party or movement. I respect those who choose this approach to life, although I do not believe that this is the only morally acceptable attitude. Partisanship and political commitment are values of a high order, but their place is outside science. Scholarship begins whenever someone tries to rise above his political commitments and to apply the criteria of scientific truth. It is clear to me, and I shall deal with this in detail below, that those active in the social sciences never entirely succeed in this, but I believe that they are at least obliged to strive to do so. I do not only accept this, but even wish to recommend it, although I know that numerous 'antipositivist' intellectual currents in the West as well as in the East, reject this as obsolete.

The researcher is neither prosecutor, nor counsel for the defence, nor presiding judge, but his role, to stay with the legal metaphor, is akin to that of the *juge d'instruction* of the continental system who, before the trial, collects all possible facts, questions witnesses, but does not himself pass any judgement. In this respect, it is in good conscience that I pass this small work to the reader for a second time; even today I think that what I wrote then was a correct report on the classical socialist system prior to the reforms.

The concrete system itself, about which this book speaks, no longer exists in Hungary; today it will be of interest primarily to students of economic history. But this past left such a deep imprint that its effects are still felt. It is impossible to truly understand the present Hungarian economy and the problems of transformation, if we are not familiar with the initial conditions. In addition, numerous relics of the overcentralized, bureaucratic economy, relying on instructions and other administrative measures, still remain. Not to mention that what already belongs to the more remote past in the Hungarian economy, is more recent in the Soviet Union or Poland, and is the present in East Germany, Rumania, North Korea, and Cuba. (Since I wrote the present Preface, East Germany has ceased to exist, and the situation in Rumania has also changed although the future system of its economy is uncertain.)

It is not only an emphasis on a descriptive-explanatory approach in scientific analyses that I consider a timely requirement; the book makes a contribution to scientific philosophy and methodology on numerous other questions as well. These I still fully accept. Here I shall mention but one range of questions—the relationship of the book to the Marxist political economy.

I ask the reader to place himself into the intellectual atmosphere of that time. Abroad, the socialist economy was of course much discussed employing a non-Marxist approach. In Hungary however, just as in other socialist countries, Marxist political economy enjoyed an officially proclaimed monopoly. Not only blind supporters of the existing system, but its sharp-eyed critics as well relied on this apparatus. Reformers demanded respect for the Law of Value, and among other things, debated whether the means of production or labour were commodities. The method, conceptual apparatus and terminology of *Over centralization* are not part of the above. As I was writing, I was not only convinced that Stalinist innovations in political economy (Basic Law, The Law of Planned Proportionate Development, etc.) were unusable and misleading, but also that the conceptual apparatus of the Marxist theory of labour value was unworkable. It provided no constructive help in the analysis of the reality of the socialist system. I did not argue against it, but simply ignored it. I have been doing so ever since.

I wished to suggest to readers that they could reach noteworthy and substantial conclusions if they avoided the texts and jargon of the anointed priests of Marxist political economy and did not get bogged down in their arguments. Instead they should try to observe reality directly and from a pragmatic perspective and then draw generalizing conclusions. What makes a work theoretical is not the number of references to *Das Kapital* or the repetition of the term 'Law of Values' but generalization based on the observation of reality. In numerous other disciplines (thus, philosophy festering in the shadow of Gyögy Lukács) not only dogmatic Stalinist social scientists but also others critical of the classical socialist system were still caught for a long time in the tight chambers of Marxist doctrine, or tried to expand its walls by cautiously exchanging a brick or two. In other socialist countries (for instance in the Soviet Union under the influence of Kantorovich and Novozhilov) a similar situation prevailed over a long time in economics as well. Perhaps I may say without appearing immodest that is was also due to this book that the profession of economics in Hungary was freed of these shackles earlier.

At the same time it is worth stressing that the influence of Marxism can still be felt in several aspects of the book, and that in these aspects I have remained loyal to this understanding of Marxist method ever since. I think, for instance, it is a fertile approach to consider that if something appears on a large scale, and goes on for some time, one should not be satisfied with seeking a superficial explanation in individual mistakes, policy errors, or in the personal characteristics of the man in power. Let us examine whether it is not the system which is the principal factor, or at least one of the principal factors, in the explanation of the problems.

Socialism, whether in its classical pre-reform shape or in the variant which came about in the course of the reforms, is not a coincidental agglomeration of individual phenomena. Regularities, general tendencies, ingrained patterns of behaviour come into being. In the fully-formed system, characteristic situations occur repeatedly and this gives rise to characteristic attitudes. The basic duty of the social scientist is to study and describe these regularities, tendencies, patterns of behaviour, and response functions, as well as to synthesize them into a theory. I am now aware that this approach is not particular to Marxist social science. Not all schools of thought may accept them; yet it is true all the same that such methodological principles form part of several respectable non-Marxist, or institutionalist research strategies.

An example of this approach in the book is the examination of how a particular system of planning, control, and financial incentives induces certain reactions in the management of firms, against the will of the allegedly almighty centre. Chapter III describes seven regularities. While the standard textbook of the time taught that the ever higher level of consumption or the planned nature of all activities were 'laws' of socialism, I tried to present what the real laws were, that is more precisely and more modestly, the real regularities. Making a fetish of the plan, plan-speculation, plan bargaining, and the rush at the end of the plan period, among others, were all inevitable under the given conditions.

Others may have learned this from other sources, but in my case it was Marxism which taught me that things occur on different levels. There are chains of causality and at the same time more superficial and deeper regularities. *Over-centralization* made several attempts at applying this approach. In fact, this first book of mine raised all the important questions that were to torment me throughout my life as a scholar. To what degrees can human action be planned? To what extent does uncertainty govern society? What is the relationship between bureaucratic control, forced growth, and chronic shortages? To what extent can the selection and behaviour of bureaucrats according to certain criteria (uncritical obedience, lack of initiative, etc.) be explained by the characteristics of the political and social system? Why does the huge bureaucratic apparatus tenaciously recreate itself? As I reread my first book after more than thirty years, I became aware that the questions which I asked were drafted in my mind as I took my first tentative steps. What has changed in my later works are the answers to these questions. On some problems, I changed my mind more than once. I cannot provide infallibility retrospectively, nor for the future. All I have done is to try to establish the truth and I will continue to do that in the future as well.

One of the sources of weaknesses in the book was ignorance, or perhaps I should call it half-knowing things. I was 28 when I wrote it. I knew a thing or two about the way the system I examined worked; I was a trained Marxist-Leninist, familiar with the debate in Hungary. Yet this was about all. The book was my dissertation for a Candidate's Degree, comparable to the thesis a graduate student has to submit to obtain a doctorate in a university in an English-speaking country. I knew virtually nothing of the literature and ideas with which a student at a good university has to be familiar if he wishes to graduate in economics. What skills I acquired in this area, I obtained after the publication of *Overcentralization*, in the years when I found myself on the fringes of the Hungarian academic community and thus had the time to spend most of my waking hours reading. Those years were my 'Universities', when I learned by teaching myself with considerable effort, many things which students at Western universities are spoon-fed by their lecturers and tutors.

The book refers to some Hungarian authors, primarily to György Péter, whose ideas influenced me very much. On the other hand, there is no reference in it to the Western literature, or in general to contemporary foreign literature on economics. This was not done to plagiarize the ideas of others or to hide my sources for tactical reasons, but simply because I was unfamiliar with those writings. I look at the man I was then with a certain astonishment and hair-raising respect: how could I attempt such neck-breaking heights with such poor equipment? And yet, I had no illusions about my knowledge at that time either. It was clear to me that I did my work almost instinctively; my only instruments were the interpretation of elementary statistics, the observation of individual cases, and the questioning of persons taking part in economic events, as well as comparing the pieces of information thus obtained. In this respect my work resembled the practice of the Hungarian rural sociologists of the 1930s and made no use of the advanced methodology of western empirical surveys. Aside from lacking methodological skills, I knew little about the results achieved by Western economists in clarifying the general problems of the working of an economic system, such as prices and markets, the behaviour of firms, risk and Uncertainty, or the theory of conflicts. I was aware neither of the debate between Ludwig von Mises, Oskar Lange, Friedrich von Hayek, and others concerning the nature of socialism and planning nor of the work done by Western students on the economic system of the Soviet Union and the other socialist countries.

Perhaps I even benefited from this situation. Ignorance sometimes acts as the midwife in the birth of original ideas. Take an example: Section IV.4 describes the 'model' of the old economic mechanism, differentiating between vertical and horizontal links, and stressing the dominant role of the former. As far as I know, this kind of differentiation was introduced by *Overcentralization* and has become part of the common knowledge to such a degree that no one now remembers the source. It is possible that if when writing the book, I had known about what economists today call a model, I would not even have dared to write those few pages.

But I do not want to make a virtue out of necessity after the deed either. I have overcome this phase, as have many other Hungarian economists. From the time that I began to become familiar with the world economic literature and its conceptual and analytical apparatus, I felt it indispensable that I too should join the blood circulation of the international professional community. I felt that we had to break out of narrow provincialism. There is no obligation to agree with the methods or theories of this or that foreign school of thought. I myself have engaged in numerous disputes. But I believe it is imperative that we familiarize ourselves with the scientific results of the time; that we take over everything that can be adapted, and reject only what, on the basis of thorough argument and not of prejudice, we do not consider workable under our circumstances. I would therefore advise readers of this second edition, and especially students and young scholars that they transcend the methodological standards of the book. What was perhaps a forgivable weakness, a pardonable sin, on the part of the early pioneers several decades ago, is an unpardonable omission today.

Regarding the length of the text, approximately ninety-five per cent is descriptive, positive analysis, and at the most five per cent falls into the category of normative theory. In my later works I strove to keep the two clearly apart, even if they appeared within a single study. At that time, however, I had not yet formulated this goal, and consequently normative arguments appear here and there, sometimes in a sentence or two, condensed into a requirement or recommendation, mainly in the second half of the book. Nevertheless, the normative arguments hang together and suggest a certain notion of reform.

The book influenced the Hungarian reform process. Among other factors this book also shares responsibility for its virtues and shortcomings—even if no one mentioned this influence at the time. Its influence was, of course, indirect. It manifested itself as an influence on the thinking of the intellectual leaders of the Hungarian reform process.

Although at the time it was not precisely formulated in my mind, I felt— and this was also expressed in the book—that the purpose of the reform was not only to improve economic efficiency but also to give more scope to other things valued by human beings, such as initiative, spontaneous action, a life free of fear and reprisals by the authorities, the opportunity to make autonomous decisions. On the level of practical economic tasks the reform here outlined is linked to the principles that in the Hungarian literature were first formulated by György Péter: greater autonomy for the firms, prices ensuring equilibrium between supply and demand, the central role of profitability in the material, and moral incentives offered to management. In addition, in some more specific proposals, *Overcentralization* contributed to another substantial idea to this system of thought: partial measures were unsatisfactory, the whole of the economic mechanism had to be changed radically, and at one stroke.

I well remember that when the manuscript was first discussed in the Institute of Economics it was precisely this message that irritated some. They objected that my book argued as follows: If we changed the mechanism this way, then this would be bad, and if we changed it that way, then that would cause trouble as well. What then did I want? Did nothing please me? A couple of years later the same objection dominated a hostile official press campaign against *Overcentralization*, alleging that it rejected the entire existing economic mechanism of the socialist economy.

The principle of a package of measures became one of the distinguishing features of the Hungarian reform process. The reform of 1968 was the first and so far the only action which produced substantial changes in almost all areas of the socialist economy at one full sweep. *Overcentralization* had pointed out many years earlier that the introduction of the profit incentive might produce scant results and might even do damage, without a simultaneous radical change in the pricing system, i.e., without introducing market-clearing prices.

It is hopeless to reduce the size of the apparatus without changing the mechanism. New ratios must be established between production and consumption, and between supply and demand; chronic shortages have to be ended so that the market and horizontal inter-firm contacts can function successfully. There is a close relationship between forced growth and overcentralization; consequently the growth policy and the economic mechanism must be changed concurrently. On all these questions the book was much more consistent and unequivocal than later 'neither-fish-nor-fowl' Hungarian (and Soviet, Chinese, Polish, etc.) practice. Within the limitations to be mentioned, it proposed that uniform and complete change should take place. Truly comprehensive changes were needed in the domain of prices, financial incentives, growth policy, and power positions in the market.

The book reflects the recognition that much had to be included in a package of simultaneous measures so that detailed measures should not run counter to each other but should have a beneficial joint effect. But as the years passed and experience was gathered, it became more and more obvious that much had been missing in the package, not only in the reform plan sketched in *Overcentralization*, but also in the points debated in later years, as well as in the practical measures of the 1968 reform. These shortcomings were exactly what I had in mind when I mentioned that *Overcentralization* shared responsibility for weaknesses which became more and more distressing in later years.

Already in the beginning of the 1970s the discussions about the reform in Hungary revealed that those who had theoretically prepared the first wave of reform and those who later carried it out in practice had thought that the 'division of labour' between plan and market would be very simple to achieve. The idea was to entrust short-term regulation, the input–output flow necessary for current production and consumption, to the autonomous decisions of profit motivated firms, while leaving long-term regulation, primarily investment decisions, in the hands of centralized planning authorities. The error is now obvious. As long as the truly vital decisions, such as entry and exit contraction and expansion of output, the changing of the product pattern, decisions concerning technical development, and investment in general are left mostly in the hands of the central authorities, it is self-deception to speak of a genuine autonomy of firms.

Overcentralization had a position on this question, though it was mistaken. But what was not even mentioned, not even in the form of a hint, is even worthier of attention. Not only this book, but all those who participated in the discussions taking place in the economic journals and the economic and business institutions of the existing system, neglected to deal with the fundamental issues of ownership, political power, and socialist ideology.

In more recent writing I have called that type of reform economist, to which I also belonged between 1954 and 1956, the naïve reformers. At that time in Hungary this group included György Péter and Tibor Liska. In the 1950s and 1960s Wlodzimierz Brus in Poland, Sun Ye-fang in China and Ota Sik in Czechoslovakia could be included with them. If we were naïve, then Evsei Lieberman who was the first apostle of the profit motive in the Soviet Union in the 1950s was ultra-naïve. (It is essential to give dates because most of the reform economists still alive have changed at least some of their views since.)

The word naïve is not pejorative. Used in its original sense, it refers to a peculiar well-intentioned childlike attitude, the stage of development of the mind in which somebody courageously engages in a task because he does not even suspect how difficult it is. He puts his hand into the fire without hesitation because he has never burnt himself. In addition naïveté is not merely a state of mind, but also a form of behaviour. A naïve person is completely outspoken, since he feels he has nothing to hide and he cannot yet evaluate the consequences of what was said. It is of course easy to be wise after the event. It is not my aim to point out old errors, including mine at the time, knowing what I know now. But is worth asking why we were not interested in the depths of the problems.

Before trying to answer, I must seek to eliminate in advance a possible misunderstanding. Naïve reformers did not keep silent about difficult and delicate questions of this sort because they exercised self-censorship. It does not mean that I condemn self-censorship. In a system in which legal publication and public lectures are subjected to formal or informal censorship, self-censorship is unavoidable if one wishes to propagate ideas in a legal way that transcends officially set limits. Those who speak and write can decide to give up legality. This choice implies much gain in speaking without self-imposed limits and at the same time loss of influence, not to speak of other gains and losses. If a scholar chooses legal publication, he faces thousands of further concrete dilemmas: how far to go in self-censorship; what to say out loud and what to throttle; how to suggest to readers implicitly what cannot be communicated explicitly. An enlightened and far from naïve critic of the existing system usually holds back a great deal. He consciously or half-instinctively suppresses much of his message. Compared to him the naïve reformer is refreshingly outspoken, since he does not even understand the grave implications of the problems he tackles. When, in later decades, there were debates among the various schools of reformers, the naïve ones were always in a more favorable psychological position. They could easily answer the questions put to them, because they simply said what they thought. Every major question confronted the 'enlightened' with complicated intellectual and moral dilemmas and forced them to decide how far they might be able to go, and how far they wanted to go, in providing an answer.

Looking back at the evolution of my own ideas, I can say that *Overcentralization* was not only my first book but also the last which I wrote as a naïve reformer. Back then the reason I omitted one or another difficult question was not because I had recognized, after much brooding and fretting, that it made sense to draw the limits at that point. I omitted them because, at the time of gathering material for the book and writing it, I simply did not sense the importance of numerous major problems. Now is the time to ask why not?

One reason has already been mentioned and that was my incomplete knowledge. My impression is that this was of secondary importance. By that time, those economists listed above and numerous others who thought along the same lines, already had the chance to read as much Western literature as they wanted to. There were certainly a few among them who then knew more economics than I did. The problem at such times is not that there is no broadcast but that the set is unable to receive it.

Anybody who tries to think about social issues on a theoretical level takes certain axioms as given, or adheres to the declared axioms of some school of thought. There are some whose minds are governed by an implicit set of axioms, unaware that a few final principles, postulates, and taboos limit their thinking. What distinguished the naïve reformers from their successors was that their axioms had not yet been questioned by anyone. These axioms ceased to function as such for the later generation of reformers.

Let me mention a single, though very important question—that of ownership. It was this aspect of the Hungarian economic reform that was most important in the formal and informal private sector's gaining as much ground as it did. By comparison, the changes that occurred in some respects in the state sector were of secondary importance. But in recalling conversations at the time I was working on *Overcentralization*, I have to admit that the problem did not even arise. The desirability of state ownership was an axiom that was not questioned either by myself or by those to whom I talked.

The system of axioms of a social scientist does not usually take shape on the basis of an individual intellectual choice. It can, of course, be imagined that an individual chooses among different possible systems of axioms, just as he chooses among television sets or suits in a store and then mentally selects the one that he finds most attractive. But I do not believe that this is the typical course. The system of axioms is already predetermined by metarational values, which are largely linked to feelings, passions, and prejudices. Those who detest private property do not compare the advantages and disadvantages of public property and private property with an open mind. They think only of how the operation of public property should be organized. Usually a trauma, a shock, or some stirring historic experience is needed for an axiom or an entire system of axioms to be suddenly shaken, for the internal taboo to disappear, and for thinking to suddenly become open to rational argument and comparative analysis. The part of the Hungarian intelligentsia which started out with a belief in socialism can be divided into many groups according to the following criteria: when and under the influence of what experience they suffered such a trauma; how thorough the catharsis was, and; which axioms or group of axioms it destroyed. Perception and understanding are selective. They are ready to expel certain impressions and ideas, and the selection is also subordinate to the system of axioms. Starting with the lifting of one or two internal barriers and the expansion of the receptivity of thinking, numerous questions which were considered uninteresting before suddenly become important. Men of science suffer shocks of recognition; all of a sudden they realize how clearly this author or that author had seen the essence of the problem twenty or one hundred years earlier.

A comparison of the reform process in the different socialist countries offers important indirect evidence for this argument. It seems that no country ever learns anything important from the experience of another. It is possible that one or another partial measure is adopted. Let us suppose that in the Soviet Union, reform economists copy the (bad?) Hungarian personal income tax. Does the first naive group of Soviet reform economists pay attention to what the second and later generations of no longer naive but enlightened, disillusioned, sharply critical, and radical Hungarian economists disclose of the failures of their first attempts? No. They start all over again. No matter how many intelligent people there may be among them, the received axioms prevent them from hearing the voice of Hungarian social scientists.

The work of social scientists is seriously limited by their inhibitions. These blunt and narrow the influence which a man can have on his colleagues, let alone on the wider public—a bitter recognition which should at least serve as a sign of caution against immodesty.

Nevertheless, without exaggerated illusions as to possible influence, or exaggerated expectations as to political impact, there is great need for more research in the social sciences. We are taking part in unique and important events in the socialist world; many kinds of duties await the economist. There is great need for what Americans call monitoring—presenting in detail on the screen of scientific works the events and processes of the immediate past and of the present. This can also provide useful help to active participants in political struggles. Researchers can help to clarify in a given situation what can be realized and what is impossible, what the options are among which we can choose, and what the expected consequences of alternative political and economic actions are. In other words, the researchers, although they do not remove responsibility from the shoulders of those who make the political decisions and who govern the country, can help to ensure that their decisions, and their governing in general, serve the progress of the country. And they can further this aim indirectly as well through educating, through adding a ferment to intellectual life.

But however many-sided the duties of the scientific researcher may be, his task is always conditioned by the fact that he has to take the positive perception and thorough analysis of reality as his point of departure. This lends credibility to his words; this is the particular job that no one can do in his place. Today the vast majority are busily preparing programmes and proposals, arguing. It is good that many do so. But I believe that it is desirable that there should continue to be some whose main activity is research—the honest, the more complete exploration of reality.

J.K.
Budapest, August 1989

CONTENTS

LIST OF TABLES

I

THE SYSTEM OF INSTRUCTIONS

1. THE PLANS LAID DOWN FOR ENTERPRISES

THE basic instrument used for directing production in a centralized manner within the framework of our existing economic mechanism[1] is the all-embracing system of plan instructions. Five-year plans and annual plans for the national economy are passed by the Council of Ministers and by Parliament respectively. These plans determine the tasks set for individual industrial ministries by way of a multiplicity of approved plan index numbers. The ministries divide these tasks between the industrial directorates which, in turn, break them down further for individual enterprises.

All this follows from a basic principle of planning which has hitherto been thought to permit of no alternatives: plans should always have the character of instructions. The doctrine taught has been that every approved plan index number should, at the higher level to which it applies, be broken down and divided up among the units of a lower level, since it was held that the execution of the government's economic plans could not be secured without establishing a closed chain of interdependent instructions.

---

[1] Frequent use is made of this concept in the present study. I would therefore like to make clear the sense in which I employ it, from the very outset. When I speak of the mechanism of the economy I mean to refer to the *methods* in use in administering the economy (i.e. to the systems of planning, money, credit, wages, and prices) and to the *forms of organization* of economic activity. Moreover, I conceive of all these as an interrelated, organic whole.

It is possible for a socialist economic system, based upon social ownership of the most important means of production and on centrally-planned direction of the economy, to employ a variety of methods of administration and forms of organization. In other words—it is possible to bring about considerable changes in the 'economic mechanism' without at the same time affecting the essentially socialist character of the economic system.

'Economic mechanism' is not really a very fortunate expression. As it appears in the literature of economics, particularly in the West (as, for example, in such expressions as 'price mechanism', 'market mechanism', &c.), the familiar concept of a mechanism carries an altogether different meaning from the above. In Poland, where there have been a number of debates about economics along similar lines to those held in Hungary, they prefer the term 'economic model' in discussions of this kind. My reason for sticking to the term 'economic mechanism' has been that my book is a contribution to a major theoretical controversy in which this term has already come to be employed rather extensively. There is, in any case, a need for a concept which refers to methods of administering the economy, and forms of organization employed in doing so, in, as it were, a summary manner, so that it conveys the fact that one is discussing a largely unified piece of machinery.

Overcentralization in Economic Administration. János Kornai translated by John Knapp, Oxford University Press.
© Oxford University Press (2023). DOI: 10.1093/oso/9780192894427.003.0001

In what follows, we shall not inquire into how plans for the national economy as a whole are prepared, into the degree to which they are well founded, or into the manner in which the National Planning Office divides up tasks among ministries, and these in turn among industrial directorates. The analysis of this chapter is confined to the study of the relationship which develops in the process of planning and administering the economy between its basic unit, the cell of the economy, which is the enterprise, and its immediate directing body, the industrial directorate.

Long-term plans

During the periods of the three-year plan and of the first five-year plan[2] our enterprises—at least in light industry—had no long-term plans. A few large enterprises, two of them in light industry, have, quite recently, experimented with drawing up five-year plans. As the present study is being written, there is talk of a number of other large enterprises in light industry being asked to do the same.

It might seem an obvious notion that one way in which the advantages of a planned economy should appear would be that enterprises could take longer views. They could plan the broad future course of some things about which it is suitable, and economically advantageous, to look several years ahead: the development of the enterprise, i.e. investment, modernization, technical development, and measures of redeployment of a general, large-scale character. Although these potentialities of operating a planned economy undoubtedly exist in theory, they have not been exploited in the first nine years of working it.

Annual plans

The plans of enterprises in light industry for the year 1955 were formulated centrally in the industrial directorates.

The requirements of home and of foreign trade, for which production caters, were not known in specific detail at the time when plans for individual enterprises were being laid down. All there was to go by were rough 'notifications of requirements' given by the two customer ministries concerned. In such cases the practice before 1954 was to prepare a 'quasi-plan' of the detailed

---

[2] i.e. from 1947 to the end of 1954.

product-mix of goods that would be produced, on a hypothetical basis, and the aggregate value of production was calculated on the basis of this product-mix, which, being hypothetical, was never exactly realized in practice. This procedure was no longer followed in the course of preparing plans for 1954 and 1955. The starting-point adopted instead was to determine the volume of production to be aimed at, reckoning in terms of natural units (metres, pairs, &c.). The figure thus obtained was, in turn, multiplied by an average price (e.g. the average price of one square metre of woollen cloth) to arrive at the value of production in terms of forints.[3] The bases for determining these average prices were actual figures of the preceding period, i.e. the average price of the product-mix of the previous year. Some slight corrections were made to this in cases where it could be taken as certain that large changes in product-mixes were going to occur.

Thus, the annual plans of enterprises have no firm foundation of the kind which would result from detailed attention to demand and to the requirements of commerce.

We must also ask whether directorates are able to gauge the production potential of enterprises correctly when they determine production targets. Experience shows that, in light industry, directorates generally know their enterprises quite well: they do not commit gross large-scale errors in the course of planning. Nevertheless, plenty of problems are met with in this respect as well. It is quite generally held that the assessment of capacity is not reliable enough. At the present moment[4] this does not give rise to concern, as production has been reduced in most branches of light industry in 1956. Indeed, steps to prevent the overfulfilment of production targets have actually been taken in a number of fields. But the assessment of capacity has been a problem during periods when it was desired to step up the volume of output in this branch of industry as well, and a time will no doubt come when this will again be the case. One does hear very many critical remarks concerning the methods of capacity measurement in use. (A criticism of present-day methods of measuring capacity would require a special detailed investigation, which is clearly not within the scope of the present study.)

However, such empirical evidence as can be obtained, e.g. from a comparison of actual figures with rated figures of capacity, does suggest that criticism is justified, for it shows measurements of the capacity of the shoe industry to

---

[3] £1 sterling = 32·87 forints at official rates. *Cf. Financial Gazette*, 11 Oct. 1957.
[4] i.e. during the summer of 1956.

have been unrealistically large, and those of the leather industry to have been unrealistically small.

Directors, chief engineers, and chief planners of enterprises play very little part in the formulation of annual plans. There was a time when enterprises worked out their own proposals for their annual plans. This has been discontinued since the rationalization drive of 1954. The earlier practice was that plans proposed by enterprises had to be submitted to their directorates, which reworked them several times before finally approving them. Only the name of this system remains: the plan documents sent by directorates to their enterprises are still called 'plan-approvals'. The part played by enterprises is now confined, at the most, to their being occasionally consulted over some minor question. Again, the earlier practice entailed that annual plans, as approved by the directorates, had to be elaborated in further detail by the enterprises themselves, before resubmission to their directorates. This used to be called 'planning back'. This has also been discontinued. 'Planning back' is no longer obligatory.

As top managements themselves play no really active part in the formulation of the annual plans of their enterprises, there is naturally no question of the specialist staffs of enterprises, or the general body of their workers, joining in the task.

Top managements do not take annual plans seriously. This is mainly due to three things:

1. Apart from minor exceptions, fulfilment of annual plans is not linked with financial incentives. The premiums are attached to quarterly plan indices.
2. Annual plans tell enterprises very little: they are couched in too general terms for them to enable enterprises to make real preparations for what they have to do on the basis of the information they contain. Let us consider a factory making woollen cloth, for example. It will be provided with the following plan indicators within the framework of its annual plan:
   (a) The forint value of total production and of finished production.[5] This tells the enterprise very little, since a given forint value can mean greatly differing quantities of cloth—depending on the nature of the product-mix.

---

[5] These terms are explained more fully below. Cf. pp. 28–29 n.

(b) The production plan by individual articles. This does not really amount to a filling out of the picture in exact terms either, as it merely defines the work to be done by categories of articles (e.g. it lays down how much woollen, worsted, or synthetic cloth is to be produced). It provides no further detail beyond that. Yet a given factory may find 10,000 square metres of cloth to be a difficult or an easy production target to achieve depending on the exact kind of cloth that is to be produced, the number of picks per unit length, &c. The plan for producing yarn is fixed in terms of tons, and that for producing cloth in square metres. Yet this defines only a part of what is required from spinning or weaving mills, since the character of their production tasks depends primarily on the length of the yarn and on the number of picks respectively.

(c) The production plan also contains techno-economic indicators— but enterprises do not regard these as being well founded either. (I shall revert to this later on.)

3. It is assumed by enterprises from the outset that the sum of their four quarterly plans will not, in any case, correspond to their annual plan, but will either exceed it or fall short of it. This view that the sum of the quarterly plans will only be equal to the annual plan by accident is unanimously held. A special decision is taken towards the end of the year as to what the annual plan 'should really be taken' to have been. In the woollen industry, for example, the following was adopted, at the end of the year, as having been the annual plan for 1955: the operative plan[6] of the first half of the year[7] plus the annual plan's breakdown for the third quarter plus the operative plan of the fourth quarter.[8]

In what follows I shall present data showing the extent to which the sum of the four quarterly operative plans has, in the last few years, deviated from annual plans as originally approved, in four important branches of industry.

[6] Operative plans are quarterly plans approved by directorates for enterprises shortly before, or sometimes even after, the beginning of the quarter to which they refer. These are the effective regulators of the activities of enterprises, since their degree of fulfilment has financial consequences. Quarterly breakdowns of annual plans do not have such consequences attached to them.

[7] The annual plan was issued late, so that its breakdowns for the first and second quarters were in fact identical with the operative plans of the first and second quarters.

[8] It was not possible to use the annual plan's breakdown for the fourth quartet because this was very considerably altered at the end of the year.

Table I Deviations of the sums of four quarterly operative plans from originally approved annual plans in selected branches of industry

Industry	1952	1953	1954	1955
Cotton	97.7	93.6	100.2	97.7
Wool	88.6	—	—	99.9
Clothing	106.0	86.4	96.7	98.2
Boots and shoes	96.0	87.5	99.4	99.6

Notes: Original annual plan = 100. The data shown represent the sum of operative plans for the four quarters of each year.
Source: Absolute figures provided by the Ministry of Light Industry. The data relate to total production values. The sign—indicates that sufficient data were not available.

Table I shows extraordinarily large discrepancies between original annual plans and the sum of operative plans in individual years in particular branches of industry.

The year 1955 appears to be an exception in this respect. But there were reasons for this, which were of a singular kind. The plan was greatly overfulfilled in the first half of the year, which implies that the annual plan was shown to have been unrealistically modest in relation to the technical potential of light industry. On the other hand, the plan and production were both radically reduced at the end of the year owing to a large accumulation of stocks of finished products and because of increasing difficulties in foreign trade. Thus a dependable basis for the year's work was not provided by the annual plan of 1955 either.

This, by the way, emerges even more clearly from Table II above. This compares the quarterly breakdown of the annual plan of each period[9] with the operative plan and with actual performance. The table shows figures for the second, third, and fourth quarters of each year only, as the operative plan for the first quarter generally corresponds exactly to the quarterly breakdown of the annual plan for that period owing to the fact that these two sets of figures are issued simultaneously to enterprises.

This table demonstrates clearly how little reliance can be placed by top managements on the annual plan as a basis for work, and how large the discrepancy is between the operative and the annual plan. We can see that 1955 is no exception, since by the fourth quarter far-reaching alterations were made in the plan. (Incidentally, the reason why the operative plans for the second quarter of 1955 agree so closely with the breakdown of the annual plan in respect of the second quarter is that these plans were, in a great many industries, issued

---

[9] These breakdowns are given at the time when annual plans are approved. They generally show a rising trend in the course of the year.

Table II Deviations of quarterly operative plans from quarterly breakdowns of originally approved annual plans

Industry	Year	Second quarter		Third quarter		Fourth quarter	
		Operative plan	Actual outcome	Operative plan	Actual outcome	Operative plan	Actual outcome
Cotton	1952	99.7	99.3	98.1	98.0	93.3	98.2
	1953	96.0	94.1	88.7	87.7	88.8	90.2
	1954	—	—	—	—	—	—
	1955	99.4	104.8	99.5	101.8	92.2	94.3
Wool	1952	—	98.1	—	88.5	73.4	79.4
	1953	92.8	105.4	—	102.2	89.9	92.3
	1954	—	—	—	—	—	—
	1955	100.0	104.7	100.8	104.3	93.7	96.1
Clothing	1952	108.1	101.9	104.6	96.9	110.8	105.8
	1953	90.6	91.9	84.8	82.0	76.2	75.1
	1954	—	—	—	—	—	—
	1955	100.0	104.1	99.8	101.1	93.6	93.4
Boots and shoes	1952	100.5	101.8	88.3	85.1	96.9	97.1
	1953	87.8	88.7	74.1	71.2	89.3	90.3
	1954	—	—	—	—	—	—
	1955	102.3	103.4	101.6	103.4	91.0	91.9

Note: Quarterly breakdown of original annual plan =100.
Source: As in Table I.

simultaneously with one another—such was the delay in getting around to approving the annual plan!).

So far I have only discussed data for industries taken as a whole. Yet, from the point of view of our present theme, the really significant data relate to plans of enterprises. Let us examine this side of the annual plans of the leather industry for 1954, asking how the sum of operative plans over four quarters of the year compared with the original annual plan.

Table III shows that the degree of departure from the plan is much smaller in the industry total than in the figures for individual enterprises. The operative plans of enterprises and their original annual plans show larger divergences— these cancel out to some extent in the average for the industry. This obviously affects the figures shown in Tables I and II.

For all these reasons the annual plans for enterprises carry no authority in the factories, in the Ministry, or in the industrial directorates belonging to light industry. As soon as these plans are received they are put away in a drawer. The fact that enterprises do not even argue about the figures in these plans

Table III Deviations of the sums of four quarterly operative plans from originally approved annual plans in selected enterprises in the leather trade

Name of enterprise	Index
Pécs Leather Factory	89.9
Táncsics Leather Factory	94.2
Ujpest Leather Factory	106.7
Pannónia Fur Factory	86.6
Fur Garment Factory	93.7
Industry total	96.7

Notes: Original annual plan for 1954 = 100. The figures shown represent the sum of the four quarterly operative plans.
Source: Data provided by the leather and shoe trades' directorate of the Ministry of Light Industry. All data refer to total production values. The enterprises listed account for about a half of the value of the industry's output.

with their directorates, and accept them without protest, is a bad sign from the very outset, for, if they took the plan seriously, they would surely have a series of either justified or unjustified questions to raise. I would like to quote two characteristic expressions of opinion in relation to this:

'There is a need for an annual plan, because it is useful politically', said the chief of the planning department of a textile factory, meaning, by 'political usefulness', that the slogan of fulfilling the annual plan can be used in mobilizing the workers and spurring them on.

'The annual plan is only needed to provide a basis for over-fulfilment pledges, and also because it is included in collective contracts.[10] Otherwise, there is no need for it'—this was the opinion of the chief of the planning department of another light industrial enterprise.

The view that there is no need for an annual plan for enterprises is widespread among top economic administrators in light industry—both in the Ministry and in enterprises. Their view is that while indices relating to an entire year should continue to be issued to enterprises, these should not be called plans (since they will not, in any case, be realized precisely) but merely 'figures for guidance' or 'rough indicators'. Enterprises should, they hold, be informed

---

[10] Collective contracts are normally signed by managements of enterprises on behalf of employers, and by trade unions on behalf of employees.

of probable volumes of production and of important technical specifications, so that managements can make the appropriate technical dispositions on the basis of these. But nothing more is required.

This view, representing the opinion of persons in leading positions in light industry, evoked much indignation in the National Planning Office; the staff of the office think it impossible for an enterprise to be without its annual plan. That is not surprising, for the practice of light industry in this matter is in sharp contrast with the teaching of the textbooks. The principle that the work of an enterprise should be based primarily, and above all else, on the annual plan, is axiomatic in the literature of planning. The truth, however, is that top management in light industry is merely giving open expression to what has, for some time now, been the prevailing state of affairs in practice, namely, that enterprises do not, in fact, find that they have annual plans having the character of instructions.

The foundations and stability of annual plans

But is the foregoing inevitable? Could it not be changed?

I have invoked three factors in explanation of the failure of annual plans to amount to effective instructions. I have put first the fact that there are no worthwhile material incentives attached to the fulfilment of annual plans. In practice, this is the main reason for failure to take annual plans seriously, but—speaking theoretically for the moment—it is just this that might be most easily remedied. It might, quite simply, be decided, for example, that the premiums of directors and higher executive staffs of enterprises should henceforth depend on the fulfilment of annual plan figures alone. Without a doubt, the authority of the annual plans of enterprises could, in this way, be greatly augmented in no time.

However, this idea is incapable of being realized within the framework of our present system of planning.

Let us look again at Tables, I, II, and III. We see that in each year and in each branch of industry there is a difference between the original annual plan and the sum of the four quarterly operative plans, and, correspondingly, completed production differs from the original plan as well. It may be said in reply to this that the differences are not very great. They would not, indeed, be great, if plans of production were regarded as programmes of work, serving as the basis, the point of departure, of the activities of enterprises. (This is what managements in light industry have in mind when they ask to be given 'figures for guidance' only.) But, on present principles, plans may not be regarded as programmes of work of this kind. They must be considered as instructions of an unconditionally binding character, the fulfilment of which to any extent less than 100 per cent, is tantamount to disobeying a command of the State, i.e. it implies an act of omission calling for both moral and material sanctions. The principles of planning make 100 per cent, into an absolute. This is the crucial point to which material incentives (premiums, &c.) generally attach. But, if that were so in this instance it would, of course, be impossible to neglect a degree of uncertainty in the annual plan which can lead to departures from it of 3–4 per cent, or sometimes even 10–14 per cent, in a given planning period. For such a degree of uncertainty can mean that, owing to no fault of their own, but simply because of inaccuracies in their plans, enterprises may be unable to fulfil them, with the result that all executives would be deprived of their premiums. Or, conversely, enterprises may receive additional premiums as a result of slack in their plans rather than owing to any additional efforts of their own.

Here, by the way, I would again draw attention to the fact that the problem really arises in a sharper form than is indicated by the figures in Tables I and II. We must not forget that these are data for subgroups of industry which summarize those of numerous enterprises. Of course, in such summary figures, which are averages, a certain levelling process is at work. We need only recall Table III! In the leather trade the degree of departure of the operative plan from the original plan came to no more than 3–4 per cent., but in individual enterprises it amounted to 7–14 per cent.

My reason for stressing this is that this aspect of the matter needs to be kept in mind throughout the remainder of this chapter. For example, I shall discuss hold ups in raw material supplies, particularly in the field of imported raw materials. To this it may be objected that it is unreasonable to make much of this particular difficulty, since we mostly fulfil our import plans for every basic commodity without being out by more than a few per cent. But here again, the reference is to global, summary figures of fulfilment! We may consider the example of imports of leather. The bodies concerned with foreign trade may fulfil their plans for the importation of leather in a global sense, with a shortfall of 1 or 2 per cent, at the most, which is not much in relation to the total of these imports. Indeed, a top executive of Tannimpex[11] has claimed great successes in the matter of plans on account of the fact that that organization often attains a degree of adherence to plans as high as 95–96 per cent. Yet, in spite of

---

[11] Tannimpex is responsible for transacting all foreign trade in leather, shoes, and furs.

this, leather factories constantly complain of the unpredictable, unreliable, and erratic character of their supplies of hides. The explanation of this is that the index calculated by Tannimpex to show the degree to which it adheres to plans is not based on orders placed by factories, but on the bulked order of the leather and footwear trades' directorate. This last already represents a 'compromise' reached by the industrial directorate and the foreign trading organization, and is substantially different from what the factories had ordered. Another part of the explanation is that, in measuring the degree of adherence to plans, the only classification of leathers which is taken into account is that by weight. Types of leather are ignored in spite of the fact that they also have far-reaching effects on production and plan fulfilment in leather factories. Finally, a shortfall in total leather imports of 1–2 per cent, can produce a shortage of material of the order of 20–30 per cent, in the production of particular types of finished leather in a particular factory, and is capable of completely upsetting its production plan.

I would like to point out here that all this would not in fact present grave problems if the objective of planning were merely to secure that the most important structural features of the economy developed more or less according to plan. But the present system of planning aspires to a great deal more: it wishes to regulate each main aspect of every activity of every single enterprise by means of binding instructions. This being the case, it is necessary to consider the degree to which the instructions addressed to enterprises are precise and realistic; and the fact that these problems show up less sharply in figures relating to whole branches of industry, or in those for the economy as a whole (i.e. in yet wider and more general averages) cannot be accepted as grounds for complacency.

I have so far discussed the uncertainty which characterizes the global, summary plan indices of an enterprise. (The tables have illustrated this in terms of the volume of production expressed in forints, but the position is similar in regard to planned cost-reductions, for example.) In order to put these summary indices on to a more reliable basis it would first of all be necessary to work out the actual production programmes of enterprises in detail.

The greater the detail in which the exact products to be made by enterprises are determined for one year ahead, the more likely it is that the planned figures of the volume of production, of cost reduction, of the wage bill, of personnel requirements, of the numerous techno-economic indicators, &c., will be firmly based. If, on the other hand, the detail of the manufacturing programme is not determined in advance, then, naturally, all these global annual targets will, to a great extent, be based on estimates. They may still play a useful informative role but cannot be regarded as fully binding instructions having absolute validity. In fact, as we shall see, the conditions which would be required for planning the production of light industry a year ahead in full detail of its actual product-mix do not exist.

What are the 'elements of uncertainty' which prevent the annual production plans of enterprises from being stable and firmly based? These elements in the situation would have a great influence on the actual course of events if important economic and moral consequences were attached to the fulfilment of annual plans.

1. *Interruptions in materials supplies.* This will be discussed in detail in a separate chapter later on. I only wish to refer to one or two broad features of the situation here. It is well known that we import a major proportion of the raw materials used by our light industry from abroad. In 1955 80·6 per cent, of all basic materials consumed in light industry were imported, and a sizeable proportion of this was bought in capitalist markets. In present circumstances—with foreign trade organizations being forced to buy spasmodically and late, owing to lack of foreign exchange reserves and other causes—this results in fluctuating, insufficiently planned arrivals of materials. Materials arrive at the last moment, or, indeed, late; their quality differs from what an industry or enterprise have been expecting.

Another part of our supply of materials is obtained from our own agriculture. Here weather conditions introduce a factor of uncertainty from the outset. In addition, however, the bulk of our farms still operate on a small scale, and the possibilities of influencing them in accordance with the needs of planning are limited.

If we disposed of substantial stocks of raw materials and semi-finished products, all this uncertainty would, of course, be very largely counterbalanced. In that event, delays in the arrival of particular consignments of imports or an occasional irregularity in the process of collecting farms products would cause no interruption of production at all, as requirements could be met by drawing, temporarily, on stocks.

Unfortunately, however, we have been in a bad way in this matter of stocks for some years now—as will be abundantly shown by the figures adduced in a later chapter which deals with this.

The halting, spasmodic character of the supply of materials, and the tight position in regard to stocks, is one basic reason for the feeling which exists among light industrial executives that it is futile to plan in detail and in a binding manner for a full year ahead. For they consider that it will in any case become necessary to adjust the actual programme in each quarter, and within that, perhaps even each month, to the real possibilities allowed by the materials supply position.

2. *Changes in requirements and in demand.* This factor is undoubtedly of most importance in giving rise to uncertainty in light industry, since the bulk of its production is for clothing purposes, where demand is rather fickle.

The first source of trouble is that trading organizations themselves are insufficiently familiar with requirements, and do not weigh their orders with sufficient care. Next comes the fact that light industry—the directorates primarily—do not hold themselves sufficiently to orders received, or, alternatively, are ignorant about them when plans are drawn up.

Over and above this, some changes in demand cannot be foreseen even if the best methods of planning are employed and no matter how carefully requirements are scrutinized. That this is so results from the course of *fashion*, for example, which often produces surprises in the field of women's wear: a mass demand will arise for some articles produced on a limited scale, while there is a sudden fall in the extent to which other articles are sought.

Another such factor is the *weather*, which has a considerable influence on the demand for consumption goods. Thus in 1955 the very rainy summer produced an unforeseeable change: bathing costumes, other articles for use on bathing beaches, &c., were sold in much smaller quantities than had been expected.

A third factor of this sort is constituted by various changes in *purchasing power*. For wage and salary earners this can be calculated in advance more or less exactly. But for the peasantry it cannot be foreseen at the beginning of the year—depending, as it does, on the harvest. Yet the demand originating with the peasants has a considerable impact on light industrial production, more particularly because the tastes and requirements of this section of the population differ from those of the urban population.

A fourth factor, which is the most important, and has more weight in most respects than any of the foregoing, is the uncertainty of *export orders*. Light industry has a sizeable job to perform in the field of exports, an important part of which are destined for capitalist markets. In 1955 we exported 22–8 per cent, of the finished products of light industry. As a rule these orders arrive rather late, and established export plans and programmes are constantly being modified. For example, the cotton trade usually receives only forty-five days' notice of the specifications of its orders from the foreign trading organization it deals with—so that enterprises cannot even get a detailed view of their tasks for as much as a quarter of a year ahead. The export obligations of the footwear trade were altered four times in 1955; on one occasion they were raised very markedly, on the other occasions they were lowered.

These problems are further accentuated by the fact that imports and exports are frequently not brought into harmony with each other; export agencies commit goods for export without import agencies having obtained the necessary materials; they undertake delivery dates which are quite unrealistic in view of late delivery dates which attach to the arrival of raw materials, &c.

It would be wrong to exaggerate the degree of variability of demand and hence of production in light industry on the basis of the foregoing. There are a great many 'standard articles'. It is estimated that 60–70 per cent, of light industrial production is fairly constant. Changes in the remaining 30–40 per cent, would not cause too much disturbance in production if material supplies were not very tight and if the hands of top managements were not tied by innumerable strict plan index numbers. As things are, however, a change in a small segment of planned production frequently upsets the whole programme, as it may necessitate the requisitioning of materials intended for other uses, as when materials for a new export order are found at the expense of a standard line of goods. It may then also become necessary to re-fashion the production programme of standard articles so as to ensure that certain basic planned figures—i.e. the index of production in terms of forints, planned reductions in costs, &c.—should still 'work out all right'. A sudden change, affecting 5–10 per cent, of production, will not infrequently upset the entire plan of an enterprise, for what one is dealing with is an interconnected system of figures.

Demand for the products of light industry can be approximately estimated within fairly narrow margins of error, especially so far as home demands are concerned. There is no need, even, for export requirements to give rise to altogether unexpected surprises if a thorough job of market research is done. The problem can be further eased by maintaining suitable stocks of finished products. But, on a sober view, one must nevertheless reckon with a certain amount of uncertainty always remaining. However comprehensively one builds up a system of instructions, one cannot direct either foreign buyers or domestic customers in the shops to buy what they do not want. This is why it is impossible to plan demand, and, with it, production in light industry, with 100 per cent, precision. An annual plan which prescribed targets for standard lines and contained a programme of not necessarily binding 'figures for guidance' in respect of the changeable portion of the output of enterprises could be realistic, since it would reckon with the fact that the latter will in any case have to be adjusted to demand in a flexible manner. But the present system of annual planning strives to 'fill' the capacity of enterprises completely, and also to define all their tasks exactly, for a year ahead—although this can only lead to unrealistic and uncertain figures.

3. *Alterations of national economic plans.* Naturally, the plans of light industry fit into the national economic plan, which is an interdependent system. There are innumerable links between the plan for light industry and other parts of the national economic plan via foreign trade, home trade, raw material supplies, power supplies, purchasing power, &c. Hence modifications of the national economic plan will mostly affect light industry as well.

The government has, in recent years, been regularly forced to change the national economic plan in the middle of its course. Sometimes this has happened more than once within a single year. Let us rapidly survey the last few years from this point of view.

At the end of 1952 stocks of finished goods began to pile up.

In the second quarter of 1953 plans for light industry were scaled down in view of the growing volume of stocks.

In the fourth quarter of 1953 the production plans of light industry were raised again, by now in the spirit of the Hungarian Workers' Party Central Executive's June decisions.

In the first quarter of 1954 light industrial enterprises fell badly behind their plans owing to trouble over electrical power supplies. This shortfall was subsequently 'piled onto' the plans of the second and third quarters of the year.

In the first quarter of 1955 the light industrial conference decided to over-fulfil the annual plan by 3 per cent. This did not, however, materialize, because the plan for the fourth quarter was radically scaled down owing to an accumulation of stocks of goods and also because of import difficulties.

Early in 1956 the plan for the first quarter was itself reduced in mid-passage.

In the second quarter of 1956 a new decision was taken to scale down that part of the original annual plan which related to the second and third quarters.

It will be argued that this uncertainty of national economic planning is not a necessary feature of it, and can be changed. But a certain degree of instability in national economic plans is, in fact, unavoidable, if for no other reason, then because the economy is affected by many factors of a kind which our central organs either cannot control at all or can only control partially at most. To list a few such factors briefly:

(i) The international situation leaves its stamp on economic policy as a whole.
(ii) The world market exerts an important influence through exports and imports.

(iii) The weather first of all determines the harvest and also influences demand and production in certain industries making seasonal products, &c.

(iv) The private sector of the national economy, which it is naturally an object of policy to influence in accordance with plans, nevertheless unavoidably generates more unforeseen changes than the State-controlled sector.

(v) Mistakes in management are made at higher levels of economic administration, as well as 'further down' at the enterprise level. It is, of course, necessary to fight against mistakes—but the fact that human beings will make mistakes and are repeatedly wrong is a feature of reality that cannot be ignored.

Of course, even though a certain degree of instability in national economic planning is unavoidable, this does not account for the large ups and downs and vacillations characteristic of planning in the last few years. This had other causes besides inexperience in planning. The frequent re-casting of plans on a considerable scale has been due to recurring lack of realism on the part of the administration in assessing the resources of the national economy, i.e. to planning characterized by 'voluntarism'[12] and also to repeated changes in policy, of a kind which entailed fairly large upheavals in the economy.

The uncertainties of national economic planning naturally have a marked influence on enterprises. They almost suffice, in themselves, to give rise to a feeling at the enterprise level that to take the annual plan very seriously is not worth the trouble, as the government itself will in any case be changing the plan in the course of the year.

In view of all this, a number of readers may be prompted to ask whether it is my view that it is impossible to plan ahead for a full year? And, if so, they will want to know why I had also found fault with the fact that enterprises have no longer range plans covering several years?

I would like to make it quite clear that, in my view, it is possible for enterprises to plan for a full year ahead. The question is merely: what should be planned, and how?

It is undoubtedly worth-while, possible, and necessary to plan a full year ahead for investment and for renewals in the first place, but also for technical development, product improvement, and large-scale changes in methods of

---

[12] 'Voluntarism' is a term used in Marxist discussions for characterizing ideas and actions which place primary emphasis on the will of human beings rather than on objective circumstances.

production and in layouts. Thus, what needs, above all, to be planned is the development and progress of enterprises—a matter which receives much less attention nowadays than the planning of current production.

By contrast, it is impossible to plan all current production for a year ahead in light industrial enterprises with absolute precision. Product-mixes cannot be laid down in advance in full detail, so that it is not possible to provide a fully exact basis for the various other indices of production, such as those of the production plan, of costs, of the planned wages bill, &c., either. Consequently, annual plans which require an exact, 100 per cent, fulfilment of these targets cannot be realistic so long as they are thought of as binding instructions. I am not yet at this point concerned with posing the question of whether it is desirable to have unconditionally binding detailed annual plans which have the character of instructions. For the time being I also leave open the question of who should decide about particular parts of the plans of enterprises—the enterprises themselves or a higher authority? All I want to stress here is that annual plans of the kind described cannot be realistic and firmly based. To attach material incentives of any importance to such plans would be a serious mistake.

All that has happened in light industry has been that this fact has been recognized as a result of sober assessments of practical experience.

Quarterly plans

The role of quarterly plans differs radically from that of annual plans. They have very great weight and authority, and are looked upon as binding instructions which really do form the basis of work in enterprises. That this is so, is very closely connected with the fact that the payment of premiums depends on fulfilment of the quarterly plan.

What kinds of target figures were contained in quarterly plans of enterprises in 1955?

Take the woollen industry, for example. The production[13] plan lays down figures for full production[1] and for corrected production[1] at constant prices, and for finished production[1] at current prices. Production plans for individual commodities are expressed in natural units by commodity groups. The techno-economic indices used are the following: kilometres of output per

---

[13] These terms are explained below, pp. 28–29 n.

1,000 spindle hours (calculated separately for mills producing tape yarns and worsted yarns); an index of output per unit of material imports; and picks per machine hour (in thousands).

These indices are for the most part in the form in which the Ministry hands them down to directorates. The directorates merely break them down.[14] (Finished output is an exception—this is not prescribed for the directorate, yet it does itself lay down a figure for firms. The explanation here is that there is always a lot of wrangling over finished output.)

I will not deal at this point with other subheads of the plan, such as those dealing with labour, costs, raw material utilization, &c.

There is one important difference in the range of plan index numbers prescribed for directorates and enterprises respectively: simultaneously with quarterly plans, the directorate also elaborates programmes for enterprises. These are integral parts of the quarterly plans. In most branches of light industry the programme details the tasks of an enterprise in terms of 'concrete products'. For example, in the woollen industry a programme will prescribe how much 'Oslo' cloth or how much 'Erőd' cloth is to be produced. A designation of this kind fully determines the composition of materials to be used in making the product, its technical properties, &c.—in fact every characteristic of it except its design and colour. It corresponds to the finest breakdown appearing in the Uniform Product and Price List. In addition, programmes designate customers or consumers as well. (They may be the wholesale trades, the clothing industry, &c.) The system in use in the cotton and leather trades is similar; it is somewhat less detailed in character, but still very finely articulated in the clothing and shoe trades.

The quarterly plan is entirely the work of the directorate; primarily of its planning department, in collaboration with the departments responsible for raw materials, marketing, and occasionally others as well. The degree to which enterprises participate in this stage of planning varies by directorates. Perhaps the most extreme example is that of the woollen trade, where the directorate

---

[14] It has, until quite recently, been a characteristic feature of planning method that indices approved by higher authorities for use by subordinate organizations were in every case broken down and passed on forthwith in the form of an instruction; e.g. from the National Planning Office to the Ministry, from the Ministry to the industrial directorate. It has, until recently, been unknown for the Ministry or a directorate to be given a plan figure, and for it to proceed to secure its fulfilment by any other means than that of breaking it down and passing it on to units subordinate to itself in the form of binding instructions.

A typical example is the index of material input-output coefficients of which I shall have more to say later on (cf. p. 169 n.). This index is also broken down and passed on in a mechanical manner, even though several other methods (e.g. the employment of materials norms, the provision of incentives to promote economy in the use of materials, &c.) are available which could secure the attainment of the figures set out in national plans more effectively.

agrees the programme for the industry in full detail with distribution and then proceeds to break the resulting figures down among enterprises. In doing so, the directorate bases itself on the established pattern of specialization among enterprises. Naturally, the directorate knows its enterprises well, but much of the process of breaking down the plan is mechanical and routine in character. In the woollen trade enterprises are presented with ready-made programmes. Enterprises are entitled to comment on these before they are finalized. But this 'comment' is usually no more than a protest against some excessively tight figure or some very disadvantageous product. Enterprises hardly ever make proposals of their own, partly because they are insufficiently familiar with demand and with the requirements of consumers, and partly because they have practically lost the habit of taking a constructive part in shaping their own programmes. The practice is for enterprises to work out even more detailed plans on the basis of the programmes they receive from the industrial directorate. This is called 'planning back' in industrial jargon—but in doing so, enterprises must keep strictly to the programmes handed out to them by the directorate. The detailed plans prepared in this way are then submitted to the directorate concerned for approval.

The position is somewhat different in the shoe trade, where enterprises are consulted at the earliest preparatory stages of the planning process. Further, before final programmes are constructed, a so-called 'bourse negotiation' is convened. This is a face-to-face discussion between representatives of commercial organizations and factories, in the course of which matters of detail are thrashed out and settled. Programmes are not finally laid down until after this. In assessing the value of these 'bourses' it should be recognized that they undoubtedly provide enterprises with opportunities for familiarizing themselves with the requirements of commerce and of consumers as well as for taking a part in the formulation of their own programmes by way of the process of negotiation. However, the degree of independence vouchsafed to enterprises in the course of all this is less than appears at first sight. Before the 'bourse', the leather and shoe trades' directorate will already have agreed in detail with the central directorate of clothing in the Ministry of Domestic Commerce about both global figures of production and about details of product-mixes (i.e. whether men's or women's shoes, boots or shoes or sandals are to be produced; the leathers to be used; the technology to be used, &c.), albeit with some attention having been paid to the views of enterprises. The topics still open for discussion at the bourse are confined to the colours of the leathers to be used, their thicknesses and grain-design, as well as the product-mixes to be produced, by models. The choice in regard to this last is, however, restricted to models already approved centrally at the model show early in the year. Thus discussions can only be concerned with the proportions in which prescribed models are to be produced. As the leather trade also participates in the bourse, instant information is at hand in regard to availability of the required quantities of leather. This also facilitates the process of constructing programmes. But the part played by leather factories in all this is practically negligible: they arrive at the negotiations bringing finished, centrally formulated programmes with them, and only modify these a little at the request of the directorate. The leather factories themselves play practically no part of substance in fashioning their own programmes. Summing up, it can be said that the bourse system does not secure significantly more independence for enterprises than, for example, in the wool textile industry, since colours and designs are settled directly between the factories and the distributive trades in that trade also. The difference lies rather in the bourse system being a cleverer form of organizing contacts between the factories and distribution; it promotes appreciation of consumers' requirements on the part of the factories and of production problems on the part of the distributive trades.

As I have already said, enterprises elaborate their plans in fuller detail, break their jobs down for allocation to individual workshops, &c. This presents a special problem where enterprises are not given their tasks in fully specified detail. In the cotton industry, for example, plans are given in fully specified detail where spinning and weaving sections are concerned, but not in regard to finishing. So far as the latter is concerned, programmes laid down at the centre prescribe the make-up of basic materials to be used, but not details of modes of finishing. Yet the prices of articles depend, in part, on these last. At this stage there begins the process of what heads of planning departments call 'totalling up'; they set about arranging their programmes in such a way as to make their total values correspond to the sum of forints prescribed in their plans. The directorate determines the forint plans of finishing sections on the simple basis of taking actual figures for the previous plan period, reflecting the product-mix of that, earlier, period. It would be in vain for enterprises to point out that, having already received 60 per cent, of their orders, it appears that, even assuming unchanged or improved technical performance, current product-mixes will 'yield less forints'. Notwithstanding this, the figures will not, as a rule, be altered.

Let us now look at annual and quarterly plans in conjunction with one another. What do they imply so far as the degree of independence of enterprises is concerned?

The production targets of annual plans are of formal significance only, while quarterly plans and the detailed programmes of production that go with them originate with the industrial directorates. The task of the directors and top executives of enterprises is thus confined to carrying out the quarterly instructions of their directorates; they can hardly play any creative part at all in shaping their own production programmes.

All this means that the industrial directorates perform some of the basic functions of directors of enterprises. The real economic unit in these respects is the directorate; the independence of enterprises is to a large extent no more than formal. It would be no great exaggeration to liken the situation to that of enterprises having geographically scattered locations and plants. The industrial directorates would correspond to the top managements of such enterprises, while enterprises would correspond to their individual plants.

This interpretation is borne out in very telling fashion by a reorganization which has been carried out in the silk industry. There used to be numerous enterprises in this branch of industry, functioning in subordination to a silk industry directorate. These enterprises have now been combined, and the directorate has been transformed into the head office of the combined enterprise.

The stability of quarterly plans and their modifications

It is clear from the foregoing that quarterly plans are much more firmly based than annual plans. The reason for this difference lies in the fairly close examination of requirements and of the materials supply position which goes into the preparation of the quarterly plan.

Yet, the various 'factors of uncertainty' of which I spoke before in connexion with the annual plan, do make themselves felt even within such a relatively short time as a quarter. Industrial directorates cannot foresee the probable course of raw material supplies sufficiently precisely and reliably even for a quarter of a year ahead; it is particularly in connexion with arrivals of imported materials that troubles arise again and again. It is quite common for the requirements of the distributive trades to be modified in the course of a quarter, exports, in particular, being a frequent cause of uncertainty.

It may be suggested that it is really not asking too much of trading organizations to expect them to say exactly what it is they will require, if not for a year ahead, then at least for a forthcoming quarter.

I do not wish to repeat here what I have already said before, in connexion with annual plans, about limitations on the possibilities of measuring requirements and laying down future demands exactly. All I would like to emphasize again here is that, under our present system of planning, there are bureaucratic obstacles which stand in the way of the ability of trading organizations to bring about even relatively small changes, affecting no more than 5–10 per cent, of production. Yet this much flexibility could be necessary even if market research were a great deal more thoroughgoing, and the planning of demand more firmly based than it is today.

The foregoing holds particularly for exports of light industrial products which, as they include fashion goods, are characterized by orders for quick delivery and by a variable demand.

We have seen that—in contrast with annual plans—the fulfilment or otherwise of quarterly plans is attended by far-reaching financial sanctions, in that the premiums of top managements and technical staffs of enterprises depend on it. In these circumstances a great deal of significance attaches to every percentage point where production plans are concerned, and to every tenth of one percentage point where plans of cost reductions are concerned, for the receipt of premiums often depends upon this. That is why the question of the degree of flexibility of quarterly plans is so important. What scope is there for modifying them in the face of changing circumstances?

Let us first look at actual practice.

By a decision reached early in 1955 by the Council of Ministers a prohibition was placed on ministries making modifications in quarterly plans during the course of their currency. This prohibition was not heeded, even for a moment, in light industry. Later, the original decision was modified by the Council of Ministers, and, by virtue of a new decree made public in September 1955 it became permissible for plans to be modified once within a quarter but only before the end of the first month of the quarter. Further modifications are only permitted if exports are involved, and this only by the 25th of the second month of the quarter at the latest. In practice, however, even this less stringent prohibition is often violated. Modifications of plans and programmes are very numerous in many quarters, more so, in fact, than was the case before the decrees limiting modifications were promulgated.

Incomplete or partially disguised modifications are frequent. For example, production figures alone are changed, while figures relating to wages, manpower, costs, &c., are not—even though consistency requires that these also be modified. (This is a matter to which I revert later.) Or, during the third month of a quarter, when, according to the decrees, plans may not be changed, the *programme* alone is changed, not the *plan*—so that the decree is 'observed'. (It

THE SYSTEM OF INSTRUCTIONS   23

is recognized, meanwhile, that a programme, so altered, will not correspond to the quarterly plan. If, therefore, an enterprise obeys its directorate's instruction in these circumstances and modifies its programme, it will usually be incapable of fulfilling its plan.) Nor are straightforward breaches of the decree uncommon; the directorate simply goes on making frequent modifications in spite of the prohibition on doing this. Economic administrators concerned with plans call this 'black plan modification'.

Thus, the decree of the Council of Ministers is not, in practice, effective. What is wrong here? Is it that the decree is ill conceived—or are we to regard the failures to carry it out as so many mistakes?

I propose to examine this question from the point of view of three criteria:

First: *the need for flexible adjustment to demand.* It is evidently preferable from the point of view of both domestic and foreign trade that quarterly programmes should be adjusted to demand in a flexible manner rather than be treated rigidly. Very often, however, the requests of commerce come up against resistance on the part of industry. This happens when modifications give rise to raw material supply problems, or to technical difficulties, &c. But they also meet opposition in cases when fulfilment of a request for modification causes no trouble in actual production, but merely in the fulfilment of some compulsory plan index figure. For example, distribution may ask for one kind of cloth to be supplied instead of another—but this may have lower raw material content. Then, if the product-mix envisaged in the programme is modified, enterprises may be unable to 'make their forints', i.e. they may be prevented from fulfilling planned production values. Or, commerce may call for the production of more labour-intensive articles—but the permitted wages funds available to enterprises may not suffice to meet this. In such cases the factors preventing a flexible adjustment to requirements are no longer real economic or other factors relating to production, but merely the fact that a fetish has been made of plan index numbers. The system of plan index numbers and its mechanism, a method of managing the economy, a set of means, has become primary and supersedes the true objective, which is the satisfaction of needs.

In such cases—i.e. when the requests of trade cannot be met within the limits set by the approved plan index numbers of enterprises—a factory will approach its directorate with a request that its plan be modified.[15] In handling the matter the directorate will tend to adopt the same attitude as an enterprise:

---

[15] In fairness it must be said that enterprises will occasionally make decisions on their own to meet the requests of commerce for modifications, even in cases when they risk their own premiums in doing so. They are led to do this by a willingness to exercise their better judgement by a clear recognition of what is in the national economic interest. But just because this involves special sacrifices on the part of the top managements of enterprises, it is wrong to turn this into a system. It is also unrealistic to try to rely on it.

if a request happens to lend itself to being fitted into the directorate's given set of figures, so that it does not risk jeopardizing the fulfilment of its own plan indices, then the directorate will agree, but otherwise it will not.

Since the decree of the Ministerial Council explicitly prohibits or else limits plan modifications within a quarter, directorates and enterprises have every legal opportunity to reject the wishes commerce expresses, and to insist on the original plan for the quarter—even though events in the real world may have made it obsolete.

Next, consider *the second criterion: the interests of enterprises.* It is true that an absence of continual modifications of plans makes production freer from disturbances and smooths the work of management in enterprises. The decree of the Council of Ministers had just this in view, among other things—to protect enterprises from being harried in this way. However, the bureaucratic restrictions at present in force have a tendency to backfire. To begin with, very often enterprises themselves would wish to initiate modifications of their plans, because fulfilment has encountered some real difficulty (lack of materials, &c.). Under the present system, agreement to such requests on the part of enterprises comes up against the same sort of obstacles as we saw confronted the satisfaction of the requirements of commerce (i.e. consideration of whether they can be fitted into the plan indices of directorates, &c.).

Besides, enterprises may come to grief for yet other reasons. Directorates are often forced to order enterprises to change their programmes—without at the same time being in a position to alter those plan index numbers of the enterprises concerned to which premiums attach. For example, the Tata Shoe Factory should have produced chrome soled ox-hide men's sandals in the second quarter of 1955. However, exports were lagging behind their planned amounts; whereupon the factory was instructed, on foreign exchange economy grounds and in the interests of the national economy, to manufacture pigskin shoes with soles made of synthetic material. This, however, is a product of lower forint value, and, as a result, this enterprise failed to fulfil the full production plan laid down for it for that quarter. It failed to obtain the premium. There are other similar examples to be found: the Duna Shoe Factory fulfilled its plan in the second quarter of 1955 to the extent of 106·7 per cent." in terms of natural units. In terms of *forints* this only came to 98·7 per cent, because—on orders from higher up—its programme had been modified and instead of box-calf it had used ox-hide in part and also leather soles instead of crepe soles, &c. As a result, it lost its premium.

Finally, take *a third criterion: the strengthening of discipline in carrying out plans.* The intention of the Ministerial Council's decree had been to contribute to a stiffening of discipline, since continual modifications are damaging to the authority of plans. Nevertheless, this was a poor solution of the problem because the authority of plans is damaged even more by prohibiting all modifications of them or by placing strict and unconditional limitations on them. For these things lead to the personnel of enterprises forming the view that higher authority is demanding the execution of plans, the feasibility of which it does not itself believe in. Invoking the nation's economic interest, the authorities may even demand that enterprises manufacture something other than their plans prescribe, but they will nevertheless saddle enterprises with the financial and moral consequences of failing to fulfil plans.

The matter is further complicated by the problem of bringing the various sections of plans into harmony with one another. A number of definite economic interrelations exist between the targets for the value of production and those of costs, the detailed manufacturing programme, the plans of materials supply, of the permitted wages fund, and of man-power requirements. Changes in the course of one index react on the others; together, they ought to form a unified system.

It is, to begin with, an extraordinarily complicated task to secure consistency between all indices when drawing up the original plans at the outset; complete success in this is never attained. But let us suppose this to be feasible. The logical corollary of modifying any basic index (e.g. changing the volume of output or the programme) would then be that every other planned target would require correction.

There are two possibilities. The first is that this would, in fact, be undertaken at the cost of enormous labour. We may imagine what would be involved for industrial directorates and enterprises in recalculating many dozens, or indeed many hundreds, of figures. If this were regularly done, even a planning and administrative machine several times as large as the present one would be insufficient for a rapid execution of individual modifications.

The other possibility is that of individual plan figures being modified in isolation, the remainder being left unchanged. The fact that these other figures would thus become more or less unreal would then be taken into account from the outset. Being simpler, this is the solution generally chosen. Yet it does do damage to the authority of the instructions contained in plans, since enterprises are well aware of the fact that this procedure implies that many of their approved targets will be unrealistic.

The lesson to be derived from all this is that if minutely detailed, and strictly binding plans are constantly modified—this is bad, because it undermines discipline. If such plans are made more rigid (and this is what the decree of the

Ministerial Council aims at) this is also bad, because it may harm the process of satisfying wants, and thus the real interests of the national economy; moreover, it is not even realistic, since real life will break through rigid plans again and again.

The nature of this contradiction is such that no regulation of plan modifications (whether strict or liberal) is able, in the present circumstances, to solve it, for its roots lie much deeper, in the contradictions of our planning methods. A contradiction exists between the method of planning hitherto in use—with its extraordinarily high degree of centralization, its instructions from the centre concerning minute matters, its unconditional demands for exact, 100 per cent, fulfilment of plan indices—and the fact that in the extremely complex and interrelated system of our national economy it is not possible to foresee and regulate every development in a precise manner by using instructions.

The dilemma of plan modifications could be mitigated to some extent by practices of a 'middle-of-the-road' character, which would avoid both excessive rigidity and excessive liberality. The point of departure of such a system would have to be a scrutiny of each request for plan modifications on its individual merits, rather than on the basis of generally binding rules. But it is only possible to solve the problem by means of deeper and more comprehensive reforms of our planning methods.

2. PLAN INDEX NUMBERS

Let us summarize our conclusions so far. We have seen that the central authorities make use of a very large number of plan indices and of minutely detailed manufacturing programmes in the course of instructing enterprises to fulfil their production targets. We have seen, also, that the indices in question are insufficiently firmly based and too rigid. The question that requires to be clarified next is the extent to which these indices succeed in giving true expression to the wishes of the State. Do they make it unmistakably clear to enterprises just what it is, exactly, that the State and central economic authorities really require of them?

This question needs to be looked into in relation to our whole system of plan indices, considering the indices contained in each separate section of the plans in turn. However, in the present study this has only been done in respect of the most important indices of the plans for (i) *production*, and (ii) *costs*. It will be the task of further research to examine other sections of plans (i.e. those concerned with labour, &c.) from this point of view.

The value indices of the volume of production

In planning practice, a number of different value indices are used for measuring the quantity of production. In most branches of light industry—in the cotton, wool, silk, flax, hemp, and paper trades—the fundamental index of quantity upon which premium payments are based is the so-called index of *corrected production value*. In two branches of industry—the leather and furniture trades—the chief index of quantity generally used in 1955 was that of *finished production*. In the remaining trades the index upon which premium payments are based is that of *total production*.[16]

(The printing industry is a special case. Here, net value added (reckoned at current prices), which excludes the cost of materials, forms one of the bases of premium payments. As the character of the printing industry differs a great deal from the trades connected with clothing which I analyse, and as I have made no separate study of its problems at all, I shall not devote space to dealing with this.)

The points to be discussed below are generally applicable to all three of the indices. I shall therefore simply speak of 'production value' in what follows.

---

[16] We may briefly clarify the meaning of the three volume indices in use in light industry, as follows: *Finished production of the enterprise* = finished output produced by the firm within a defined period (month, quarter, or year) *plus* the value of industrial services performed for other enterprises. From the point of view of an enterprise, products are to be regarded as finished when

(i) no further work is to be done on them by the enterprise in question;
(ii) they have been vetted by the MEO;* and
(iii) they have been taken into stock as finished products.
   (Industrial services include repairs and work done for other enterprises, &c.)

Total production of the enterprise = finished production of the enterprise in a given period plus the value of work in progress and of stocks of semi-finished products at the end of the period, *minus* the value of work in progress and of stocks of semi-finished products at the beginning of the period.

Thus total production measures the actual productive activity of a given period, in contrast to finished production, which includes the results of the activity of the workers of an enterprise in the previous period as well (in so far as this appears as finished output in the present period), while it excludes present output which is only due to appear in the finished product of a future period.

Thus, for example, activity devoted during the first quarter to the making of a piece of furniture which will only be completely ready in the second quarter will be included in the *total* production, but not in the *finished* production of the first quarter.

Corrected production value, or in other words *accumulated production value within the enterprise* = total production *plus* the value of staple, characteristic semi-finished manufactures made in the enterprise, irrespectively of whether these semi-finished manufactures are to be worked up further within the enterprise, or in another factory. Hence, e.g. in a textile factory, corrected production value = value of yarn *plus* value of grey cloth *plus* value of finished cloth plus services, &c. Incidentally, all three of the above indices (or, rather, whichever serves as the basis for premium payments in the branch of industry in question) are reckoned at constant producers' prices (excluding turnover tax).

The index of production value makes use of prices in trying to indicate the mass, or quantity, of material goods. The nation's economy gives rise to the production of the most highly variegated material goods: furniture and tractors, shoes and coal, &c. The production of each one of such articles can be expressed in terms of natural units of measure: e.g. we can say how many tons of steel, pairs of shoes, or calories worth of coal we have produced. But it is impossible, in practice, to measure the combined quantity of a highly heterogeneous collection of goods otherwise than by indices of production volume expressed in forints.

It follows that the use of this index in planning and in the presentation of statistics has undoubted justification. The study of many other indices is necessary in addition in analysing and planning the quantitative contours of production, but study of the course of total production and of finished production is clearly indispensable. (Even for purposes of measurement this index must be used with due awareness of its imperfections.)

However, we are not here interested in the role of the index of production value as a measure, but rather in an altogether different question. What part does this index play in the process of the central direction of production in enterprises, through either stimulating or controlling it? For, at present, this index plays a crucial part in the production plans of enterprises; it is one of the two fundamental indices upon which premium payments are based.

It is the evident purpose of this index to stimulate enterprises to raise volumes of production. It is unquestionably successful in this respect. (We shall see on pp. 118–20 that the system of plans, of indices, and of premiums does exert a very powerful stimulus in the direction of raising the quantity of production.) As and when the authorities tighten this index from time to time, they impel enterprises to increase the quantities of goods they produce. Moreover, an indirect stimulus towards raising labour productivity and better utilization of the machine capacity of enterprises is generally exerted in this way.

Thus, this index has a favourable influence. At the same time, however, it must be realized that the index of production value can also be raised by methods other than the right and proper ones of raising actual production and productivity, or making better use of capacity. These other methods are the following:

1. The magnitude of the value of production is greatly influenced by the composition of production, or product-mix. The problem involved in this is widely known, and the story of it has been told very often. It has, by now, a large critical foreign and Hungarian literature. Yet, the scope of the problem remains undiminished, for all that. The plans prescribe certain forint sums that must be

attained by enterprises in the course of production. This sum can be fulfilled the more easily the more expensive, or 'forintful', the goods produced, and with more difficulty the cheaper they are. For example, in the Hungarian Posztó Factory one square metre of woollen cloth may yield anything between 20 and 100 forints in terms of production value. According to what the product-mix is, production values of enterprises can fluctuate to the extent of several hundred per cent., even if productivity and the degree of utilization of capacity are constant.

This characteristic of the index of production value leaves its imprint on planning. I mentioned in connexion with the annual plan[17] that the point of departure of planning at the directorate level is the production plan given in terms of natural units. For example: suppose that a total production of x square metres of worsted cloths has been decided upon at the directorate level in a given year. This quantity will be multiplied by an average price based on the average price of the actual product-mix of the previous year. This gives the value of the finished product in this industry. But what if this does not suffice to cover the sum appearing in the national economic plan as representing the share of total industrial or light industrial production value falling to be covered by this particular field of industry? The cry then becomes: 'raise the average price'—that is (prices being fixed), transform the planned product-mix in the direction of goods of higher value. At the time of the preparation of the 1956 plan, for example, requests to do just this arose in a number of fields.

There are two possible ways of attaining a higher average price. Either enterprises devote more labour to production; that is, products are made more elaborate so that wages costs are raised. Or, the materials used per unit of output can be increased in value or quantity. Possibly the two methods can be used in conjunction. In any event the higher production values obtainable by raising average prices constitute an incentive for the National Planning Office, the Ministry, and the directorates to try to shift product-mixes in the direction of more valuable goods, i.e. products containing more labour, more materials, or more expensive materials.

A further consideration relating to this stage of planning is that the plan of the product-mix is influenced by the so-called 'optique' of the plan relating to labour. Here the two methods of raising average prices which have just been described act in opposite ways. The more highly priced and valuable the articles manufactured by an enterprise, and the higher their raw material content (given the size of the labour force and the wage bill), the 'better' the indices of the labour plan (production value per hour worked, production value per 100 forints of wages, &c.) will look. In other words, 'productivity

[17] On p. 3.

improves'—without the least change having occurred in the performance of enterprises. Conversely, if product-mixes are shifted towards articles having higher wage costs, then all these indices will 'deteriorate'.

The expression used above, the 'optique' of the plan, is a very character-istic one; the fact that it is frequently used in our economic parlance is not to be wondered at. It is an accurate reflection of an outlook which thinks of the course of indices, of their 'optique', rather than of actual economic results, as being of primary importance, even though the former only provide some-what inexact and often strongly distorted indications of the real processes of the economy. This fetishization of indices has permeated economic thinking in our country so strongly that it exerts a serious influence on the planning activities of industrial and economic bodies. (This fetishized outlook is further strengthened by certain amateurish manifestations of agitation in the field of economic policy. These suggest that the values of indices of this kind must constantly increase, under all circumstances and in every field, for otherwise something must be wrong. Yet no such rule can be valid.) Serious battles are often fought over securing the acceptance of plans which prescribe reduc-tions of production value (say, because product-mixes are to be shifted towards cheaper articles), or falls in productivity indices (because articles having lower raw material content are to be produced).

Naturally, what matters most to top managements is that they should be able to fulfil their plans. If their plans are framed to prescribe lower production val-ues than in a previous period, managements will find nothing objectionable about this from their own point of view. However, there is a certain moral pressure which weighs not only upon higher authorities but on individual enterprises as well; it gives them a bad name if 'their production diminishes' or if their 'labour productivity' stagnates at a given level. For this reason enter-prises are happier with plans which shift their product-mixes towards articles having a higher raw material content, for they can then boast of 'results' which are easy to come by: production will tend to grow and productivity to rise.

So far we have considered only the process of drawing up plans: but their execution is also affected. Once enterprises have been given their targets of production value, their interest is to overfulfil them by as much as possible, for their premiums will grow correspondingly.[18] It is, therefore, in their interest to modify their programmes, so far as is possible, in the direction of producing

---

[18] There are (in 1956) numerous measures in force in light industry designed to limit the overful-filment of plans. But this is an exceptional state of affairs. It is, after all, a characteristic feature of our system of planning that its intention is to provide ample incentives for overfulfilling production plans. (In other branches of the economy, i.e. outside light industry, this, in fact, remained so even in 1956.)

more expensive articles having higher raw material content. This tendency is strengthened by the fact that permitted wages funds and man-power establishments are strictly limited and controlled from the centre; top managements have an important stake, financially speaking, in observing economy in their use. On top of this, the more expensive types of raw material are more often than not technically easier to work up (e.g. when better cotton is used there are fewer thread breakages, &c.) so that indices improve all the more with the use of these, and the positions of enterprises as regards wages are improved at the same time.

I have so far discussed the 'interests' and tendencies evoked and encouraged by this index. The question of how far these tendencies can gain actual expression raises a different issue.

Calculations showing changes in the share of materials in costs tell us little about this. For costs are reckoned at current prices and wages, and these have changed several times in the last few years. Hence, comparisons of data of this type provide no real basis for coming to any conclusions on this point.

All the same, experience shows that, in practice, the tendency to be drawn towards articles making heavy use of materials can hardly become effective in light industry. The reasons for this are as follows:

First and foremost, there is the shortage of materials, and our difficult foreign trading position. The desire to shift product-mixes towards more expensive articles making heavier demands on materials is in vain: foreign currency and raw materials are not available in sufficient quantities.

Next, managements of enterprises are alone in having a direct financial interest (premiums, &c.) in the fulfilment of plans. In this respect, anyway, the industrial directorates are in a position to assess the true national economic interest in a more disinterested and objective manner, since they, at any rate, do not have premiums providing them with direct incentives to raise the raw material content of production. (As we have seen, however, industrial directorates are not entirely free from bias either. In any case the comparatively disinterested directorates are responsible for making up detailed programmes, which in turn determine product-mixes.)

Further, the nature of the orders placed by commerce are an additional limiting factor on the possibility of arbitrary decisions being made in this matter in industrial enterprises.

It may be asked, in the light of the foregoing, whether it is worth wasting so much breath on this problem in view of the great strength of the forces acting against the tendency we are considering? The answer to that is 'yes', and this for a number of reasons.

First, planning is complicated by it, even in the circumstances referred to in the foregoing. For example, as I have already said, attempts to secure a 'raising of average prices' were made in 1956. Soon afterwards it was discovered that the plan was excessively ambitious, and that for the reason just mentioned, as well as others, it had to be scaled down. (The Ministry for Light Industry had come to the conclusion that the average prices used in arriving at production values in the 1956 plan were too high. This was also revealed by study of the detailed requirements of commerce. For this last reason alone it became necessary to effect a reduction of 80 million forints in the target figure of production value appearing in the annual plan of light industry.) Moreover, even if the tendency we are considering here cannot prevail generally, it can come to the surface partially in individual fields, at particular enterprises, and in relation to particular products.

Thus the Chief Planning Division of the Ministry of Domestic Commerce reports that light industry is reluctant to produce a number of articles on the ground that they require too much labour, thus worsening indices of labour productivity, and are 'not bringing in enough forints'. Such articles include: certain types of coloured woven flannels, checkered buckram canvas, pure shantung silk, pure silk twill, print matelassé, 'Diana' woollen cloths, 'Rába' trousers for young 'pioneers', men's zipper jackets, good quality clothes-hangers.

These articles are either programmed in insufficient quantities by light industry from the very outset or else enterprises show themselves reluctant to enter into contracts involving these items. Hence there is a shortage of these goods. Incidentally, the Ministry's report is confined to articles, shortages in which are primarily due to holding back connected with 'unfavourable indices'. Causes of a real, tangible character (like shortages of capacity or materials) are not involved in these shortages.

Secondly, the forces counteracting the tendency we are discussing are not of a necessary character: they may weaken or even cease altogether. For example, it is imaginable that the raw material supply position might improve a great deal. Indeed, every effort should be made to bring this about. In that event— assuming that powerful financial incentives continue to attach to bringing about increases in production value—the existing tendency to produce articles of greater raw material content would suddenly express itself much more strongly.

Thirdly, expressions of this tendency would increase even more if a hybrid type of reform which at present enjoys the support of many people in light industry were adopted. The proposed reform would have the effect of leaving the whole present-day set-up of planning and administering the economy intact—with enterprises continuing to be under an obligation to fulfil production plans and, indeed, having an incentive to overfulfil them. However, they would be given a much freer hand in making up their detailed programmes and determining their product-mixes. It is clear from the foregoing analysis that half-hearted reforms of this kind may do more harm than good. The tendency under discussion here—the propensity to shift production towards articles requiring more materials—is perhaps least noticeable in light industry because it is here that centralization has been carried to its greatest lengths and is much stronger here than in the machinery industry, for example. It is this difference that would be removed if enterprises were simply given a freer hand in constructing their programmes, without this being linked with other changes of a far-reaching character. Hence it would contribute to an accentuation of the harmful tendency for the product-mix to be shifted in an unbalanced manner (and this all the more, if it were associated with an improvement in the raw material supply position).

2. It is necessary to mention a different problem in connexion with this question of articles 'bringing in forints'. Of two articles making equal demands on materials and labour, and having identical costs, one can 'bring in more forints' than another—if it shows a higher profit. It is clear that enterprises or branches of industry can produce more 'production value' with a given amount of effort if their programmes contain articles carrying higher profit margins.

Nevertheless, top managements are not particularly interested in the profits to be had on particular articles. This indifference on the part of enterprises is not due solely to the fact that top managements have no worthwhile financial incentives to increase profits. It also results from the fact that the difference in profit between articles does not amount to much from the angle of production value either, since in most cases it is merely a matter of differences of 1–2–3 per cent, or, perhaps exceptionally, of 5–10 per cent. This matters precious little compared to the fact that the inclusion in the programme of an article made of more expensive raw materials can mean a two-to fivefold increase in 'forints coming in'. Price variations of articles due to differences in profits are completely dwarfed by this! In fact, when the object is to step up production value by changing the product-mix, the question of whether some commodity 'brings more forints' on account of higher profits, as against higher costs, is never even gone into, as a distinct question. The profits on the articles which are to be fitted into programmes are not even considered at the directorates in the course of planning.

It is necessary to lay some stress on this, because in discussions of the distorting influence exercised by the index of production value, it is often said that this is a question of price. In my view, however, this is not a question of price at all, or else it is that to a very limited extent only. Our system of prices does give rise to many difficulties, as is well known. But these difficulties are distinct from the problems presented by the production value indices in the plans of enterprises. The state of affairs in which firms or industrial subgroups can attain higher production values by turning out articles having a higher raw material content would persist, even if the price system were different.

3. 'Production value' will go up if division of labour between firms is artificially increased. This, too, is a well-known problem, especially as it appears in the machinery industry. In light industry the problem has, to all intents and purposes, been solved. I have already referred to the introduction of the measure of accumulated production value within the enterprise, or 'corrected production value', and, since quite recently, premium payments are being based on this. On this measure it is always necessary to add the value of the staple, characteristic semi-manufactures of enterprises to the value of their finished outputs when arriving at their total production. The value of semi-manufactures must be added in, irrespectively of whether they are worked up further within an enterprise, or sold. Hence, enterprises no longer have an interest in artificially and superfluously raising the degree of their interdependence with other firms.

This system of measurement has been introduced in every branch of light industry in which the problem arose. It has, generally, succeeded.[19]

It may be noted that in many other fields of industry this method provides no solution. It can only be applied where there is comparatively little vertical integration, and what there is of it has to be stable, as in textiles: yarn—greycloth—finished cloth, or, e.g. in metallurgy, where the position is similar. But in the pharmaceutical industry, for example, the problem is insoluble. For in that industry inter-firm dealings are on a very extensive scale. Every factory produces hundreds of articles of different kinds. These are both finished and semi-finished products and the degree and direction of interdependence between firms is in constant flux. There are no staple lines of semi-finished products. Thus, except for light industry (and some other trades) there are

---

[19] The introduction of this index has been under discussion in light industry for some time. See, for example, the article by Sándor Fülöp, 'The measurement of production volume in enterprises of the textile industry', *Iparstatisztikai Értesítő*, May 1954). In that article the author recommended that the main index used for measuring the volume of production in the textile industry be based on measurements of accumulated production value within enterprises.

many fields of industry in which this fault persists—the index of production value operates so as to promote a superfluous volume of interdependent production among firms.

Even in those branches of industry in which the perfected index does function, it remains possible to get around it to some extent. If an enterprise is behindhand with its plan for finished products it can make up for this by manufacturing more yarn or grey cloth within the period of the plan. It can secure the fulfilment of the accumulated production plan, and thus its premium, by producing the constituents of the final product in amounts out of proportion to each other and to the plan. Indeed, it is not even necessary to produce more yarn or grey cloth in the course of a 'finishing spurt' of this kind—it will usually suffice to go ahead with the more expensive, 'forint bringing' varieties alone. Actions of this kind do not alter results by very much, but they can certainly yield 2–3 per cent., and this is sometimes just the amount by which production is short of its planned amount. Hence the remark of one chief of a planning department, concerning the accumulated production plan: 'The gaps in the regulations are there to enable one to dodge them'. In general, as soon as a new index or regulation is adopted, with the intention of putting a stop to one dodge, several new dodges are promptly invented.

4. It is also possible to 'juggle' to the tune of a few per cent, by manipulating stocks of semi-finished products and work in progress. For example, in the leather trade, permitted outlays on wages and salaries are related to total production. If, therefore, enterprises run into trouble over these outlays towards the end of the plan period, the way out is for them to dump large amounts of raw hides into tanks for soaking. In an hour they can throw as much as two wagonfuls into their tanks and these hides immediately appear in total production as work in progress. Net value added is practically nil, but the material thrown into the dipper instantly assumes a value equal to 75 per cent, of that of finished leather for the purposes of reckoning total production. It is true that a regulation now exists according to which the 'input plan' (i.e. the plan which prescribes the amount of raw hides to be fed into the production process in a given period of time) must not be exceeded by more than 2 per cent. This prevents major abuses at the price of a fresh restriction, but it still leaves scope for minor abuses, for it is often just this missing 1 or 2 per cent, that must be forthcoming if wages funds are not to be overstepped and if plans are to be fulfilled.

5. Finally, it is also possible to raise production values simply by producing unnecessary products. All that is required for a product to be 'reported finished' is that the factory MEO accept it, and that it be put in storage with

other finished products. Whether consumers want the product or not is a matter of complete indifference from this point of view. If a product is later found to be faulty, or of poor quality, then a corresponding price reduction will be deducted from future production value at that time. But if the article happens not to be faulty (i.e. is free of defects in materials and in workmanship) and is nevertheless not wanted by anybody, then this has no consequences. It does not affect the fact that it will be counted as part of the 'production value' credited to the enterprise concerned.

In what ways can production of unwanted articles arise?

(*a*) From time to time enterprises will produce articles in respect of which they have no contracts; possibly, they may overfulfil their plan in articles, the excess production of which was not contracted for. There was a time when this matter was dealt with fairly liberally, with the consequence that excess production of articles was a frequent occurrence. Nowadays a strict instruction prohibits the production of anything in light industry that has not been contracted for. In some fields this is taken into account in connexion with the payment of premiums.

This, however, is not an ideal solution, and should at the most be regarded as a necessary evil, for it implies yet another restriction of a rigid character. Let us take a capitalist factory for comparison. Much of the capitalist's production was in fulfilment of orders. But if he saw fit (e.g. so as to use capacity more fully, to achieve longer runs, or steadier working, &c.) he would also produce, in the absence of orders, for his own stock. This, however, he did at his own risk. If he succeeded in selling at a good price, he did well out of it—if he got left with the goods, then sooner or later he had to sell at low prices and made a loss. With us, in former days, when this problem was not yet taken seriously, the chief trouble was not that an enterprise could produce even if it had no contract to do so, but that it was able to do this without incurring any financial risk. In determining production value and premium payments products were valued at the same price irrespectively of whether or not they were adapted to what was in demand.

(*b*) Frequently, the products of industry turn out to be unwanted because they are not of a prescribed standard of quality, or of the desired variety, or because they do not meet an agreed delivery date. (Frequently commerce, the recipient of the goods, is ready to make concessions in such cases, for reasons to be discussed presently.)

(*c*) Demand may have changed since the date of authorization of plans and the placing of contracts, but industry may have refused to consent to modifying its programme. (This has already been discussed on p. 24.)

(*d*) In some cases industry can force commerce to sign contracts for certain articles even when the latter would not wish to do so. The Central Arbitration Committee has made decisions in such a sense more than once. This will occur, for example, if some article had figured in the annual statement of requirements put out by the Ministry of Domestic Commerce,[20] and had been correspondingly taken into the production plan of the Ministry of Light Industry. In such cases commercial enterprises are made to sign contracts, even if they do not themselves wish to place orders. A similar position exists in regard to products which figure in the commodity balance sheets prepared by the National Planning Office[21] or in the industrial plans authorized by the Council of Ministers. The distributive trades can be compelled to take these products even if, in their own view, there is no need for them.

(*e*) In fulfilling export orders factories often produce excessive 'safety reserves'. In fulfilling an export order for, say, 100 pairs of shoes, a factory will produce 120 pairs for safety's sake, so that, in the event of some of the shoes turning out to be of imperfect quality, it can still meet the order in full. The surplus is called the 'safety reserve'. Thus these are goods against which no orders have been placed. It is not at all certain that there will be a demand for them, either at home or abroad. Especially in textiles, foreign requirements (e.g. the orders of Far Eastern and African countries) differ drastically from what is acceptable to our own tastes here at home. In these articles the safety reserves are simply unsaleable. Moreover, these reserves are frequently very sizeable; they are greatly in excess of what would be warranted by technical considerations alone.

Naturally, a number of factors damp and limit the tendency towards the production of unwanted goods. One of these is the conscientiousness and sense of responsibility of top managements. The financial and credit systems work in the same direction. If, for example, stocks of finished products accumulate at the enterprise level, this gives rise to financial problems; credits must be obtained to finance excess stocks, &c.

Now, how serious is this whole problem?[22]

---

[20] This is used in preparing the annual plan of light industry.

[21] Commodity balance sheets are planned input–output tables prepared for major materials and finished products.

[22] Two important and instructive articles on this topic have appeared in economic journals. One is the article by Miklós Somogyvári 'On the unnecessary products of industry and its unsold stocks', *Statisztikai Szemle*, May 1955. The other is the article by Sándor Gergely and Vilmos Wesely, 'Unsold stocks: an important reserve of raw materials', *Közgazdasági Szemle*, Feb. 1956. Both articles contain interesting analyses of the causes of the emergence of unwanted products and of unsold stocks, and provide a wealth of data from the field of light industry among others.

It is difficult to give an unqualified answer. The notion of 'unwanted prod-ucts' is a relative one. A product will be unwanted—at a particular price; if the price of an unsold product is drastically cut it is generally possible to dis-pose of it sooner or later. Again, a product may be unwanted from the point of view of immediate sale-ability; but in the course of a year or two it may be possible to get rid of it, albeit with much difficulty. Moreover, in the event of a shortage of goods developing it may be quite easy to find customers who will accept it.

Unsold stocks can accumulate in other ways besides those I have already listed. They may simply reflect bad estimates of requirements, or ill-advised orders on the part of the distributive trades. This adds to the difficulty of assess-ing the extent of this problem. The volume of stocks of finished products laid up in factory warehouses is, in general, comparatively small. Unwanted prod-ucts mostly get into the hands of wholesalers, and possibly also into those of retailers. So-called specialist warehousing enterprises are particularly favoured dumping grounds of such products. As these are administered by the pro-ducing ministries, goods can be freely transferred to them from the factories. And this is worth doing, for unsaleable, or hardly saleable stocks of goods will attract less notice if left to lie for a long time at specialist warehous-ing enterprises, rather than at the factories themselves. Incidentally, the fact that warehousing enterprises only pay 0·5 per cent, interest while factories pay 3 per cent., itself makes it worth-while to dump these articles on to the former.

Let us consider just one figure which indicates the proportions of this prob-lem. It is well known that by the end of 1955 and the beginning of 1956 stocks of clothing had assumed a very swollen state.[23]

Now, according to estimates of experts in the distributive trades, 15 per cent, of these stocks can, on average, be regarded as 'unsaleable'. There is no way of going further and establishing what part of this originated in mis-takes of industry, as a result of bad planning methods, as against the part due to faulty ordering of the distributive trades, or other causes. Of course, even these articles are saleable if sufficient price reductions are made. But such price reductions mean reduced State revenues as compared with ordi-nary sales, since a part of the turnover tax on these articles will not, in fact, be collected, and some articles may even have to be sold at a sizeable loss. This, however, is of no concern to enterprises, for, upon completion of their pro-duction programmes, they will already have received the full producers' price

---

[23] Cf. Tables XXVIII and XXIX, pp. 148–9 below, showing data which illustrate this.

for such articles. They will already have included them at these prices in the 'production value' they have been responsible for, and indeed may even have *over*fulfilled their plans by this means.

In the aggregate, such 'unwanted products' are clearly not a large part of production in light industry: they probably amount to a few per cent. only. But, as with stocks of unfinished goods, or distortions of product-mixes, in this case also the attainment of 100 per cent, and thus of the premium frequently turns on just these few percentage points.

Two things follow from the analysis so far made of the index of production value.

One is that there are a number of methods, or tricks, for raising production value by one or two and indeed occasionally more percentage points, and this in ways which not only fail to connote a real improvement in the work of enterprises, but may even do damage to the national economy. This in itself suffices to make it irrational to employ a planning and premium system which makes a fetish of the 100 per cent, fulfilment of plans of production value. It is quite possible that enterprises attaining 100 per cent, work no better, but are merely 'cleverer' than those attaining 98 per cent.

The second point which emerges is this: production value is no longer the dominating index number these days, but it is still one of the two crucial indices to which payment of premiums attaches. (In branches of industry other than light industry this is so to an even greater extent, for in these, premiums are also attached to overfulfilment of the index. Moreover, in light industry itself, the arrangement by which no premiums are paid for overfulfilment is evidently no more than temporary.) This is a harmful state of affairs. For the index of production value does not merely instruct enterprises to perform what the national economy and society really do demand of them—it also, and unavoidably, provides incentives in directions which are harmful. For this reason, while it is possible to make use of this index in the practice of planning, its dominating role must, in my opinion, undoubtedly be ended. To attach decisive financial incentives to this index is, in my view, wrong.

The production plan by commodities or programme

The function of the production plan by commodities is to secure that enterprises really do make available the use values required by the country's economy besides fulfilling the plan in terms of forints. Two problems arise in connexion with this part of the plan.

One is: how detailed should this plan be? Should it lay down the tasks to be performed in terms of broad commodity groups containing several dozens or perhaps several hundreds of individual products (e.g. worsted cloths), or should it prescribe the actual article in fully specified detail (e.g. 'Oslo' cloth)?

The more minutely detailed the breakdown of actual production programmes prescribed by plans, the more unambiguous they are, but they correspondingly fetter enterprises more. If, in the example just given, a factory in the wool textile trade is asked to make x square metres of 'Oslo' cloth—then this is a completely unambiguous instruction, and the enterprise cannot shirk this task. Nor, on the other hand, can it produce something else instead, even if its own special characteristics, the wishes of its distributors, and the raw material position all made the production of a different article desirable.

Yet this last can happen in practice. However well industrial directorates may know the enterprises belonging to them—they can never know them as well as do the men working in the enterprises themselves. A directorate, in deciding upon programmes itself, is undoubtedly in a better position to survey the situation as a whole than its separate enterprises are. And this has great advantages. If enterprises dealt separately with their customers, orders would become more fragmented. As things are, the directorate, acting as a sort of joint marketing agency, is in a position to bulk these orders into larger lots. Having knowledge of detailed product-mixes, it can also ration out scarce materials more exactly. But I must repeat that these advantages are coupled with serious disadvantages. The operational efficiency of directorates is not such at the present time as to enable them to rival the day-to-day managements of factories in making reliable estimates of their specific capabilities (i.e. their technical equipments, expert staff, experience in various lines, &c.).

In constructing the programmes, directorates do not, in present circumstances, have the time or the opportunity to make an analysis, by individual articles, of the costs of each factory in producing them, and of what the most economic distribution of the product-mix may be.

The allocation of products to enterprises is decided in the light of their established pattern of specialization. In this process, technical characteristics are weighed up with a certain amount of care, but other economically relevant considerations are not examined comprehensively. Nor can this be held against the directorates: the central elaboration of detailed programmes for a whole branch of industry is such an enormous job that, given the present-day working methods of the authorities, matters of detail must necessarily go by the board.[24] In any event, the result is that programmes frequently force enterprises to turn out articles for the production of which they are ill suited, and for which they could substitute others in regard to which they are well placed—these latter products being, at the same time, at least as acceptable to their customers as the prescribed ones are.

What would happen if plans in respect of individual commodities were framed in a much broader way, e.g. in terms of commodity groups? (This, incidentally, is what happens outside light industry in several other branches of industry, e.g. in many parts of the machine-making industry.)

The answer depends on what assumption is made about the mechanism of the economy in other respects. If everything apart from this one change continued as before, then it is possible that the increased independence of enterprises in shaping their programmes would be associated with the emergence or strengthening of a series of harmful tendencies. For example, enterprises might go in for the 'cream' among articles and push the production of those which have the highest content of raw materials (so as to attain high production values more easily, and to make a better showing with their wages funds), or they may concentrate on those which are technically the least trouble, or on those which lend themselves best to cost-reductions, &c. In general, the harmful tendencies I discussed in connexion with the index of production value—which are at present partly counterbalanced by the detailed character of programmes—would be strengthened. This striving of enterprises towards some articles and their tendency to shy away from others would frequently fail to correspond to the real course of demand and to the needs of society.

Thus, within our present economic mechanism serious disadvantages attach both to very minutely strict programmes and to much looser and less specific commodity plans. Of these two sets of evils, the first set has been chosen in light industry—and it is not possible to say which is in fact the lesser evil. It must be conceded that the path chosen in light industry is at least consistent, and carries the logic of centralization through to its ultimate consequences. In any event, the fact that both alternatives involve serious disadvantages does show that this problem also derives from the inner contradictions of our present-day economic mechanism. Inner contradictions of this kind can be mitigated even within the present set-up, but a true resolution of them requires

---

[24] In some Western countries use is made in economic analysis of certain mathematical methods—known as linear programming—for the solution of problems of this kind. These methods are, however, not used in the practise of planning here.

that the economic mechanism which lies at the root of these contradictions should itself be improved by being overhauled in a comprehensive manner.

The second problem connected with plans by commodities is the question of units of measure. (This is, of course, much less important than the former problem.) In light industry, the production plan by commodities generally defines tasks to be done in terms of natural units of measure. This often opens the way to various anomalous tendencies. For example, in the various branches of the textile trade the plan of yarn production is laid down in terms of tons. This provides enterprises with an incentive to manufacture a thicker yarn of low count, so far as is possible—even though this may conflict with the interests of the economy as a whole. The plans for production of sacks, of knitwear, and of paper are also fixed in terms of tons. Here, again, incentives exist for producing heavier sacks, knitwear of larger sizes, thicker paper, &c., so far as may be possible.

The index of adherence to plans

The name here is not a very happy one: the purpose of the index is to provide incentives for keeping enterprises to their prescribed product-mixes.[25]

This index raises the same problems as does the plan by commodities. Enterprises could pursue a comparatively flexible policy in regard to production if the index of adherence to plans were calculated with respect to broad commodity groups, or (what comes to the same thing) if the required degree of adherence to plans were only 70–75 per cent, rather than 90–97 per cent, as

[25] Plan fulfilment is measured by the following method:

Name of article	Prescribed plan figure	Actual production	Allowable for calculating adherence to plan
A	2,100	2,300	2,100
B	800	600	600
C	2,400	2,800	2,400
D	—	600	—
E	—	500	—
Total	5,300	6,800	5,100

In this case adherence to plan is 5,100÷5,300 = 96·2 per cent. In other words, in this calculation the value of actual production over a given period is aggregated in such a way that any excess of the value of production of articles specified in the programme over the prescribed amounts, as well as the value of production of articles which do not appear in the programme, is deducted from the value of the actual total. The sum thus obtained, expressed as a percentage of the planned production value of finished articles, gives 'the degree of adherence to plan.'

is the case at present. In this case, however, the production plans by individual articles, i.e. the programmes, would have little effective binding force, since enterprises would be able to make up any shortfalls in their production of particular articles by overfulfilling their output of other articles within the same commodity group. The broader, and less specific, the commodity groups serving as the basis of the index of adherence to plans, the more its significance dwindles towards being of merely formal importance. (This is in fact the case in some fields outside light industry, e.g. in the pharmaceutical industry.)

What is measured in light industry is really the degree of adherence to programmes, since the index has to be calculated on the basis of the fully specified detail of output. On top of this a very high degree of adherence to programmes, amounting in most fields to 90–97 per cent., is demanded as the qualification for premium payments. This certainly provides a strong incentive towards disciplined fulfilment of programmes, but it imparts a great deal of rigidity to the work of enterprises. It also gives rise to some definitely harmful tendencies, of which I shall mention two.

One of them is 'adherence to plans'—*at all costs.* As this is a part-condition for the receipt of premiums, production spurts towards the end of plan periods are concerned with the observance of indices of adherence to plan, as well as with targets in terms of production value. Thus if, for example, a factory making woollen cloth sees that it has still to polish off one or two further articles if it is to fulfil the prescribed degree of adherence to plans, then, in the 'finishing stretch' there will be a rush to produce the missing articles, even at the cost of removing from machines whatever material happens to be in process of being worked upon—and this even in circumstances when customers are in no particular hurry and could be left to wait. But such a switch will raise costs, since it involves rendering machines idle, increasing waste, &c.

In most branches of industry the exact detail of what is demanded in regard to adherence to plans depends on the number of distinct articles an enterprise has to produce. For example, in the woollen industry an enterprise manufacturing five articles is required to adhere to plans to the extent of 97 per cent.; another, making thirty, is asked to attain 94 per cent. This easement of 3 per cent, is far from being proportional to the increased difficulty of holding to a programme exactly in the course of making a number of articles which is six times greater. For this reason the index of adherence to plans provides enterprises with an incentive to strive to narrow their range of production as much as possible, even when this is harmful to the interests of consumers.

Quality indices

As is well known, a high proportion of products is graded according to quality. This is done in two distinct ways: first, via production plans, and second via methods of recording results achieved.

(i) In some branches of industry a minimum proportion of first-class products appears as one of the approved plan indices. (Possibly, the maximum proportion of fourth-class and even lower-grade products will also be prescribed.) In some fields the fulfilment of these 'quality indices' is a condition for the receipt of premiums.

(ii) Factories are bound to reduce prices on second, third, &c., class articles on a predetermined scale. (For example, third-class woollen cloth costs 15 per cent, less than first-class cloth.) This is called 'marking down'. In calculating production value, articles of lower grades must be reckoned in at these reduced prices.[26]

The view that the foregoing methods are sufficient to stimulate enterprises to improve quality is pretty widely held. It is thought that the quality of an article is sufficiently expressed in the grading I have mentioned, i.e. by whether the article is first or third class.

In my opinion this view is false. However, in order to rebut it, the question of what is to be meant by this concept of the quality of a product must be examined more closely.[27]

In part, the quality of a product depends on the material used and the amount of work expended on it. For example, the quality of woollen cloth will be better the higher its content of live wool and the less refuse wool and 'synthetic fibre' there is in it. A shoe will be better if more work is spent on making it, if time is devoted to adding decorations and finishing touches to it. A product which is better for such reasons will evidently also cost more.

---

[26] Products count as finished when factory MEOs have received them; any mark-downs resulting from quality control activities within enterprises can, therefore, still be taken into account in valuing output under current plans. But in cases when complaints originate with purchasers, any consequent price-reductions—or deductions of the full price in the case of returned articles—can no longer be effected in retrospect, so as to diminish production value of a past period of manufacture. It is customary, instead, to reduce the production value reckoned for the current plan period by the amount involved.

[27] The present study does not go into the problems of producers' prices in any detail. But at this point, and in a few other places in this study, certain aspects of our price system must unavoidably be touched upon.

However, other quality differences, which are unrelated to varying amounts of inputs having been devoted to a product, but depend exclusively on its utility, also exist.

The system of grading by quality referred to in the foregoing is designed to take account of one aspect of differences of this latter kind. The system of grading is based on so-called quality standards. The standards define certain objectively measurable technical characteristics of a commodity: e.g. the tear resistance and thickness of weave of cloths, &c. In the course of the grading process, special attention is paid to faults in technical execution and in materials, e.g. in the case of shoes, to scratches on the leather, or perhaps to quite small differences in the sizes of identical component parts of the left and right shoe, &c.

The significance of the quality standards upon which the grading process is based is precisely that its criteria for judging quality are objective and measurable technical characteristics.

It would be wrong to overrate the degree of objectivity of even this kind of judgement of quality. There is much arbitrariness in it. Thus, when improvement of quality is the order of the day, because agitational activity or some resolution of the government has placed great emphasis upon it—then the MEOs become more strict, only to slacken off and become gradually more liberal later, until the next campaign. A given article is correspondingly sometimes reckoned to be of better and sometimes to be of worse quality.

In any event, a system of grading based on these quality standards is necessarily one-sided, for the subjective judgement of the buyer always has a very important part to play in the evaluation of quality.

Let us consider these subjective elements in turn. First of all, where consumer goods are concerned, aesthetic requirements, like the need for pleasing form, colour, design, and fashionable execution or style, will always count for a great deal. Yet tastes vary; there exist no 'objective' criteria here on which it would be possible to base standards for use in grading.

Nor is this a matter of aesthetics alone. There is the question of usefulness in the widest sense of the word. Let us take two slippers, for example. Suppose both to have been made of identical materials with an equal degree of care; both are flawless, 'first class'. Yet a buyer will not consider them to be of the same quality if he finds one to be more comfortable than the other. In the slipper example it is sufficiently obvious that every purchaser will consider the question of comfortableness of fit when buying. But the criterion need not always be as unambiguous as this. For the usefulness of an article is mostly very much bound up with circumstances, i.e. with the precise use to which the article is intended to be put by the purchaser. Suppose, for example, that two women both buy printed summer cotton frocks. One of them wants to wear hers at work and therefore attaches importance to its being durable, i.e. to its having great resistance to wear and tear, &c. The other woman intends to use hers for beach-wear and sport, during a single season only, and therefore requires principally that the frock be colour-fast, light, &c. It is possible that the same dress will be felt to be 'good' by one and 'bad' by the other woman. The first woman will, in fact, attach importance to certain objective qualities prescribed by the standards (e.g. a specified degree of tear resistance), but for the other these will be fairly unimportant.

Quality grading does provide consumers with something to go on; it can prevent their being deceived in regard to such characteristics of the product as they are unable to judge reliably at sight (e.g. durability, &c.). Nevertheless, it is the consumer's own subjective wants that weigh most with him and he will gladly buy an article he likes, even if it should, for example, be second class. (This, moreover, independently of the reduced price, which will often not even be noticed!) Every salesman engaged in the distributive trades will confirm that the first thing a customer considers is whether a piece of cloth appeals to the eye, what it feels like to touch, and to grip it, whether a suit fits, whether a shoe is comfortable, and so on. He will be much less concerned about small faults in the weave or small scratches on the leather.

It must not be thought that there is no scope for subjective judgements outside the consumer goods field (although it is naturally true that they play most part in that field). When, for example, a productive enterprise judges the quality of a raw material, it is again not a matter of going by quality requirements, all of which are eternally valid and fixed once and for all. Rather, it is a matter of enterprises going by their own 'subjective' requirements: things will turn on what enterprises themselves want to manufacture and to achieve by their use of a material.

An actual case reported by the management of the enterprise Tannimpex, which is engaged in foreign trade in leather and footwear, is very characteristic in this connexion.

The West German leather factory by the name of Freudenberg is renowned the world over. Its finished leathers are counted among the best in the world market. There have, however, been occasions when consignments from that factory have been classed as 'sub-standard' on the basis of our grades. The leathers of the Freudenberg factory excel, among other things, by virtue of their beautiful colours—of which no grading system can of course take account.

This example shows that it is not possible to use technical criteria which are fixed once and for all for arriving at judgements concerning the quality even of such a raw material as leather. In the case just cited, our inspection staffs did not give sufficient weight to the aesthetic qualities of the material nor, generally, to the question of how it would shape up in the course of working on it and making something out of it. They judged instead by rigid and probably excessively strict standards.

To sum up: the quality of a product is an exceedingly complex concept. It depends partly on the quality of inputs expended on making the product, but is partly independent of this. It is partly capable of being measured by 'objective criteria'—and partly not measurable. Objective and subjective elements are intertwined in any evaluation of it.

We may now pose the question of how far our system of plan index numbers is sensitive to the various aspects of quality which have just been discussed. How far do our production plans provide a stimulus in the direction of improving quality?

1. Products incorporating costlier materials or more skilled workmanship, and thus costing more, must, according to the rules, carry higher producers' prices.[28] Thus in this case production value will be raised. A brief reminder of what has been said before[29] in this connexion is appropriate here. On the one hand, enterprises have an interest in making improvements in quality of a kind which are based on the use of more expensive materials. However, opportunities for actually doing this are very limited. On the other hand, enterprises are definitely averse to increasing labour input per unit of output as a method of raising the quality of products. In any case, they do not have much say in these matters, since it is the industrial directorates, and not enterprises themselves, that make up the programmes of enterprises.

---

[28] Even this is not quite so simple in practice. Our system of producers' prices does not reflect actual input differences in a sufficiently differentiated manner. Products which count as individual 'concrete articles' for the purposes of the Unified Product and Price List (e.g. welted women's shoes with chrome soles and box-calf uppers) actually contain entire groups of numerous different articles (i.e. different shoes). These may vary in style, finish, &c. But according to the Unified Product and Price List individual 'concrete articles' may only have a single, uniform price. Consequently, enterprises have an interest in providing, for this price, whatever variety of the concrete article in question is flimsiest, and requires least by way of inputs, while still answering to the specifications prescribed in the Unified Product and Price List for shoes of the type under consideration.

The lack of price variation by individual models—and generally, the fact that our price system is insufficiently differentiated—provides a real temptation to indulge in hidden price increases, for it tempts enterprises to make products of relatively poorer quality at a given price.

[29] On pp. 27–42.

2. Now consider quality differences of articles costing the same to produce, but having varying utility. A part of these differences will be reflected in prices, namely, those which are capable of being measured by the quality standards which are used in the grading of products. As we have seen, mark-downs involve reductions in production values. This undoubtedly stimulates quality improvements in certain respects, primarily by penalizing faults in material and workmanship. They thus have beneficial effects to this extent.

3. The position is very different where quality differences which turn on subjective preferences are concerned. Individual judgements of quality made by consumers in the light of such preferences gain expression in the course taken by demand. However, in our system, producers' prices of light industrial products are entirely independent of the relationship which exists between supply and demand.[30] Consequently, these prices are completely insensitive to the subjective aspects of taste, even though it is precisely in light industry that these have especially great significance.

To sum up:

(i) The true course of change in regard to quality is not reflected adequately by the proportionate importance of first-, second-, and third-class products. Correspondingly, the indices of the quality of products described in the foregoing are one-sided in their operation, and the degree of their fulfilment reflects results in a one-sided manner. It is perfectly possible for the quality of articles to deteriorate in a broad sense (i.e. taking the factors mentioned in points 1, 2, and 3 above into joint consideration), while 'indices of quality' improve, and conversely. Hence, to view the course of quality changes primarily in the light of these 'indices of quality' is definitely misleading.

(ii) The incentives which are designed to lead to quality improvements are one-sided. They act in the direction of reducing faults in materials and workmanship—which is, in itself, desirable and useful. But

---

[30] We may here ignore the fact that, owing to the operation of a multiplicity of factors, net producers' prices can differ from costs in widely varying degrees, even though, according to the rules, net producers' price = costs plus 2 per cent. This much is certain: whatever the difference between price and cost it is not connected with the relationship of supply to demand. The distinct problem of the extent to which supply and demand affect consumers' prices is not examined in the present study. It is, in any case, clear that producers' prices are supposed to be entirely independent of consumers' prices.

they do not do anything to stimulate attainment of the broader, more comprehensive objective of satisfying consumers' preferences better. Yet the former requirement is only a part, and a subordinate one at that, of the latter.

Techno-economic indices

These are coefficients indicating either the level of technique or that of productivity attained in production (e.g. picks per machine hour in weaving mills, the proportion of hides dried on glass sheets in the leather industry) or techno-economic aspects of the product-mix (e.g. proportion of shoes having soles made of synthetic materials); or the use made of important inputs (e.g. materials used per unit of output). Such indices do, undoubtedly, represent a contribution to our statistics and our planning. They assist the central authorities in following and keeping a check on the levels of technique attained in individual enterprises and branches of industry; they facilitate the performance of certain calculations.

The question, however, is whether it is right to communicate these indices to enterprises as so many binding instructions? For at present the production plan of every enterprise contains a whole series of these techno-economic indices, and, in principle at least, their fulfilment is no less obligatory than the fulfilment of the other plan indices.

What needs to be said here first of all is that the business of prescribing some of these techno-economic indices, in the form of instructions, is simply superfluous. This because some indices are bound to be realized anyway. (For example, the proportion of shoes to be produced by assembly-line methods is compulsorily prescribed even for factories which are not in any case in a position to produce in any other way.) In other cases, the instructions are superfluous because the indices merely prescribe what their plans or programmes have already laid down for enterprises in a different form, and in terms of different figures. For example, a shoe factory will be instructed to devote a given proportion of its output to making shoes made of synthetic materials by means of a techno-economic index, even though this already emerges with unmistakable clarity from the programme.

All this side of the problem is comparatively trivial. Such obviously superfluous techno-economic indices can simply be dropped; or, more precisely, they can be taken account of in the statistics without being prescribed in advance in the form of a binding instruction.

Undoubtedly, however, other, more important techno-economic indices exist as well. The trouble with these is that they are often determined in a mechanical and hence unrealistic manner. Suppose, for example, that a techno-economic index laid down for a directorate is tighter by 3 per cent, than in a preceding period. The practice in such cases is for the directorate to fix this index, in the course of breaking it down among enterprises, at a level 3 per cent, tighter than the level actually achieved by them in the preceding period. This the directorate does in a uniform way, even though it is clear that the potentials of enterprises differ; moreover, the values of the techno-economic indicators are affected by current changes in the detail of product-mixes, and this also varies by enterprises.

With such methods of planning it is not to be wondered at that the plans of enterprises, their programmes, and their techno-economic indices do not always square with each other. This is another frequent ground for complaint at the enterprise level.

In its decree of 1954 concerning the simplification of planning, the Council of Ministers laid it down that: 'A state of affairs needs to be attained in which the indices hitherto appearing in plans for technical development become primarily a means of providing firmer foundations for production plans.'[31] There is, however, no question of this being the case in practice. Production plans and programmes are drawn up without any reference to technical indices, and are not based on them in any way. Production plans are drawn up by the planning divisions of directorates, and programmes by planning and trading divisions acting in collaboration. The technical divisions frequently work independently of these former divisions, and the process of reconciling their several figures may not take place until after the work of each is finished. (Even this does not always happen.) But it is also fairly common for the technical indices to be prepared by the planning division itself, which it does by simply calculating the figures from others already given in production plans and programmes. This, however, is the exact opposite of what the decree of the Council of Ministers enjoins.

As a result of all this, the directorates and the Ministry are frequently accused of 'bureaucratic administration' by many irate managers working on the economic side of things at the enterprise level. Yet this is not a matter of bureaucracy in the directorates. For directorates cannot be expected to attempt to weigh the specific circumstances of each factory and the probable effects of their product-mixes in a forthcoming period in connexion with every

---

[31] *Collected Decrees Concerning Simplification of Administration in State and Enterprise Affairs,* p. 80.

techno-economic index of each factory. This would require special study in arriving at every single figure—a procedure for which there is obviously neither time nor man-power available. The attention of the staffs of directorates is concentrated primarily on preparing programmes and plans of raw material supply, labour, and costs, so that little of their energy is left over for the technical indices. The course of the trouble here does not lie in 'bureaucratic administration' but in methods of running the economy which demand the impossible: namely, the detailed planning, from a single centre, of the activities of a whole host of enterprises in all their technical and economic aspects, and this by the use of instructions of a compulsory character. It must, by the way, be said, in addition, that these techno-economic indicators are in any case only compulsory 'in principle'. In practice they are taken much less seriously than is fulfilment of the targets of production value or of cost reductions. The financial incentives held out to top managements are generally not bound up with techno-economic indices. Consequently, these indices are comparatively ineffective, even though personnel in charge of individual departments may sometimes receive premiums based on these indices.

It is clear from all this that these techno-economic indices very largely fail in fulfilling the function originally envisaged for them, which was to convey the instructions of the State and central authorities to enterprises in so far as they concerned improvements in technique and economy in production. These indices carry little weight as they are not endowed with much force as incentives and are insufficiently well founded on facts. They command no authority.

Indices of costs

In the last two years[32] indices of cost have come to be numbered among the basic plan indices to which premium payments are related. By now these plan indices rank equally with those of production value—at least in light industry. This makes an appreciation of the true nature of these indices the more important.

The plans relating to costs have three main parts:

   (i) the plan of cost reduction for standard products;
   (ii) the plan of production costs;
   (iii) the plan of costs in respect of major product lines.

---

[32] I was assisted, in writing this chapter, by the results of studies carried out for the Institute of Economics by Mrs. László Tüü.

As only the first two categories of plans have financial sanctions attached to them, attention will here be confined to these.

The plans of cost reduction for standard products prescribe, in numerical terms, the average proportionate reductions which enterprises are required to make in the costs of their standard or 'comparable' products, i.e. in products they have had in regular production during the current and previous plan periods. Rather inexactly, it is this index that is commonly thought of as the 'plan of cost-reductions'. This part of the plan—like that of production—is drawn up after detailed preliminary study in extraordinarily minute detail; cost reductions are planned in respect of every single standard article.

The only compulsory part of the plan of production costs (also known as the production budget) is the so-called *cost quotient*. This is the ratio of total production costs to total production value at current prices net of turnover tax, expressed as a percentage. (For example, the cost quotient may be prescribed at 96 per cent, or 101 per cent., &c.) Once costs have been fixed, the profitability of the enterprise is also determined, up to a point, since the difference between production value and production costs determines the magnitude of what is called the *plant result*. This may be a profit, or a loss. (In the examples just given there would be a plan profit of 4 per cent, and a plant loss of 1 per cent, respectively.)[33]

The first of the two indices under discussion here has been the more important one during the period we are studying. For where the proportionate importance of standard products has exceeded 50 per cent., the size of premium payments has been made to depend on cost reductions attained in respect of standard products. Elsewhere, premium payments have been based on cost quotients. The former index was in fact the basis of payments of the premiums related to costs in about two-thirds of light industrial enterprises, and the latter in about one-third of them. During the first quarter of 1955, for example, these proportions worked out at 65 per cent, and 35 per cent, respectively.

In general the statements to be made in this section of my discussion apply to both of the indices to which premium payments attach. Problems peculiar to one or the other of these indices will only be referred to occasionally, as and when this is required.

[33] It is necessary to distinguish what is known as the *enterprise result* from this. The latter is obtained by setting the revenues obtained by enterprises from actual sales of their products against their costs in producing them, account being taken of all the various receipts and purchases of enterprises. It thus expresses the profitability of enterprises in terms of actually realized financial results.

When cost reductions were given prominence by having premium payments attached to them the lopsidedness which had characterized our system of financial incentives until 1954 was undoubtedly mitigated.[34]

Cost figures provide much more comprehensive indicators of the various facets of the activity of enterprises than do the indices of production value which were formerly given such exclusive prominence. Costs react to output changes indirectly; they generally fall as production increases. Costs also reflect the course of variations in labour and material inputs employed, and they also indicate, up to a point, the extent to which enterprises fulfil their financial and delivery obligations (via interest, costs, penalty payments, &c.). There is, therefore, every justification for paying particular attention to the course of cost changes.

Yet, at the same time, indices of cost do not mirror every aspect of the activity of enterprises, and they cannot be regarded as an all-inclusive index of it as is often supposed. What things are not shown by costs? First and foremost, changes in indices of cost reductions (like those of production value) are completely unaffected by the degree to which the products of enterprises are adapted to satisfying the requirements of society to the greatest possible extent, that is, the extent to which they correspond to the course of the demands of customers (i.e. to both personal and producers' demand). Enterprises may turn out articles at lowered costs which are less in demand, so that cost reductions attained in this way may nevertheless be wasteful from a social point of view. In other words, cost reductions do not depend on sales except at best indirectly (by way of interest and penalty payments). This is true of both of the cost indices upon which premium payments are based, and also of plant results but not of enterprise results, which have special significance precisely because of their close connexion with the course of sales.

Furthermore, when the process of attaching financial incentives to cost reductions is pressed, it produces some definitely harmful effects as well.

1. Costs can be reduced at the expense of quality. Indeed, this happens to be one of the easiest ways of doing so, for it requires little technical ingenuity or organizing ability. In past years this kind of cost reduction has been going on steadily in light industry, partly with the knowledge of the authorities at the centre, and partly behind their backs, on 'local initiative'.

---

[34] For a time, in addition, limitations were imposed on the permitted degree of fulfilment of production plans owing to difficulties in foreign trade. Thus during this period cost reductions became the chief method for obtaining premium payments. The limitations on production increases must, of course, be regarded as having been temporary in character.

Costs fall when cheaper materials are used instead of more expensive ones. This will be associated with a deterioration of quality, since better quality materials—especially imported ones—are, as a rule, more expensive. The scope for cost reductions of this kind is increased in branches of industry which mix a number of materials together in the process of turning out their product, for example, in the woollen industry. (Any tendencies in this direction are hampered by the circumstances that lower-grade materials are, as a rule, more difficult to work up. They thus increase wage costs, which is a serious matter, as particularly powerful financial incentives have, until now, always attached to keeping within the limits of permitted wages funds.)

Occasionally, good organization of the work to be done can lead to the omission or simultaneous performance of some industrial operations. But in our light industry, operations indispensable for the achievement of good quality, of pleasing execution, and good workmanship have often been skipped. In many fields quality has suffered from an excessive tightening of norms which, of course, also reduces costs. This has happened in many shoe factories for example.

Measures such as these, which lower quality, have in quite a number of factories been acclaimed and considered to be great achievements at the time of their being accomplished because they were regarded as successful economy measures. It was this sort of thing that gave birth to the ironic expression often heard in industrial and trading circles: this or that necessary operation or valuable material has, it is said, been 'innovated out' of a product. Buyers have every right to describe this process as one of 'disguised price increases', since it is of the essence of it that they receive an inferior product at an unchanged price.

It is not easy to restore the position once quality has been lowered for the sake of reduced costs. This is because past performance is incorporated into subsequent plans, so that enterprises which have indulged in this practice will find their next plans of costs to be drawn up on a lower cost basis. If they now wished to improve quality that would involve raising costs, and it is not easy to arrange for plans to envisage higher costs. Thus the *modus operandi* of planning costs actually fixes and stabilizes reductions of quality once they have taken place.

It is not, in general, possible to demonstrate the effect of cost indices in reducing quality in quantitative terms. This is because there are several factors in the present economic set-up which push enterprises in the direction of lowering quality: pressures to increase production value, omissions of necessary operations so as to effect savings in wages bills, unbalanced aspects of piecework payments, the lack of stocks, &c. It is consequently impossible to establish the part played by any one factor in causing a deterioration in the quality of a product once this has taken place.

It must be noted that the part played in all this by the two indices of cost reduction in which premium payments depend is not identical. The plan of cost reduction of standard products provides every opportunity for, and indeed definitely stimulates, the process of lowering quality. The other index, the cost quotient, does not operate in quite such a clear-cut way from this point of view. The calculation of it is based on the level of production value attained by an enterprise. But goods graded second class, third class, &c., can only be taken into account at reduced prices. If enterprises get into the position of having to make numerous price concessions on grounds of quality, they will at the same time be worsening their indices based on the cost quotient of production. This may therefore deter them from lowering quality in this particular direction. But—as has already been pointed out—the system of grading of products which comes into this gives no more than a partial picture of their quality. Enterprises are thus left free to pursue the object of reducing their cost quotients by neglecting those sides of the quality of their products which (like pleasing appearance, &c.) escape measurement on the basis of the 'objective criteria' prescribed in the system of quality standards.

The only possible remedy for this state of affairs would be for producers' prices to be made sensitive to quality differences of other kinds as well, which would involve that they would no longer be independent of the course of demand. Given our present, rather insensitive price system, it is clear that there is an at least partial tendency for enterprises to be driven, by the indices of cost, and also by the figures calculated for plant results, in the direction of deliberately lowering quality.

All this is the more dangerous because—as we have already seen—important forces which would stimulate enterprises to improve quality continuously do not really exist, while at the same time a whole series of factors tempt them to worsen quality. Thus, the conflict of cost with quality is now seen to take its place alongside other conflicts, that of quantity with quality and that of labour-intensive, careful workmanship with the desire to economize on wages bills. Quality is usually the loser in all these conflicts.

2. Closely connected with the question of quality is the *problem of variety.* Their indices of cost provide enterprises with incentives to narrow the range of their products and to avoid new products. The greater the number of products made by a firm, the smaller the quantities in which it is able to produce any one

of them. It is a familiar fact that production in small lots is more expensive than production in large quantities—hence their indices of cost provide enterprises with an incentive to shun the former.

This effect must not, of course, be regarded as an unmitigated evil. The true social interest is of a twofold character here, and it entails conflicting requirements. One requirement is that inputs per unit of output be minimized. From this point of view longer production runs are, indeed, in the social interest. The other requirement is that wants be satisfied to the greatest possible extent. This, however, calls for an ample range of goods to choose from. The attractions of women's fashion goods, in particular, are enhanced when they are only produced in small quantities. In foreign markets, too, it is easier to sell comparatively small, varied collections of goods. What we should therefore aim at is that enterprises be interested in achieving an optimal adjustment of these two conflicting requirements.

The trouble with our present arrangements is that everything combines to draw enterprises in a single direction—towards longer runs—and nothing pulls them in the other direction. (It is, for example, an unknown thing for enterprises engaged in foreign trade to offer factories higher prices as an inducement for them to produce smaller, more varied assortments of goods, which it would be easier to market abroad.)

As things are, the indices of costs act in such a way as to hamper not only a broadening of choice, but also steady introduction of new varieties of articles. If an enterprise wished to adjust itself to changes in demand in a flexible manner, then this would necessitate a reorganization of production. But reorganizations of this kind always give rise to additional costs.

The introduction of new articles leads to additional expenses under a number of heads. This is true even when it is not a question of introducing what are called 'socially new commodities', i.e. entirely new types of product, but merely a matter of introducing new, so-called 'assortment-broadening' products, the object being that of laying in fresh stocks of goods corresponding to new fashions. For money must then be found for new models and patterns; installations and equipment of certain kinds have to be bought (new lasts, new patterns, &c.). Nor is it merely a matter of once-and-for-all outlays of these kinds. Enterprises will have become experienced in producing their previous products, but now production flows will have to be interrupted it will be necessary to get accustomed to the performance of new operations, &c. All this will be reflected in profit rates on most established articles being higher than on new lines, the prices of which will have, according to the rules, to be fixed so as to yield profits of merely 2 per cent. Thus, given our present pricing system, new products worsen the cost quotient of production, and thus plant results.

There are certain factors at work which, in practice, counteract the force of the tendency towards a narrowing of variety. Such are the central determination of the programme and the orders placed by commerce. But the strength of these factors is not very great because the industrial directorate itself also lacks any considerable interest in the enlargement of variety. A certain dullness and uniformity of the assortments of our light industrial production is the final result. Both domestic and foreign customers often complain about this.

The process of planning and determining the costs to be prescribed for enterprises is extraordinarily unreliable. It requires a great deal of administrative work both at higher levels and, even more, at the enterprise level. Even in its present form, the work involved frequently amounts to a multiple of what is done on other parts of plans. In many enterprises the preparation of this plan involves work-spurts reaching far into the night. Precision in planning is nevertheless not achieved, because numerous factors which make for uncertainty are in play.

(i) There is a great deal that is imprecise in the data calculated *ex post*; yet it is these *ex post* calculations in respect of the preceding period that serve as the basis of determining planned costs of standard products.

(ii) Cost targets proposed by enterprises form the point of departure for planning. Much depends on whether the proposals made by enterprises are realistic, or whether they are loose and too favourable to themselves.

(iii) The proposals made by enterprises are added together by the directorate, and in case their sum total does not match what is prescribed for the trade as a whole, the directorate will 'tighten' them. The latter is not in a position to judge how far this procedure yields realistic targets for individual enterprises. From the point of view of enterprises, there are evidently numerous chance elements in whether or not such a tightening process occurs.

(iv) It is difficult to take account in advance of all the effects of changes in production volumes, in product-mixes, and in other factors influencing costs, with a sufficient degree of realism.

(v) Programmes may include new articles. The effect of the future production of these articles or costs is difficult to measure realistically in advance.

(vi) Actual levels of costs attained in the previous plan period, the so-called 'base period data', are one of the points of departure in planning. What these previous results were like counts for a great deal. It is easier to achieve progress in relation to bad base period results and vice versa. Even if attempts are made to take this into account in advance in drawing up plans, this factor will still be responsible for a certain amount of uncertainty.

The fact that considerable divergences regularly appear between planned and actual figures of cost at the enterprise level is proof of the unreliability of planning. Divergences of this kind weigh heavily in the scales in this part of the plan, where the payment of premiums may be affected by differences of one-tenth of 1 per cent.

Let us first consider planned and actual figures relating to cost reductions of standard articles in the woollen industry for the year 1955 and the first half of 1956 (Table IV, p. 62).

We obtain similar results if we consider individual enterprises one by one rather than examining results in respect of the directorate as a whole. Take the results of enterprises in the woollen industry in respect of the fulfilment of their plans of cost reductions of standard products for the fourth quarter of 1955 (Table V, p. 62).

These two tables provide further support for the unanimous expressions of opinion of planning officials at the Ministry and in enterprises, to the effect that it is impossible to draw up exact plans of costs for enterprises. (Indeed, as we have seen, uncertainty also attaches to the fulfilment of the plan of the directorate itself, even though the averaging effect of the 'law of large numbers' is already in play here.)

Table IV Degrees of fulfilment of plans of costs in the woollen industry

	Period	Plan (%)	Actual (%)	Per cent. plan-fulfilment
1955	1st quarter	97.5	95.6	102.0
1955	2nd quarter	96.5	93.7	103.0
1955	3rd quarter	96.3	92.6	104.0
1955	4th quarter	94.2	92.2	102.2
1955	Total	96.7	93.5	103.4
1956	1st quarter	97.1	99.8	97.3
1956	2nd quarter	96.7	97.8	98.9

Source: Data of the Wool Trade Directorate.

Table V Degrees of fulfilment of plans of costs in individual enterprises in the woollen industry

Name of enterprise	Plan (%)	Actual (%)	Per cent. plan-fulfilment
Bajai Gyapjúszövő	97.8	95.4	102.5
Gyapjúmosó	94.2	89.6	105.1
Győri Gyapjúfonó	93.5	95.5	97.9
Hazai Fésűsfonó	93.6	93.6	100.0
Kalapgyár	101.8	95.3	106.8
Kistarcsai Fésűsfonó	97.5	99.9	97.6
Kőszegi Textilművek	94.5	94.5	100.0
Lóden Posztógyár	80.0	74.3	107.7
Magyar Gyapjúfonó	94.2	91.2	103.3
Magyar Posztó	94.8	93.0	101.9
Pomáz-Budakalászi	96.2	93.5	102.9
Soproni Fésűsfonó	99.4	100.4	99.0
Soproni Posztó	95.0	98.5	96.4
Szombathelyi Takarógyár	95.5	94.0	101.6
Tatai Szőnyeggyár	95.0	92.0	103.3
Ujpesti Gyapjú	91.3	91.2	100.1
Váci fonó	91.4	91.9	99.5

Source: Data of the Wool Trade Directorate.

The fact that the two authorized indices—the plan of cost reduction of standard articles and the cost quotient of production—are frequently out of step with one another is also a reflection of the uncertain character of planning. This last fault is the more troublesome because generally, as we shall see, there are financial consequences attached to both of these indices in most enterprises. Observing the lack of precision and reliability of the planning process, light industrial directorates keep changing planned targets all the time in an attempt to make them more realistic. Modifications of cost targets have become standard practice in a number of branches of light industry. As a rule, this is done well after the start of the relevant quarter, generally towards the middle of its second month. The basis for it is provided by the actual balance-sheet figures of the preceding quarter. (Thus, for example, the plan for the third quarter of 1956 for enterprises in the woollen industry was modified on 28 August.) This procedure of immediately translating past results into plans puts a strong brake on the efforts of top managements to reduce costs, since any result once attained is immediately made into a performance demanded by the next plan. Besides, all this chopping and changing makes for uncertainty.

Conversely, when the production programme is altered in the course of the year, cost figures are often left unchanged, even though these also should clearly alter.

So far, I have stressed only the unreliability of planning. There also exist several well-known methods of 'window dressing' the degree of plan-fulfilment achieved. To give some examples:

(i) Enterprises can turn an established product line into a 'new article' by means of insignificant alterations of a technical character, thus shifting it out of the category of standard products, into the group where cost comparisons cannot be made. Or, conversely, a product can be so changed that its classification as a new article would be warranted—but it may nevertheless be continued under its old name if that is more advantageous for a factory.

(ii) In one quarter an enterprise can turn out individual products in small lots and at a high cost in order that it may achieve a good result in relation to this base period figure in the next quarter, &c.

Thus, here also, in measuring the costs of standard production, we are faced with a phenomenon having contradictory aspects. If the criterion of standard products is defined in too strict a manner, then the proportionate share of these articles will become too small, and, conversely, a definition which is too broad means that we are not really comparing identical articles.

The technical problems of cost accounting are not as acute in light industry as they are in several other branches of industry; accounting work is well developed and reliable in this field. But such 'dodges' as the above can nevertheless be used here also.

To sum up. The prominence accorded to indices of cost reduction undoubtedly stimulates economy-mindedness. At the same time, obtaining the premium—which depends on a 100 per cent, fulfilment of these indices—hinges on a number of chance and accidental factors, since the cost indices cannot be planned accurately. Thus, in fulfilling this particular premium requirement, managements of enterprises can easily find themselves in positions of undeserved advantage or of unwarranted disadvantage.

In addition, these indices also lack the property of unambiguousness: besides their positive and healthy effects they also have undesired, unregulated, 'wild' effects as well. The indices of production value and of costs have in common an insensitivity to demand and to sales problems, and a tendency to release stimuli working in the direction of lowered quality and of restricted variety.

3. OTHER INSTRUCTIONS REGULATING PRODUCTION

The two preceding sections have dealt with plan instructions, i.e. the system of plan indices. There are, however, other ways besides plan indices which can be used by the authorities to issue instructions and binding prescriptions to enterprises. These must on no account be omitted from an examination of the system of government instructions regulating production, since the work of enterprises is influenced, and their independence greatly limited, by a multiplicity of instructions, decrees, and restrictions of these other kinds.

I shall give some examples of these. I should add that the orders and instructions I mention here are chiefly those which serve to complete the part of plans which is concerned with production. Innumerable additional instructions are used to regulate raw material utilization, personnel and wage issues, work arising in connexion with cost reduction, &c.

(a) Authorization of monthly production rates

In March 1955 it was decided, by decree of the Ministerial Council, that, within the quarterly plans of enterprises, binding monthly rates of production should be prescribed by the ministries. Thereupon the Ministry of Light Industry instructed its enterprises to break their quarterly plans down into time periods on a *pro rata* basis, that is, the total forint value of quarterly production was to be apportioned in three equal parts over three months. This decree hampers enterprises and their directors in making dispositions of their own. Moreover, it can clearly not attain its objective, which is to secure an even flow of production. For this last depends on even conditions in the technological aspects of performance (e.g. in picks per machine-day), rather than on a rate of production resulting in identical forint values month by month. This is so, because the latter depends, among other things, on the product-mix, the value of materials used, &c., as well.

Thus the rhythm of production and the fulfilment, on time, of customers' orders, tend, in fact, to be interfered with by the decree. More precisely this is what its effect would be if it were not the case that this instruction of the Ministerial Council and of the Ministry is hardly ever carried out.

(b) Centralized design and planning of models and patterns

In many lines of industry enterprises have no opportunity of planning their models and designs by themselves. For example, in the shoe trade a central department of model design is at work. A collection of models is prepared here from which commerce makes its choice of the items that appeal to it, whereupon the factories are asked to manufacture these. Naturally, however, there is, in the course of planning, insufficient opportunity to take account of the specific characteristics of individual factories, of their equipment, of the habitual ways of operation of their specialist staffs and workmen, their raw materials supply position, &c. The result is that the models produced without the collaboration of the factories look altogether different from the shoes subsequently produced on the basis of them. It is really astonishing that large 'independent' enterprises employing many hundred workers are not entrusted with turning out models—a task which every small shoemaker takes in his stride! Recently, one or two of the largest factories have been granted the right to prepare their own models, but the rest had still not come 'of age' from this point of view. From time to time models are prepared even by the smaller factories, but they do this entirely off their own bat, flying in the face of all regulations in doing so.

In 1955 the situation was similar in the manufacture of woollen cloth. The Central Office for Planning Designs produced designs which were then passed on to enterprises for manufacture. The factories only produced designs of their own when it was a matter of working up their accumulated stocks of waste materials. Even then the approval of the Central Office for Planning Designs had to be obtained. All this had a hampering effect on rational utilization of raw material supplies, for, in the production of woollen cloth, a very close connexion exists between design and the particular combination of the various varieties of wool and waste materials and artificial fibres to be used. Hence, designs ought to be adapted to the prevailing raw material position in a flexible manner.

The foregoing state of affairs proved so unworkable that these severe restrictions have since been eased. Nowadays, enterprises are allowed to produce their own designs, but these have still to be submitted to the Central Office for Planning Designs. Thus, the system has undergone change. Yet it is worth providing a reminder of the position in 1955, for it shows the tendency towards 'centralization at any price' in operation in a clear manner.

The planning of designs has, on the face of it, been 'decentralized' in the cotton industry: factories have design offices of their own. But, in practice, the responsibility for presenting collections falls to the Central Textile-design Producing Company; it places orders for work with design offices, and approved designs are subsequently handed out to enterprises quite irrespectively of whether these were designed in the design offices of the enterprises in question or not. Thus, the factories have nothing to do with producing their designs after all.

The idea, by the way, that every trade should have an institute of its own concerned with models and designs should not, of course, be thrown overboard. Their employment should, however, be put on to a 'business footing' rather than being compulsory. Enterprises could then suit themselves about whether they wished to buy models or designs from the institute rather than making them up for themselves. If the central institutes were to be manned by persons of outstanding ability, then many enterprises would, no doubt, place orders for models and designs with them voluntarily.

(c) Profiles

One advantage of the social ownership of the means of production is that it renders planned specialization possible. The development of 'profiles', i.e. of specialization, which was put through in the wake of nationalization, has produced numerous good results.

In several fields, however, the process has been carried too far. The profiles developed have been so rigid that, instead of rational production being promoted, it is, rather, hindered. This is the case most notably in the leather industry. Here the types of finished leather to be turned out by each individual factory have been laid down; every factory has its own permanent profile. It occurs very frequently, however, that a factory finds itself the recipient of a type of raw leather which it would be more rational and economic to convert into a different type of leather from that prescribed by the profile of the factory. It is, nevertheless, required to adhere rigidly to its permanent profile.

In the shoe industry, factories have been made to specialize by sizes of shoes as well as by production processes and the chief varieties of products. For example, there are three factories engaged in making children's shoes: one makes sizes 19–22, another 23–28, &c. This hampers attempts to effect economies in cutting up leathers. While the rigidity of profiles in the leather industry causes serious harm, specialization by sizes of shoe does not pose serious problems in the shoe industry. I only mention it because it is characteristic of the tendency to bind enterprises hand and foot. But it has also become characteristic, lately, for shoe factories to simply break loose from these rigid restrictions; they will accept orders placed by commerce which depart from the size category prescribed for their factory.

(d) Quality standards

It is not possible to think of modern industrial production dispensing with the widespread application of quality standards. Their use can promote economy in production and the assessment of quality.

A critical evaluation of our present system of quality standards is, of course, beyond the scope of this study; it would require wide-ranging research of a technical character. All I wish to recall to mind here is the economic aspect of the matter, which has already come up earlier on, in connexion with quality indices of the production plan.

Standards which prescribe criteria of a technically controllable character necessarily provide one-sided characterizations of the quality of articles. Thus, while they exert great pressure on enterprises in causing them to observe quality standards (this naturally has its own healthy and beneficial effect)—they deflect attention somewhat from other elements in quality and the factors determining these. They also divert the attention of enterprises from trying to do their best to adjust themselves to the changing real requirements of buyers in regard to quality as these enfold themselves with the passage of time—the more so as no serious incentives exist to provide inducements towards a flexible satisfaction of demand and careful attention to consumers' requirements.

All this needs to be emphasized because there exists a school of thought according to which it is possible to ensure substantial and continuous improvement in the quality of products by way of a further extension of the scope of the system of quality standards and by tightening up on the degree to which they are enforced. This view is yet another instance of over-estimating what instructions coming from the centre can do, for quality standards must also be thought of as having the character of binding instructions emanating from the centre.

(e) Operative instructions and decrees

Over and above the foregoing types of standing regulations there are also innumerable individual instructions regulating the course of production at the enterprise level.

An analysis of the number of instructions addressed to an enterprise by its directorate, in matters relating directly to production,[35] was prepared at the Ujpest Leather Factory. According to this, 102 instructions were received between 1 September and 31 December 1955—not counting plan figures with related documents and modifications of these. The number of decrees published in the *Magyar Közlöny*[36] and the *Könnyűipari Értesítő*[37]—the

---

[35] i.e. not including instructions relating to accountancy, statistics, labour, and personnel matters.
[36] *Hungarian Gazette.*
[37] *Light Industrial Gazette.*

official organ of the Ministry—each one of which contain further instructions addressed to enterprises, would deserve separate study.

The instructions and indices which go to make up plans are evidently in a different category from the kind of instructions, restrictions, and regulations listed in the foregoing. Nevertheless, it is not the legal line of demarcation which separates plan instructions from an order issued by a ministry or a circular put out by a directorate that is felt to be important by top managements in enterprises. After all, they are, in principle, in duty bound to carry out each of these types of instructions without fail. What matters to top managements is the distinction between demands made upon them which they feel to have been made in a strictly serious way as against those about which they do not feel this, and the distinction between those demands to which financial consequences attach, as against those to which no such consequences attach. It is, moreover, not uncommon for a directorate to insist more strongly upon some special instruction of its own, of the kind I have just discussed, than, say, upon some plan figure of a not very prominent character.

II

INCENTIVES FOR TOP MANAGEMENTS

The previous chapter contained a brief review of the system of instructions. We have seen that this system embraces all of the processes of the economy in an extraordinarily comprehensive manner. All aspects of economic activity are regulated by means of instructions consisting of plan index numbers, and of prescriptions, regulations, and restrictions not contained in the plans.

The amount of detail contained in these instructions is by no means a reflection of the degree to which they are well founded; and besides, most of them fail to express the real wishes of the central authorities. These wishes are often distorted in the process of their transmission by way of the instructions, so that they may in fact be instrumental in causing enterprises to move in what are definitely undesirable directions.

The question which next arises is: what induces top managements to carry out instructions? The fulfilment of each authorized plan index number is equally obligatory in principle. This, however, is not how things work out in practice: the weight given to different plan index numbers and their actual influence on events varies a great deal. The differences which exist in this respect are intimately bound up with the question of what material and moral consequences attach to the fulfilment, as against the non-fulfilment, of particular indices.

It is also necessary to ask what inducements exist to impel top managements to make decisions to act in directions required by the good of the economy where no instruction exists in relation to the matter concerned?

I would stress that what is under examination here is the system of incentives affecting top managements, that is, principally the directors of enterprises and their top-ranking technical staffs. I shall also be concerned, to some extent, with incentives designed to apply to entire enterprises in their collective capacity.[1]

---

[1] Problems of the remuneration of manual workers and of persons engaged in administrative occupations below the top levels are, therefore, examples of matters outside the scope of my study.

Overcentralization in Economic Administration. János Kornai translated by John Knapp, Oxford University Press.
© Oxford University Press (2023). DOI: 10.1093/oso/9780192894427.003.0002

1. FINANCIAL INCENTIVES

The connexion between the interests of individuals, of enterprises, and of society

To say that the achievement of a harmony of individual and social interests which is as complete as possible is required if our economic activities are to run smoothly and successfully, is a truth so constantly voiced that it has, by now, become platitudinous. However, in discussing the question, many articles and lectures neglect to deal with an indispensable link in the chain which exists between the individual and society—the enterprise and 'the interest of the enterprise'.

The social process of production can evidently not be considered analogous to the activity of a single gigantically large concern—even if our attention is confined to the nationalized sector of the economy. We should regard enterprises as being the basic cells of the social production process if we are to reckon with the facts as they really are. That enterprises should form economic units which are to some extent independent is a matter of necessity. This results from the contemporary state of productive forces and the relations of production flowing from these, which are characterized by a high degree of specialization and division of labour, within which large productive units occupy a position of dominance. The requirement that factories or enterprises should have autonomy flows from the circumstance that large-scale, complex, and manifold production processes need to be co-ordinated on the spot and directed within the framework of large productive units. The extent and character of the autonomy to be possessed by enterprises is, of course, a matter which needs consideration separately in the light of the character of production processes, prevailing methods of administering the economy, &c. But the feature of autonomy itself is a matter of economic necessity.

Any well-designed system of economic incentives must, therefore, take full account of this necessary feature of economic reality. Our present system of incentives makes an attempt to do this, but it does not do so consistently or with sufficient success.

The problem has two sides to it: one is that enterprises (regarded as more or less united collective bodies, and as groups each having a responsible director and a staff of top managers at their disposal) must be provided with incentives to serve the national economy and society as effectively as possible. With this object in view, a direct connexion needs to be established between the rate at which enterprises develop and the degree to which they satisfy the interests of the national economy. This happens, for example, when the growth and technical development of enterprises depends on the results of their own work, at least in part, or when the benefits derived by the workers from collective social and cultural facilities provided by enterprises (i.e. lockers, baths, canteens, cultural and holiday centres, &c.) expand at a rate which is related to the achievements of their enterprises.

That the earnings of individual workers should depend on the position and the results attained by their enterprises as a whole, as well as on their personal achievements, is the other *desideratum*. Incentives are needed which will stimulate the personnels of enterprises, and top managements in particular, to do their utmost to serve the interests of their enterprises effectively, and thus, in the last analysis, the social interest as well.

Briefly, it is necessary to connect the interests of individuals, of enterprises, and of society to each other in a harmonious whole so far as possible. The establishment of these connexions is best thought of as occurring in a system of transmission of interests operating through a number of gears.

Since in practice, conflicts and contradictions of interest will inevitably arise, one must, of course, think in terms of establishing a harmony of interests which will be less than complete. But it matters a great deal whether these conflicts are numerous, sharp, and of a recurring character, or relatively infrequent and muted. At present the former tends to be the case, and this is something we cannot view with equanimity.

In what follows I shall discuss the various incentives in succession. In examining each I will attempt to consider separately how far they serve the objective of securing a harmony of the interests of individual workers, of enterprises, and of society as a whole.

The parts played in total earnings by basic pay, premiums, and bonuses

We must first clarify the manner in which earnings are made up in terms of their various constituent parts. Let us first look at the ratio of regular premium earnings[2] to the amount of basic pay in light industry as a whole in 1955 (Table VI).

---

[2] This should be understood to refer to the premiums received by technical personnel and administrative employees in leading positions; it is the premium regularly received by these workers, quarterly as a rule, if certain definite conditions and plan index numbers are met and realized. In what follows it

Table VI Premium payments as a percentage of basic pay in light industry

Quarter	Number of technical personnel receiving premiums as a percentage of all eligible technical personnel	Premium payments actually received as a percentage of basic pay
1st	95.7	28.1
2nd	94.2	26.5
3rd	87.4	23.2
4th	88.9	22.7

Source: Central Planning Division of the Ministry of Light Industry. Data shown refer to premiums received by technical personnel only. Premiums received by administrative employees are not shown.

The proportion of total earnings which consists of premiums varies as between different groups of technical personnel and for different categories of higher administrative personnel. The class of workers eligible for premium payments are divided into three categories labelled A, B, and C; category A consists of top management personnel (directors, chief engineers, chief accountants); category B of persons in less responsible positions; and category C of those in the least responsible ones. Let us examine the magnitude of premiums in the third quarter of 1955 in five enterprises, three of which belong to the woollen industry, one to the leather trade, and one to the shoe trade (Table VII).

The table shows quite clearly that the part of earnings which consists of premiums is, in general, largest in the case of those employed in top-ranking

Table VII Premium payments as a percentage of basic pay in individual enterprises, by premium categories

Name of enterprise	Category A	Category B	Category C
Hazai Fésűsfonó	36.9	22.3	23.1
Magyar Posztógyár	36.8	27.6	34.3
Magyar Gyapjúfonó	54.8	36.4	34.0
Táncsics Bőrgyár	10.8	13 6	14 6
Minőségi Cipőgyár	39.6	34.6	29.6

Note: The table shows the value of premiums paid expressed as a percentage of basic pay.
Sources: The data were furnished by the planning divisions of each enterprise. The figures include data in respect of eligible administrative employees and technical personnel.

will be these payments and not the various special premiums, bonuses, &c., that I shall have in mind when I refer to 'premium payments'.

positions. (This only works out otherwise when certain basic indices of the plans of enterprises are not fulfilled. When this happens, top management forfeits a considerable part of the premium, while heads of sections, foremen, &c., may nevertheless fulfil their own indices, and may thus obtain their premiums. The Táncsics Leather Factory is an example of this.)

It is worth looking at the premiums of the directors of enterprises separately (Table VIII).

The above table, supplied by the Labour Division of the Leather and Footwear Trades' Directorate, provides data on premiums earned by directors of enterprises in the fourth quarter of 1955. It can be seen that, here and there, individual directors fail to earn their premiums, but that those who do earn it receive a good deal more than technicians do on average.

The data given so far are all concerned with the relative magnitude of regular premium payments and of basic pay. Unfortunately, overall figures showing the relative importance of other supplementary bonuses and of special premiums are not available. It will, however, be seen in a subsequent part of this discussion that the importance of these payments is much smaller than the importance of regular premiums. According to expert estimates the former account for only 2–5 per cent, of the earnings of technical personnel at the most. (Of course, they may amount to much more than this in the earnings of individual workers in particular periods—but relatively few people receive

Table VIII Premium payments to directors as a percentage of their basic pay in selected enterprises in the leather and shoe trades

Name of enterprise	Premium as percentage of basic pay
Pécsi Bőrgyár	22.7
Táncsics Bőrgyár	(did not receive a premium)
Ujpesti Bőrgyár	34
Pannónia Szőrmeárúgyár	50
Rákospalotai Bőrkonfekció	45
Average premium received by all technical personnel in the leather industry as a whole	23.8
Duna Cipőgyár	48
Tisza Cipőgyár	34
Szombathelyi Cipőgyár	(did not receive a premium)
Bonyhádi Cipőgyár	42
Bőrtex	45
Average premium received by all technical personnel in the shoe trade as a whole	18.6

large bonus payments in this way.) Thus, this constituent of earnings is quite overshadowed by the 20–30 per cent, which is characteristically derived from regular premium payments.

Special premiums and bonuses really are regarded as extraordinary sources of income. Things are very different where the regular premium is concerned. This is regarded as an integral part of earnings and not as an occasional bonus, precisely because of its large importance, on average, and particularly in the case of personnel in top positions. Domestic arrangements and modes of life are adjusted to a firm expectation of receiving premium payments. Family budgets are badly upset by failures to earn the premium. Hence, top managers of enterprises take it for granted that the premium must be earned—and its incentive effect is correspondingly exceedingly strong.

Let us now take a look at the constituents of individual earnings, one by one.

The regular premiums of top managements

Let us first of all examine the actual conditions of obtaining the regular premium in light industry. Since this study is mainly concerned with the situation that existed in 1955, I shall describe the rules of the premium system in force during the fourth quarter of 1955. We must first consider the conditions attaching to the payment of premiums to persons in top managerial positions (directors, chief engineers, chief accountants).

Premiums consisted of two parts at that time, the receipt of one part being conditional on fulfilment of production plans, and that of the other on fulfilment of plans of cost reduction.

1. To earn the first part of the premium it was necessary to fulfil the target of production value to the extent of 100 per cent. Overfulfilment of the plan was not rewarded by additional premium payments, as, towards the end of the year, a desire had already emerged on the part of the authorities to put a brake on further increases in light industrial production. (But, as I have already mentioned, this can, of course, be regarded as having been an exceptional state of affairs; generally speaking, the basic principle of our system of premiums is for the premium to increase when the production plan is overfulfilled.)
2. The premium on cost reductions could still be earned, even when the production plan was not realized. This premium rose proportionately with results achieved by way of cost reduction. As I have already

explained, where the share of standard products in output amounted to 50 per cent, or more, the plan of cost reduction in respect of these products constituted the basis of the premium system. Budgeted costs of production, and the degree to which actual costs were within prescribed cost quotients were the basis of premium payments where the share of standard products in output was less than 50 per cent.

3. A so-called corrective condition was that planned outlays on wages and salaries were not to be exceeded. Enterprises had certain sums at their disposal, which were available for making premium payments. These sums had to be made use of to the extent that the limits set on planned wage and salary bills had been overstepped. This in turn led to corresponding all round reductions in premiums. The task of fulfilling this condition was made even more difficult by a rule laid down at the end of 1955 which provided that, in cases of underfulfilment of the production plan, the planned amounts of the wage and salary bills were to be calculated on a relative basis (i.e. if the degree of plan fulfilment was 97 per cent., then the permitted degree of utilization of planned amounts of wage and salary bills was reduced to 97 per cent.)—whereas in cases of overfulfilment of the plan, the absolute amounts of planned wage and salary bills were to be relevant. (That is, even if the degree of plan fulfilment came to 102 per cent., the permitted wage and salary outlays of an enterprise remained at 100 per cent, of their planned amount.[3])

4. Certain so-called 'conditions of payment' were also laid down, their application to the top managements of enterprises being in the hands of the directorates. The sums due in respect of fulfilment of the tasks described under points 1 and 2 above could only be paid out if these 'conditions of payment' had also been met. These conditions were not themselves prescribed uniformly and compulsorily; they varied in different trades.

---

[3] To prohibit outlays on wages in excess of their planned amounts in absolute terms is an exceedingly rigid method of preventing overfulfilment of production plans. It is very difficult for enterprises to control the degree to which they fulfil their plans to the nearest percentage point, and—as I have already emphasized in the course of discussing the index of production value—there is, in any case, not much sense in making a fetish of 100 per cent, in connexion with this index.

Enterprises can, in these circumstances, easily find themselves overstepping the limits of their planned outlays on wages and salaries—unless they have preferred to fall short of attaining their production plans instead—in which case they will have forfeited their premiums for the latter reason.

This rigid rule was relaxed in respect of most of light industry early in 1956, when the criterion used for calculating permitted outlays on wages and salaries reverted to a measure taken relatively to production even in cases of overfulfilment of production plans. Since that time, limitations in terms of absolute amounts have only been left in force in enterprises specially singled out by their industrial directorates.

The following are examples:

In enterprises in which the task determining eligibility for the premium in respect of cost reduction was fulfilment of the plan of cost reduction of standard articles, the condition of payment prescribed was fulfilment of the overall plan of production costs, as budgeted—and vice versa.

In a number of fields of industry, payment of the premiums due on fulfilment of production plans was conditional on some given degree of fulfilment (e.g. 95 per cent.) of what was called the index of the degree of adherence to plans.

Frequently, some index of quality[4] formed the basis of yet another condition of payment.

All of the foregoing relates to the premiums of top managements. The other recipients of premiums may be divided into two large groups. The first of these consists of personnel whose premium receipts depend on results achieved by their enterprise as a whole. Persons employed in departments concerned with the overall activity of their enterprise would be members of this group. (For example, the chief technologist or the head of the personnel division.) In 1955 the two tasks determining eligibility for premiums and the corrective condition (cf. the points listed under 1, 2, and 3 above) were the same for persons in this category as for top managements. While the conditions possibly preventing payment could, in principle, be different, these also were at least partly the same in practice.

The other group of recipients of premiums were the personnel of individual plants, sections, and other parts of enterprises whose premium determining tasks were based on plan indices relating to their own sectors of activity, and not on those of their enterprises as a whole.

This, then, was the system of premiums in force during the fourth quarter of 1955.

A detailed evaluation of the advantages and disadvantages and of the economic consequences of this system of premiums will be found later on in what follows.[5] The ground for postponing this discussion is that it is inseparably bound up with providing an evaluation of our whole system of planning and administering our economy. This in turn requires previous clarification of a number of further questions, and this is undertaken in the following pages. However, I would like even at this stage to point out some characteristic

[4] e.g. the proportion of grade I articles produced, or some scale of maximum values of reductions granted in respect of grade II and grade III articles.
[5] Cf. pp. 117–46.

general features of our present system of premium payments, since appreciation of these will be important subsequently when it comes to evaluating the
system and assessing its consequences.

(a) The system of premiums has, for years, been subjected to an incessant
process of modification. This is not merely a simple matter of the conditions for
earning premiums changing, as the tasks confronting the economy changed
from time to time. The system itself was also altered again and again. I have
just described the rules in force in 1955. But I had to add that this referred
to the situation in the fourth quarter, for there had been a number of important changes in the course of the year. Within a single year there appeared as
many as five decrees, each of which effected widespread changes in the system
of premium payments in light industry. And this takes no account of modifications effected by individual directorates in their own particular branches of
industry.

Since then, and up to mid-1956, further changes of varying importance have
taken place. An example is the abolition of control over the absolute level of
outlays on wages and salaries, which has already been mentioned. Again, a new
set of rules relating to premium payments, superseding all previous instructions, was issued by the directorate for the wool trade on 3 April, to be effective
as from the second quarter of 1956. But this did not last for long either. By
virtue of a decree of the Ministerial Council made public at the time of writing this study, the system of premiums in light industry is to be regulated in
accordance with a fresh set of rules of yet another kind.

Naturally, this multiplicity of modifications and changes produces uncertainty among potential recipients of the premiums, and reduces their effectiveness as incentives.

(b) The degree of independence enjoyed by enterprises and their directors
in the matter of premium payments is very limited; here, too, excessive centralization is very much in evidence. It is, in principle, the job of directors of
enterprises to determine the conditions in which premium payments are to
be made to all members of their staffs other than the personnel holding the
three top managerial posts. However, this is not what happens in practice. For
example, in the woollen industry, the directorate prescribed a total of six factors relevant to premium payments payable in respect of the fourth quarter
of 1955, each of which had to be incorporated in the conditions laid down
by directors of enterprises for determining eligibility for the receipt of premiums by all persons whose premiums depend on results achieved by their
enterprise as a whole. In such a situation, directors can do nothing but pass on
these premium-determining tasks in a mechanical manner. The requirement

that as many as six factors be involved in determining eligibility for receiving premiums is excessive. It does not permit the directors of enterprises to make allowance for special characteristics of their own set-ups or in the responsibilities of individual members of their staffs. And the case of the wool trade is not exceptional. It is normal for the Ministry and directorates to prescribe various conditions for the receipt of premiums centrally for personnel whose eligibility turns on results shown by their enterprises as a whole. Again, there are special regulations covering premium payments to MEO workers and to technicians concerned with gas and electricity supply. It is only in respect of the remaining categories of workers (plant managers, foremen, &c.) that directors are in a position to define the tasks determining eligibility for premiums in a more or less independent manner.

(c) Closely connected with the foregoing is the fact that premiums of subordinate employees are very often based on factors which are completely incapable of being influenced by their own work.

(d) The premiums of different categories of workers are related to different sets of plan index numbers. For example, directors of enterprises, chief engineers, and chief accountants, and also other technical and administrative personnel assessed on the basis of results shown by their enterprises as a whole, are so placed that their premiums act as a stimulus to attaining the target values of production laid down for enterprises. On the other hand, fulfilment of the various techno-economic indices is promoted by making these one of the premium-determining tasks of personnel (e.g. plant managers, foremen, &c.) who are employed in constituent units of enterprises. In this way the various premiums do, in fact, complement one another. There is, however, no doubt that the premiums offered to the former group exerts the stronger pull. As the chief planning official of one enterprise revealingly put it: 'It frequently happens that directors secure their own, and other top managerial personnel's premiums at the cost of subordinates, even if they have to "ditch" the latter in the process.' Thus, for example, a director will cause some part of his enterprise to produce a more expensive, 'forint-producing' article for the sake of fulfilling his target of production value without regard to the fact that this may have deleterious effects on the techno-economic index which appears among the determinants of the premiums of technical personnel in charge of particular plants. A director can do this with a fairly easy conscience, since he will consider that the higher authorities will evidently have built the indices which are of most importance for the national economy into his own premium. Therefore, other requirements can be subordinated to these without undue qualms.

This kind of thing is probably not a general phenomenon in quite such a crude form. This much, however, is certain: top managements and personnel whose activity is evaluated on the basis of results achieved by their enterprise as a whole, have, for the most part, identical interests so far as premiums are concerned. If these interests should come into conflict with those of subordinate personnel, the interests of the former group will tend to prevail. It follows that it is the plan indices governing the premiums of personnel whose activity is evaluated on the basis of results achieved by their enterprises as a whole, and the premiums of top managements in particular, which will play the dominating part and have maximum effect in the life of a factory.

(e) The system of premiums constitutes an extraordinarily powerful set of financial incentives. It follows from all of the foregoing that the effect of this system is at present concentrated primarily on promotion of the fulfilment of two plan indices, namely, those of production value and of cost reduction. The system also provides a strong incentive to keeping within the bounds of planned outlays on wages and salaries, and to the observance of what is called 'adherence to plans'. We may conclude that these are the dominant indices in the system of plan instructions.

Special premiums and bonuses

We may distinguish several varieties of special premiums and of bonuses:

1. Bonuses awarded to top managements by higher industrial authorities, e.g. the Ministry or an industrial directorate. If an enterprise achieves the title of a 'leading enterprise' or if it wins the pennant awarded by the Ministerial Council and the SZOT,[6] it is customary for its director, chief engineer, and chief accountant to receive personal bonuses. This naturally has the effect of increasing the incentive force of these awards. The size of the bonuses is mostly in the region of 1,000–2,000 forints.

Certain directorates have adopted the practice of compensating top managerial personnel in cases when they have failed to earn their regular quarterly premiums owing to causes originating outside their enterprise. An example is provided by the shoe trade. The better the results achieved by a shoe factory in improving the quality of its products and in economizing on materials, the larger will be the premiums it pays on this account to its own employees. In

---

[6] National Council of Trade Unions.

this way a factory may easily exceed its planned outlay on wages and salaries. In such cases, top managements will forfeit their premiums precisely because they have done good work. In cases of this sort, or of others of a similar nature, this directorate makes special 'compensatory' awards. The managements of the Duna, Szombathelyi, and Divat shoe factories were, together with some others, recipients of bonus payments on the above grounds at various times during 1955. The magnitude of the awards concerned amounted to 6–18 per cent, of basic pay in this trade.

Fundamentally, this form of compensation implies a criticism of the rigidity of the system of ordinary premium payments.

2. A distinctive type of special premium is encountered where this is offered by a body outside the industry. This is most frequently found in relation to transactions involving exports: an enterprise will be promised a special premium by some organization engaged in foreign trade on condition that its order is dealt with satisfactorily. But it is possible to find instances of this type of premium in other connexions as well—especially outside the field of light industry. For example, in cases of extensive inter-firm collaboration, the contracting factory will pay a special premium to sub-contracting enterprises if they effect their deliveries on time, &c. Special premiums of these kinds undoubtedly have sizeable incentive effects: they mostly amount to fairly substantial sums, and are capable of influencing the trend of the entire activity of enterprises.

These premiums entail two dangers. One is that, by offering pecuniary rewards, an outside body may arbitrarily distort the course of work of an enterprise, relatively to its plan. If, for example, a large special premium were to be in prospect in respect of the fulfilment of a particular order, all efforts will be concentrated on this, even at the cost of neglecting other orders and tasks prescribed in the plan. It may even pay to leave the plan unfulfilled, for the special premium may exceed the ordinary premium attached to fulfilling the plan.

The other danger lies in the possibility of corruption. It has become the vogue, in many quarters (mainly, so far as I know, in the machinery industry) to ask, as soon as a particularly important and urgent task crops up: 'And how much do we get by way of special premiums?' There is a tendency to go so far as to make delivery dates and other terms of fulfilling orders dependent on the magnitude of these special premiums. A peculiar distorted form of 'competition' among buyers develops in this way: whoever promises the largest amounts by way of special premiums can count most confidently on having his order fulfilled.

The proportion of the total earnings of technicians accounted for by special premiums of these kinds is very small. For example, in the woollen industry the prospective total of special premiums to be paid in connexion with orders for export in 1956 may be put at about a quarter of a million forints. If technicians receive, say, one-half of this amount, then the sum involved will amount to less than a half of 1 per cent, of planned outlay on technicians' salaries.

3. Another source of awards, besides the higher administrative organs of industry and customers, is the director of the enterprise. The source of these awards is the director's fund. The larger this fund is the greater the scope for awards. Special premiums provide a particularly happy channel for the use of these funds: a director can promise an award for the execution of particular tasks. This has proved a great success in providing a strong incentive. It is, unfortunately, not made use of sufficiently widely and regularly.

Basic pay

In the literature of material incentives, discussion is generally confined to consideration of various types of premiums. Demands for improving the system of economic incentives are implicitly equated with the idea of perfecting the system of premium payments.

This way of looking at things is erroneous. Economic incentives are determined by total earnings, and the larger part of these is, after all, made up of basic pay.

Moreover, the premiums attainable on fulfilment of various conditions are generally expressed in terms of appropriate percentages of basic pay rather than in terms of fixed amounts. To this extent, the magnitude of premiums are themselves a function of the size of basic pay.

In our practice, however, variations in basic pay are hardly used at all for the purpose of providing economic incentives. (It is just because this way of going about things is held to be both natural and necessary that discussions of material incentives tend always to be confined to the topic of the system of premiums.)

There are three characteristic shortcomings in our system of basic pay which I would like to discuss.

1. The difference in pay as between higher posts entailing greater responsibilities and simpler jobs of lower grades is too small in our system.

It is worth making a comparison with capitalist systems of pay in this connexion.

I would like to comment here on the fact that I shall, in what follows, repeatedly refer to the way in which technicians were paid under capitalism. Naturally, various well-known undesirable features of capitalist systems of remuneration existed in this field, as in others. But it is not these things that I wish to analyse just now. Rather, I shall draw attention to those aspects of capitalist experience in wage and salary payments which provide valuable food for thought. They may possibly contain one or two features which it would be worthwhile to use in our own conditions as well.

Detailed data concerning salaries of technicians and of managerial employees which are of a kind relevant to our theme—as distinct from summary figures of an overall character—are only available in scattered form so far as the pre-1945 period is concerned. For this reason, I have only been able to rely partially on material in the form of written records. In part, I have had to depend on the recollections of experts engaged in the relevant fields during the period of capitalism. As a result of setting the written records side by side with these recollections, it is possible to form a picture of the pattern of remuneration of technicians and salaried staff in those days. It is necessary to remember that there were, of course, no uniform and binding regulations in force in relation to this matter at that time, so that forms of remuneration varied in different enterprises. Consequently, in what follows, I shall attempt to bring out what may be regarded as generally prevalent characteristics.

Reverting, then, to the question of differences in pay: under capitalism, scales of pay showed a much broader spread than is the case today. Differences between the salaries of lower grade technical and other staff, on the one hand, and of top management, on the other, were much greater than is the case at present. Let us consider the example of the Pannonia Fur Factory, for a start (Table IX).

Unfortunately, there were no data available on the earnings of plant managers and foremen in the Lóden Felt Factory for the period before 1945. But the following data (Table X), comparing the pay of office staffs, show the same features as those observable in the Pannónia case: differences in earnings used to be greater than they are nowadays.

The table shows most strikingly how much nearer to each other salaries are nowadays than they were earlier, when the director's salary, in particular, used to stand out from the rest much more than now.

Instead of growing in recent years, the gap between the remunerations of personnel in senior and junior posts, doing jobs requiring higher and more modest qualifications, respectively, has diminished.

Table IX Earnings differentials of technical personnel in the Pannónia Fur Factory before 1945 and now

Post	Basis for measuring differential	1942	1955
Chief engineer	As percentage of total earnings of foremen receiving lowest pay	456	272
(i.e. managing director in 1942)	As percentage of the average of total earnings of plant managers	184	146
Plant managers	As percentage of total earnings of foremen receiving lowest pay	248	187

Note on sources: Data for the period before 1945 are taken from material in the Central Economic Record Office. This contains statements of earnings of the staff of the Pannónia Factory prepared for taxation purposes. If tax evasion was attempted, it is probable that the high incomes of the top management were understated to a greater extent than the incomes of persons in positions lower down. At the same time, the progression of income tax had the contrary effect of reducing differences in net earnings. Hence, the proportions of relative incomes shown in the table do, on the whole, reflect relativities in actual earnings. At any rate, they do not exaggerate them significantly.

The data in respect of the period before 1945 are based on total annual earnings, which include the so-called rent rebate, the annual year-end bonus, &c., as well as basic pay. The data for 1955 were provided by the management of the factory. Here also, total earnings for the year include premiums and bonuses as well as basic pay.

The present-day functions of chief engineers roughly correspond to those performed by the managing directors of factories before 1945. (The duties of the directors of the present were carried out by general managers at that time.) For this reason I have matched up the pay of present-day chief engineers with that of managing directors.

This is also shown by a comparison of the earnings of manual workers and technicians, for example. In the course of the last six years the movement of the relative monthly average earnings of technicians and of manual workers in light industrial employments has been as follows:

A position has arisen in which it is possible for outstandingly efficient craftsmen to suffer a loss of earnings in the event of their being promoted to supervisors or foremen compared to what they would have obtained if they had stayed at their benches. For this very reason there is a fairly widespread reluctance to take on the position of foreman. Similarly, there is a tendency to hang back when it comes to appointments to the posts of chief engineer or director, not to mention the amount of reluctance shown by plant managers when the question arises of 'promoting' them to some post in a ministry. The additional worry and the disproportionately greater amount of responsibility which goes with higher positions is very far from being matched by increased pay. Indeed, a post at a ministry may actually involve a reduction in earnings consequent upon 'promotion'.

Let us, for example, think of the position of an engineer who already has a certain amount of experience and is a functionary at a medium level of

Table X Earnings differentials of office staff in the Lóden Felt Factory before 1945 and now

Post	1943	1955
Director	1,938	300
Head of Costing Department	372	210
Dispatchers	325	133–9
Costing clerks	289	111
Material blenders	270	200

Notes on sources: In this table, the pay of subordinate clerks is taken as 100, and the pay of other grades is expressed in multiples of this. The source of data for the period before 1945 is the Central Economic Record Office, while data in respect of 1955 were provided by the management of the factory. Posts are designated in accordance with present-day terminology. (For example, in 1943 the 'director' referred to in the table would have been designated as the general manager, but his position corresponded to that of a director of the present time.) The data relate to monthly basic salaries; owing to lack of data, I was unable to add in sundry additional remunerations and subsidiary payments of various kinds. I therefore correspondingly excluded premiums and bonuses from data for 1955.

Table XI Earnings differentials of manual workers as against technical personnel

	1949	1955
Increase in earnings of manual workers	100	181.0
Increase in earnings of technicians	100	157.5
Technicians' earnings as a percentage of manual workers' earnings	200.1	182.8

Source: Based on data of the Central Planning Division of the Ministry of Light Industry.

responsibility, a deputy plant manager shall we say. As his abilities are not exceptionally outstanding, he cannot expect that he will eventually rise to a very elevated position. But he has good grounds for thinking it probable that he will sooner or later become a plant manager, or that he will be asked to take over the direction of a department of his enterprise. Now, this technician— and there are many such—has an insufficient prospect of being able to advance himself significantly in terms of the financial rewards he can look forward to. His present earnings, including premiums, will be in the neighbourhood of 2,000 forints—and, on a realistic estimate, he must recognize that it will hardly rise above this if he is promoted.

The present-day tendency towards the levelling and equalization of basic pay in respect of posts carrying differing degrees of responsibility is, in my opinion, mistaken, and very harmful. It puts a brake on people's desire to achieve promotion and correspondingly higher financial rewards by doing outstanding work and by perfecting their knowledge of their trade.

An ascending 'career' (in the healthy sense of the word), gradual advances in seniority, and gradual, regular, and worth-while rises in basic pay constitute an enormous and irreplaceable financial (and, let it be added, moral) incentive force in the lives of people generally, and particularly in the lives of the technical intelligentsia and of salaried staff.

The fact that our present economic administration makes such slight use of this incentive, and then does so in a way which is neither widespread enough, nor sufficiently well thought out, is a big mistake.

2. A second characteristic shortcoming of the system of basic pay is closely linked with the problem just discussed: experience in a trade and length of service are not taken into consideration at all, when decisions have to be made about whether remuneration in respect of the performance of a given function should be fixed at the maximum, medium, or minimal rates laid down for it in our scales of pay. No rules or even customary practices exist which would enjoin that length of service and experience in the trade must be taken into account.

Exceptionally talented people, who are capable of achieving remarkable results with very little experience, do exist, it is true. But the general experience is that 'practice makes perfect'. Experts of several decades' standing know more than beginners. Moreover, people who have worked in an enterprise over a long period get to know local conditions much better, and acquire a degree of familiarity with every person and machine in their factory which makes it much easier for them than for new staff to take the lead in work. Enterprises thus have a definite interest in attaching their employees to themselves, and forming a corps of workers loyal to themselves among their office staffs and technicians as well as among their manual workers.

Although these truths are widely appreciated, they are, unfortunately, left out of account in connexion with the aspect of the determination of pay which is here under consideration.

I spoke before of the type of employee who can count on being promoted in minor steps, even if not on making a breath-takingly rapid career. I said of this type of person that his expectation of material advancement is inadequate. It is necessary to distinguish another type of person as well. Very many people fairly rapidly reach a position beyond which they do not advance any further for the rest of their lives because they have reached the limit of their abilities. A sure knowledge on the part of such people that, if they do an honest job, their pay will rise from time to time as they are up-graded while continuing to carry out functions no more responsible than before, would stimulate them to greater industry and more enthusiasm in the performance of their tasks. Yet this group of people have not even the prospect of a slight increase in pay possessed, in case of promotion, by the type of person described earlier. The present system of pay involves that a foreman who attains this position at the age of 30, and may reach the maximum pay for foremen in the space of five or six years, will stay at this same level of pay even to the age of 60 if he continues, for decades, in his post of foreman, except, of course, in the event of a general increase in the pay of foremen. But, if this should happen, our man will still not feel himself to be the recipient of any additional financial acknowledgement of his work of several decades, because the same increase in pay will also accrue to any colleagues working alongside him who are no more than 30–35 years old.

Let us glance briefly at capitalist experience in this matter as well. In many capitalist factories pay was subject to annual review. Those whose work was considered unsatisfactory were dismissed, but those whose work was satisfactory were given pay increases of a greater or lesser amount annually by capitalist managements. This had been the case at the First Pécs Leather Factory, for example. Pay was raised at each year-end. It was the practice to raise the pay of every salaried employee—if only by 10 pengős. This was done in order to fortify the feeling that it was worth-while to stick to the enterprise and to serve the interests of the firm faithfully, as this would lead to larger earnings each year. Those whose work was considered to have been of particular merit had their pay increased by larger amounts. It was precisely by this test that technicians and salaried staff were able to tell the extent to which the managements of their enterprises valued their work.

The Pécs Leather Factory was, of course, a very prosperous enterprise, the staff of which was better placed than that of other factories. But the policy of pay increases at fixed intervals was far from exceptional. It was accepted as customary in a number of other factories as well. It is, therefore, worth reflecting upon.

3. The third characteristic shortcoming of the system of basic pay is this: the limits within which it is possible for the pay of personnel engaged in performing identical functions to vary are very narrow.

Here again, let us make a comparison with capitalism. There is a story told, for example, about the plant manager's post at the weaving mill of the Gyapjúmosó és Finomposztó Factory. At the end of the 1930's the salary attached to this post was 400 pengős. But when the management succeeded in obtaining the services of a new man for this post, who was a well-known and respected expert, they gave him a salary of 1,000 pengős, or $2\frac{1}{2}$ times the former amount. By contrast, the maximum permissible difference in basic pay in respect of a given job in our system is 50 per cent.

Or let us examine the salaries of plant managers in the Pannonia Fur Factory in 1942 (as shown in Table XII) and make a comparison with the position at present.

These comparisons also go to show that there is very little 'scatter' in the basic salaries of persons holding identical posts, although it is obvious that the quality of work done in a given post can show very great variations indeed.

It may be said, against this, that, in our system, it is the role of the premiums to reflect just these variations.[7] But this leads us on to the theme of the next section, which is to inquire into the question of whether the sum of all of the

Table XII Variations in earnings among plant managers in the Pannónia Fur Factory before 1945 and now

1942 Name	Total earnings in pengős	1955 Name	Basic salary in forints	Total earnings in forints
Ferenc Bőhm	7,377	Ferenc Bőhm	14,700	18,223
István Mormer	10,306	István Morvai	15,900	22,339
György Steiner	5,492	Vilmos Terzich	15,900	19,329
Aladár Tauber	9,821	László Simonfi	13,200	14,826
Antal Vas	6,659	Géza Vörös	15,050	18,956
Ferenc Zémann	10,924	Kálmán Karika	14,700	17,965
Earnings of highest paid plant manager as a percentage of earnings of the lowest paid 199%		Total earnings of highest paid plant manager as a percentage of total earnings of the lowest paid 151%		151%
		Basic salary of highest paid plant manager as a percentage of basic salary of the lowest paid		120%

Note: For source of data, see note to Table IX (p. 84). The names juxtaposed in identical lines of the two columns of the table—for 1942 and 1955 respectively—are those of persons who carried out exactly the same functions at these two dates. (For example, László Simonfi now performs the work once done by Aladár Tauber.) The data relate to annual earnings.

[7] Table XII is, incidentally, worthy of notice from this point of view as well. For it can be seen from it that even total earnings in 1955, as augmented by premiums, show a lesser spread than those for 1942. Against a spread, in basic salaries, of 20 per cent., we at present have a spread in total earnings of 51 per cent., but even this is only about a half of the pre-1945 spread of 99 per cent.!

The experience of the Pannónia Factory does not, of course, in itself constitute a yardstick which must, at all costs, be copied. It is not a highway to salvation. Nevertheless, in view of the fact that experience elsewhere was similar, it does provide food for thought. It helps, I think, to bring out the general picture of our system of remuneration, which is characterized by a certain levelling tendency.

component parts of earnings do jointly provide a true reflection of the varying performances of individual technicians and other members of salaried staffs.

The joint effects of the constituent parts of earnings—and the principles of socialist remuneration

Many of the problems I have mentioned in connexion with premiums and basic pay are related to a certain lack of clarity in some aspects of the theory and principles of our system of remuneration. 'Equal pay for equal work' is one of the basic canons of socialist income-distribution. The trouble is that this canon has been applied inappropriately in the matter of fixing the remuneration of responsible economic and technical personnel engaged in directing enterprises. The view held hitherto has been that a correct application of this basic canon requires that two principles be followed:

(i) roughly the same amount must be paid to persons holding identical posts; and
(ii) payment of the variable part of earnings must always be bound to 'objective' conditions of a kind which are linked to plans and are statistically measurable.

There follows from this the practice which entails that if two technicians hold equivalent posts and fulfil the conditions of their premiums to an equal degree, they will earn sums which are practically the same, irrespectively of their personal qualities. The usual way of putting this in the literature on incomes is to say: 'We pay for the work, not for the person.'

This, however, amounts to the creation of an inflexible and nonsensical antithesis between the job of work and the person who does the job of work. Of course, it is work and the result of work that is remunerated in a socialist enterprise. The problem, however, is: *how is this work to be measured?* The more complicated the work in question is, the more impossible it becomes to measure its results, its standard, and its quality by means of one or two 'objective indices'. It is clear that payment by results is the obviously suitable form of remuneration for very simple forms of physical labour, e.g. that of digging and moving earth without machinery. If a worker fulfils his norm to the extent of 150 per cent., he is paid wages of $1\frac{1}{2}$ times the amount he would have received if he had merely achieved 100 per cent. However, as soon as one comes to deal with more involved forms of physical labour, certain well-known complications arise: simple systems of payment by results, such as simple piece-rate payments, provide a one-sided incentive for augmenting the quantitative aspect of production in a way which may lower the quality of work. It is a familiar fact that many workers are neglectful of the quality of products, waste materials, and drive their machinery ruthlessly, &c., for the sake of achieving a higher quantitative percentage result.

This problem obtrudes itself even more when it comes to brain-work of a complicated character. No one would go so far as to pay premiums to doctors on the basis of one or two 'indices', like the number of his patients who died, the number cured, &c. Rather, an attempt is made to weigh the quality of a doctor's work in its entirety, in a manifold and complex fashion. Moreover, this is done on the basis of several years' experience rather than after a short period of time, until the judgement emerges that X is a first-class doctor and Y a doctor of average ability. By then, everybody will think it only natural that the first-class doctor X should earn more than Y—although the number of operations he has performed or the number of patients he has examined is no greater. He will be earning more because his personal qualities guarantee that work done by him will be of superior quality.

Now then, technical personnel are also workers by brain, and their job involves work of an extraordinarily complex kind, having a number of facets to it. This is doubly so in the case of technical staff entrusted with executive functions. Owing to its complex and manifold nature, the character of work of this kind is nearer to that of, for example, a doctor, than to simple physical labour which is measurable in terms of piece-work.

In spite of this, in remunerating work of this kind, something reminiscent of piece-work is employed, and an attempt is made to assess its value on the basis of 3–4 'objective indices'.

It might be said in reply to this that the analogy is misleading because—it will be maintained—the work of economic administration is a hundred times easier to measure by statistical indices than is the work of a doctor.

This counter-argument appears at first sight to be very convincing, and yet it contains no more than a half-truth, and is therefore misleading. For the question needs to be framed in practical terms: exactly whose work is it intended to measure by means of indices? What posts do they hold, and what is the nature of the indices the use of which is proposed?

It may be possible to find individual workers within the ranks of technical and administrative personnel engaged in management whose performance would be fairly unambiguously indicated by certain indices. But very few such can be found. It is, simply, an impossibility to evaluate the work of most technicians and salaried staff on the basis of one or two index numbers.

For example, while the work of the chief technologist of an enterprise affects the volume of production and must contribute to any reductions in cost which are achieved, yet the effect of his present work may not be felt for a year or so. And the considerable pains he may have taken, for example, over the training of those working with him, or over securing the acquisition of experience in the use of some new techniques, may not itself be capable of being measured directly in the future by means of these indices. The work of most technologists and administrative and managerial employees in responsible positions is of such a composite nature that it cannot be gauged by means of a 'thermometer' of 2–3 indices, but must rather be evaluated in a many-sided complex manner.

If the indices upon which premium payments are based were at least 'tailored' so as to suit individual workers, matters would not look quite so bad. But there is no question of this being the case; as we have seen, the excessive centralization of the system of premium payments causes these indices to be pretty rigidly uniform. In addition, these rigidly uniform indices (production value, &c.) do not even succeed in characterizing the sum total of the activities of enterprises adequately. We saw that these indices are one-sided; they provide a distorted picture in many cases, and indeed induce developments to take place in wrong directions. Hence exact fulfilment or overfulfilment of them provides no guarantee of the social interest having been well served. In this way the earnings of technologists and of administrative workers in responsible positions become partly divorced from what they accomplish. Yet this flatly contradicts the principle which forms the point of departure of the system, according to which the distribution of the product should be in accordance with work done, so that there is 'equal pay for equal work'. The earnings of technicians will in fact depend not only on their talent, diligence, devotion, and good work, but on such factors besides as whether they were 'lucky enough' to have got a loose plan or not; whether they are good enough at 'moaning' in pursuit of lower plan index numbers; whether they are adept in the performance of tricks which make it possible to slap 2–3 per cent, on to results achieved in proper ways; whether they are capable of neglecting important interests of the national economy for the sake of current premiums with an easy conscience, &c. The fate of the premiums is already partly decided as soon as plans are to hand. They are also undeniably dependent on real difficulties of an objective character which may crop up in the course of putting plans into effect. That is why technicians often feel that 'the premium does not depend on themselves'.

Let us take another example. Consider two plant managers working on similar tasks in factories of a similar character. Their basic pay is therefore the same. In addition their premiums are also the same because they have fulfilled the indices prescribed for them to the same extent. Is it certain that their work has been of equal value? Not at all. It is possible that one of them has manufactured fictitious results to 'improve the indices' while the other has not. One may have been lucky in being given a loose plan while the other may have been weighed down by the burden of a much tighter plan. One factory may be doing well, with everything ticking over nicely, while the other may be in need of having its affairs put in order just at the moment, and so on. In sum, it is possible for one of the plant managers to be much less talented, diligent, and technically well equipped than the other, but for their being equally remunerated nevertheless—merely because their jobs, and the degree to which they fulfil their respective plans, are the same. It is for this kind of reason that so many complaints are made of the injustice of the system of premiums. As the chief planning officer of one leather factory put it, exaggerating somewhat, of course: 'The premium is smallest when our technicians are sweating most, trying to fulfil a tight plan.'

Let us sum up what has been said. The basic pay of technicians and of administrative personnel in responsible positions shows a pattern of equality and levelling which is harmful. But the premiums, equally, fail to reflect differences in standards of performance sufficiently. This is partly because premium scales are always related to what we have already seen to be insufficiently differentiated rates of basic pay. Partly, it is because the size of premiums depends not only on the performance of the people receiving them, but also, to a fairly significant extent, on factors beyond their control. And, finally, it is because the indices which form the basis of premiums are insufficiently indicative of work done, and, moreover, also generally fail to provide unambiguous indications of the national economic interest.

From these conclusions there emerge clearly the reasons why the serious problem of providing adequate financial incentives would not be solved by simply reducing the proportion of the variable element in total earnings.

Such suggestions have been made. For example, an article by Jan Toronczyk entitled 'Are premiums too high?' appeared in the 20 January 1956 issue of the Warsaw newspaper *Trybuna Ludu*. A number of harmful features of the Polish premium system, which resembles our own closely, were pinpointed in this substantial and thorough article. Now the article attributed the harmful effects of the system very largely to the proportion of premiums in total earnings being too high. They are certainly higher than in our system. For example, a manager of a plant in the textile industry will be awarded 45 per cent, of his basic salary as his premium in the event of his plan being fulfilled to the extent of 100 per cent., and more in the event of overfulfilment of the plan. Hence the author recommended a reduction of this proportion to 15–20, or at most 30 per cent. Now, then, it so happens that this is just about equal to the prevailing size of the corresponding proportion in our own system, and yet the harmful features of the premium described by the author (e.g. the way in which the indices not connected with premiums are neglected in order that premium conditions may be fulfilled, &c.) still make their appearance in our system just the same. Our 'smaller' premiums give rise to much the same consequences as the 'excessively high' Polish premiums.

Thus it is futile to seek for a solution of this problem by way of an alteration of the quantitative proportions of material incentives. A transformation of their structure and system is what is needed.

Collective rewards received by enterprises

Enterprises may be awarded bonuses by the Ministry or the Ministerial Council for outstanding performances. Examples of such bonuses are the rewards to leading enterprises and the bonuses which go to holders of the pennants awarded by the Ministerial Council and the SZOT. (Both are mentioned here in their aspect as financial incentives. I cannot digress here to discuss the stimulating force of socialist competition and of the political agitation connected with it.)

The conditions for the award of the title of a leading enterprise differ by branches of industry and they also vary from time to time. In principle, enterprises competing for this title must fulfil every approved target index and must, in addition, overfulfil most of them in some stated proportion. If, therefore, the plan is at all tight, winning this title is rather difficult. In practice these standards are not rigorously adhered to in full, and the exact fulfilment or overfulfilment of each index is not demanded.

Experience shows that the prospect of winning the title has a certain tendency to act as a spur in enterprises which have a real chance of accomplishing this, e.g. where the title has already been won several times in succession. But where this looks hopeless from the start (even if this is only because one or two indices appear to be beyond the reach of an enterprise) the incentive effect will

Table XIII Rewards payable to leading enterprises

Numbers engaged in the enterprise	Reward (in forints)
–100	3,000
101–500	5,000
501–1,000	10,000
1,001–5,000	25,000
5,001–10,000	50,000
10,001–15,000	75,000
15,001–20,000	100,000

be absent. This is very understandable, since the reward attached to the title of leading enterprise is extremely small. Its size is as follows:

The reward is thus degressive; the larger the factory the less the amount received per head of personnel.

The average *per capita* figure this would work out at in light industry is 5–10 forints—which is too little to have a significant mobilizing incentive effect.

The bonuses attached to winning the pennants of the Ministerial Council or the SZOT are twice the size of those attached to attaining the position of a leading enterprise. The financial incentive effect of this is also rather weak.

Punishments inflicted upon enterprises

These are the obverse of the rewards. They include penalties, compensation payments, storage charges payable on omitting to load at the railhead, the so-called penal interest charges in the event of failure to observe prescribed conditions in regard to credits and finance, &c. Of these I shall only discuss penalties here.

The literature dealing with autonomy in accounting and with the correct allocation of economic responsibility repeatedly emphasizes the important role of the penalties payable in the event of breaches of contracts concerning conditions of delivery. In practice, however, their effects are rather small. The main reasons for this are the following:

(i) The amounts involved are very small, and have hardly any influence on total costs. For example, in 1955 the total of penalties paid out amounted to 0·24 per cent, of total costs in the shoe trade. Frequently penalties paid and received offset each other—at least in part.

(ii) Directors of enterprises and top managements generally are only affected very indirectly by penalties via their premiums on cost reductions. If enterprises reduce their costs in the process of falling foul of customers' requirements (e.g. by a process of continuous gradual impairment of quality)—then this can easily compensate for the cost-raising effects of the penalties they incur. Indeed, from the point of view of premiums it may even pay to let quality deteriorate.

(iii) There are cases of injustice which arise from firms being held responsible for faults beyond their control, when, for example, these result from bad planning on the part of the authorities, or from external obstacles of a genuine character.

(iv) Customers who have suffered losses do not always display a high degree of consistency in pressing their claims. If they are interested in being on good terms with an enterprise (e.g. because supplies from it are scarce), they will prefer to forgo their claims and will not take their case before the Central Adjudicating Committee.

Directors' funds and the funds for enterprise development. The part played by profits in our present system of financial incentives

Special significance attaches to directors' funds and to funds for enterprise development. At present these constitute the only two sources of incentives related to the profitability of enterprises in the whole of our system of financial rewards and punishments.

The question to be clarified in this connexion is: how effective is this relationship? Do profits exert a substantial influence on the work of enterprises through these two funds?

Now, our various textbooks on political economy, and the studies which deal with the subject of autonomy in accounting, never tire of stressing how important is the part played in the lives of enterprises by directors' funds, what a great stimulus they exert on the entire personnel of enterprises, &c. However—at least in the field of light industry—actual practice turns out to be rather different. Let us again begin by describing the rules now in force.

What are the sources of the directors' funds in light industry?

1. Enterprises have cultural and sports funds, which are controlled by their directors, and appear as constituent parts of directors' funds in the accounts. Directors' funds are not, however, the actual sources of these

moneys financially speaking, as they are provided for in the budgets of enterprises. Their amount is a fixed sum, unrelated to the results achieved by enterprises, and is equal to 0·6 per cent, of planned outlays on wages and salaries. These sums may only be used in the furtherance of cultural and sports objectives.

2. (*a*) Directors' funds in the narrower sense of the term. The greater part of these is a fixed sum in contrast with views commonly held about this. These funds do not vary with the achievements of enterprises, as their amount depends only on the size of personnels and on certain conditions, laid down in advance, being met. The Ministry determines a quota for the fund on a per capita basis. This averages 101 forints in the case of light industry.

Enterprises obtain this sum in the event of their fulfilling the following targets: the production plan, the plan of cost reductions, and the plan for surrendering profits.[8]

This fixed sum may be further supplemented as follows:

(b) Five per cent, of the quota is added in the event of the plan of cost reductions being fulfilled. (It is hard to see the reason for this being treated as a supplementary sum, as the payment of the quota itself already requires that the plan of cost reductions be fulfilled so that the quota could be fixed at 106 forints from the outset.)

(c) Ten per cent, of profits earned in excess of their planned amount. This is not paid until after the end of the financial year. It can be a very substantial sum. This is the part of directors' funds the size of which really does vary with the size and rate of increase of profits.

The sum of the various amounts listed under 2 (i.e. quotas plus the two supplementary payments) may not exceed 2·1 per cent, of planned annual outlays on wages and salaries.

The whole of the sums received under this head must be devoted to (i) staff welfare purposes to the extent of 55 per cent., and to (ii) bonus payments to the extent of the remaining 45 per cent.

3. A payment is made into directors' funds in respect of savings of circulating capital effected. This payment derives from a fund established by the Ministry of Finance, which is divided out among enterprises. The whole of this part of directors' funds must be devoted to bonus payments.

---

[8] This is a part of the financial plan prescribed for enterprises. The proceeds form a part of the State revenues.

4. A part of the proceeds of sales of idle fixed equipment. This also must be paid out in the form of bonuses.
5. A part of profits on articles of mass consumption produced from waste materials goes into directors' funds. (A further part goes into development funds.)
6. The fund for payments to outstanding workers. This is merely booked through directors' funds. Its source is the budget. It is established to provide awards to outstanding workers on a basis regulated by standing rules of competition. (The rules governing the award of the titles of outstanding worker, outstanding worker of the trade, &c., are laid down in precise terms by the Ministerial Council and the SZOT.)
7. Bonus payments to leading enterprises, and bonuses received together with the pennants of the Ministerial Council and the SZOT—if and when these distinctions are won. Sixty per cent, of the sums so received must be paid out in the form of bonuses, and 40 per cent, must be devoted to welfare purposes.

Table XIV gives details of the composition of directors' funds in light industrial enterprises in 1955. The allocation from budgetary funds listed under 1 above is not included here.

Let us now survey the regulations surrounding the development funds of enterprises. The chief source of this fund is a 25 per cent, share of profits in excess of their planned amount. For example, enterprises in the woollen industry obtained a fund of 8–4 millions for this purpose in 1955, and 6.2 millions or 76·2 per cent, of this was derived from profits earned over and above their planned amounts.

Other sources of this fund are:

(i) That part of depreciation allowances earmarked for investment which may be devoted to minor purchases.
(ii) Seventy-five per cent, of the net proceeds of sales of articles of mass consumption made of waste materials.
(iii) Proceeds from the sale of fixed equipment which has been replaced, if less than 25,000 forints.
(iv) Proceeds of sales of items of fixed equipment which are of minor value.
(v) Fifty per cent, of savings resulting from self-financed additions to capacity.
(vi) Fifty per cent, of savings resulting from the purchase of second-hand fixed equipment instead of new.

Table XIV Sources of directors' funds in light industry

Source of funds by the listing given in the text	Explanation of source of funds	Amount (in forints)
2 (a)	Part of directors' funds calculated on basis of per capita quota	17,540,100
2 (b)	Sums due in respect of fulfilment of plans of cost reduction	764,400
2 (c)	Part proceeds of profits in excess of their planned amounts	18,881,100
3	Sums in respect of savings on circulating capital	500,300
4	Sums in respect of sales proceeds of idle fixed equipment	193,800
5	Part proceeds of profits on articles of mass consumption made of waste materials	777,100
6	Outstanding workers' bonus funds	8,218,200
7	Bonuses going with title of leading enterprise or with holding pennants of Ministerial Council or SZOT	2,381,000
TOTAL		49,256,000

Source: Data of the Central Accounting Division of the Ministry of Light Industry.

The first among these latter sources of the fund (described under (i) above) amounts to a fairly impressive sum (1.1 million forints in the woollen industry, to put it in terms of the example given above). The remainder are fairly unimportant as sources of funds.

Disbursements from the development fund must be confined to the following:

(i) Investment outlays in excess of amounts provided for in the plan. Expenditures under this head below 50,000 forints do not require authorization by the Ministry.

(ii) Sums up to 25 per cent, of the value of the fund may be devoted to welfare expenditures without authorization on the part of the Ministry. Investment expenditures of a welfare character which are larger than this require special authorization.

(iii) Renewals in excess of planned amounts.

(iv) Reorganizations, the promotion of specialization.

(v) Outlays on research and experimental work.

(vi) Investments or renewals serving to safeguard social property. In practice, most plants utilize this fund chiefly for warehouse construction,
investment in health and safety devices and often also for purchases of
trucks.

We are now in a position to attempt an evaluation of the part played by these
two funds. I would like to raise the following problems in this connexion:

1. Directors, and other persons engaged in top management in enterprises,
have no direct interest in enlarging these two funds. The conditions which
determine whether or not they receive their premiums differ from most of the
conditions which govern the receipt of moneys for directors' funds and development funds. What matters most, moreover, is that individuals engaged in
top management have no personal interest in increasing the profits of their
enterprises.

A director will, of course, be glad to have larger sums at his disposal for
making bonus payments and will want to be in a position to develop his enterprise. He will therefore welcome increases in these two funds. This, however,
evidently does not count for as much as having a direct, personal financial
interest in them.

This is a characteristic and very important example of a situation in
which the interests of individuals and their enterprises are not sufficiently in
harmony.

2. The sums available in directors' funds for bonus payments to individuals
are very small. Yet these might be another channel by which a direct connexion
could be established between the interests of subordinate employees and the
interests of their enterprises as a whole.

Let us examine the data shown in Table XIV, which furnish us with figures
in this connexion. If we divide the grand total shown in this table among the
employees of those enterprises which had actually qualified for the receipt
of moneys for their directors' funds in accordance with the conditions listed
under points 2 (*a*), 2 (*b*), and 2 (*c*), then the amount available in the aggregate of director's funds per head works out at no more than 290.5 forints per
annum. If, further, the total amount in directors' funds were divided among
all enterprises instead of only among those which qualified for the fund in the
sense defined above,[9] then the amount available per head would become even
less—259.1 forints.

---

[9] This last calculation is not an unwarranted one since, by virtue of the conditions listed under points
3–7 above, the remaining enterprises also received some part of the total.

Thus the grand total of directors' funds equals 2·1–2·3 per cent, of average annual earnings of persons engaged in light industry. It must, further, be noted that a sizeable part of this sum is devoted to outlays of a social or cultural nature. The part of these sums available in 1955 which was left over for making payments to individuals amounted to 27,851,520 forints, or 146.5–164.2 forints per head per year—according as one or the other of the two bases of calculation I have employed above is used. This is equivalent to 1·2–1·3 per cent, of annual earnings. In other words, the sums available from directors' funds for making financial awards to individuals amounted, on average, to the equivalent of 3–4 days' earnings in light industrial employments! This may be sufficient to enable directors to make occasional distributions of bonuses. (We saw in the section dealing with target premiums that it can be used effectively for this purpose.) But it is far too little to secure that the workers of an enterprise have a personal stake in their collective achievements and in the profits earned by their enterprises.[10]

3. That the growth of enterprises, their progress in technology, and the extent of their socio-cultural equipments should—at least to some small degree—depend upon their own achievements rather than exclusively upon decisions of higher authorities and on centrally planned investment outlays, is, at present, already secured by the existence of the directors' funds and development funds.

But the extent of this connexion between the development of enterprises and the work they do is still very limited. However, if the establishment of a more substantial connexion of this kind were to be desired, then new and far-reaching problems would be posed. For the first question which would arise is this: what proportion of investment is to be carried out on the basis of plans of a strictly centralized origin, decided, or at least approved, by the higher authorities—and what part is to be decided upon by local bodies, including enterprises, in a decentralized fashion? It is clear that basic investment outlays, which largely determine the main contours of the national economy, must certainly be planned and decided upon at the centre. At present, however, the great bulk of enlargements and reconstructions of plant are decided upon centrally, and not at the enterprise level, even when they are on a partial and small scale. At the least they require the sanction or knowledge of the directorate or the Ministry. It seems to me that a considerable amount of decentralization

---

[10] It is true that the position varies by branches of industry. The total of directors' funds spread over the entire man-power engaged in the shoe industry works out at 376·5 forints per head per annum. This is above the average by about one-third, but is extremely little even so. On the other hand, in the cotton trade the figure works out at 121·01 forints, which is well below the average.

could be undertaken in these fields without in the least endangering the central determination of the overall balance of the economy. At the same time, this could provide very powerful incentives for enterprises.

However, this leads straight away to another problem. If the proportion of investment outlays which is arrived at locally, in a decentralized fashion, come to be of importance, it would then become wrong to pre-empt the entire capacity of enterprises engaged in producing investment goods, or in importing, for the purposes of centrally determined and planned investments. For if this were done, then the right of enterprises to develop autonomously would have no more than formal significance, since there would be no one to accept the investment orders enterprises would wish to place.

This problem is already with us, even though the proportion of investment which is decentralized is still rather small.

The rules governing the development fund allow an enterprise to utilize 5 per cent, of its profits in excess of their planned amount during the course of the year, but the full amount accrueing to it under this head is only at the disposal of the enterprise after its accounts for the year have been closed. The exact size of the sums at its disposal do not, therefore, become known to the enterprise until the beginning of the following year. But at that time it will already have missed the opportunity of placing an order, say, for a large machine with one of the machine-making factories—because the right moment for placing such orders would have been during the previous autumn, at the time when annual plans are in course of preparation. The acquisition of some piece of equipment from abroad presents even greater difficulties. Partly it will be late in the day for such orders also. In addition, foreign exchange resources will be fully taken up with orders necessitated by investments to be made within the framework of plans, and no foreign exchange will be available for investments 'outside the plan'. Enterprises may find it relatively easiest to spend money on investments in buildings, although it may easily happen that they can no longer locate free capacity for this either.

In spite of all these difficulties the most skilful enterprises may succeed in using their funds for the purposes they themselves regard as most important. But many enterprises will be unable to do this, and particularly just those which have the largest funds. These may then decide to spend their money on investments which, while being less essential than those which are most desired, are still of some use, or, alternatively, they may leave the money unspent for a year, 'frozen' from the point of view of the enterprise.

4. The system of directors' funds and development funds is extraordinarily complicated. We saw what a multiplicity of sources they are derived from.

It is significant that the personnel of enterprises whom I questioned about the directors' fund, invariably gave inaccurate and incomplete answers to my questions concerning the composition of the fund. Most of them only mentioned the personnel quota listed above under 2 (*b*), and, at the most, the 10 per cent, share due on excess profits in addition. The specialist expert at the Ministry was alone in being able to give an accurate answer. The attempt to provide separate incentives through these two plans to secure the fulfilment of particular tasks (e.g. savings in circulating capital, scrapping of worn-out machines, &c.) is, in these circumstances, unsuccessful. For, owing to the extraordinarily complicated character of the system, all separate incentives become blurred and lack effectiveness in practice. No one is induced to struggle for the achievement of economies in the use of circulating capital in order to increase the directors' fund by this means. The sums concerned are added together in practice in any case and the director (or, rather, the 'triangle'[11]) will start by considering what is the total sum available to him.

We have also seen that a large number of regulations and instructions exist to prescribe the exact proportions in which enterprises may make use of the various sources of finance which go to make up the two funds. The sums yielded by one source of finance has to be fully devoted to bonus payments, those by another only to the extent of 60 per cent., &c. Here, too, the influence of excessive centralization is very noticeable: the hands of directors and of enterprises are completely tied in the matter of how they are to use funds which are supposed to be disposed of at their own discretion.

5. The main source of both funds is to be found in profits, or, rather, in profits in excess of their planned amounts. Thus the size of these funds depends not only on how enterprises have functioned, but also on the sizes of profits planned for. If these are tightly set, the size of the funds acquired by enterprises will be unjustly small and, conversely, unmerited advantages will flow from plans that are drawn up in too loose a manner.

The planning of profits is at present completely unreliable, so that expectations in this field are constantly being upset.

For example, the extent to which enterprises fulfilled their profits plans for 1955 in various directorates of the Ministry of Light Industry are shown in Table XV:

There is not much point in talking of 'planning' when degrees of fulfilment vary between 87 and 400 per cent.!

---

[11] Of top management cf. p. 73.

Table XV Degrees of fulfilment of profits plans in light
industrial directorates

Branch of industry	Percentage fulfilment of profits plan
Cotton Trade Directorate	287
Flax and Hemp Trades' Directorate	175
Woollen Industry Directorate	163
Hungarian Silk Co.	137
Haberdashery Directorate	139
Knitwear Directorate	137
Clothing Directorate	125
Furniture Trades' Directorate	156
Wood and Timber Trades' Directorate	144
Paper Trades' Directorate	157
Printing Trades' Directorate	118
Leather and Footwear Directorate	156
MEH Office (By-products)	127
Investment Directorate	400
Wool Producers' Trust	87

Source: Data provided by the Central Accountancy Division of the Ministry
of Light Industry.

Seeing this, industrial directorates and the Ministry effect regular transfers between the development funds of various enterprises, on the one hand, and of industrial directorates, on the other hand; they take funds from one and hand them over to another, siphoning them off from where funds are abundant in order to supplement them where they are insufficient.

Thus, for example, in 1956 the transfers of 1955 development funds arranged by the woollen trades' directorate were as shown in Table XVI.

Such surpluses as are left over after these transfers within a directorate have been completed are subsequently drawn off by the Ministry into a so-called 'Ministry development fund'. The amounts so collected from development funds, in the light of results for 1955, were as shown in Table XVII.

The unreliability of profits plans provides a real justification for 'virement' within trades and by ministries. But this procedure also undermines the original purposes of development funds. This was to make the size of these funds, and, through these, to some extent also the growth of enterprises, dependent on *their own profitability*. But the transfer procedure may cause enterprises to develop doubts about the worthwhileness of overfulfilling their plans of profits by large margins, since such results merely lead to larger transfers of funds

Table XVI Transfers effected between the development funds of enterprises in the woollen industry

Name of enterprise	Supplements to development funds	Deductions from development funds	Deductions as a percentage of size of funds
	(thousand forints)	(thousand forints)	%
Bajai Gyapjúszövő	8	—	
Gyapjúmosó	—	158	24
Győri Gyapjú	—	30	4
Hazai Fésűsfonó.	90	—	—
Kalapgyár	—	—	—
Kistarcsai Fésűsfonó	—	13	6
Kőszegi Textil	67	78	17
Lóden	—	300	22
Magyar Gyapjúfonó	—	87	6
Magyar Posztó	70	—	—
Pomáz Budakalászi	71	—	—
Soproni Fésűs	8	—	—
Szombathelyi Takarógyár	—	27	11
Tatai Szőnyeggyár	500	—	—
Ujpesti Gyapjúszövő	—	220	20
Váci Fonó	—	91	24
Lőrinci Vatta	—	—	—
Gyapjubegyűjtő	—	2,000	43

Source: Data provided by the Central Accountancy Division of the Woollen Trades' Directorate.

away from them. At the same time, other enterprises feel less concerned about serious shortfalls in their profits—since they rely on their directorates and the Ministry to provide them with development funds.

6. The last question we need to consider here is whether profits provide an accurate and reliable reflection of the economic performance of an enterprise. How far do variations in profits reflect variations in performance as against the influence of circumstances outside the control of enterprises?

The answer is that our price system and general economic mechanism being what they are, profitability is an insufficiently accurate measure of the effectiveness of work done in enterprises. I shall revert to this later. Meanwhile, I would like only to indicate my views on this in order to avoid giving the impression that I regard profitability as a reliable measure of work done by enterprises, in present circumstances*

Table XVII Sums collected from enterprise development funds of individual trades in light industry

Branch of industry	Sum collected	Sum collected as a percentage of development fund of directorate
	(thousand forints)	%
Cotton Trades' Directorate	3,120	18.4
Flax and Hemp Trades' Directorate	760	16.8
Woollen Trades' Directorate	2,038	15.9
Paper Trades' Directorate	350	7.7
Printing Trades' Directorate	180	17.5
Leather-Footwear Trades' Directorate	2,200	16.7

Source: Data provided by the Chief Accountancy Division of the Ministry of Light Industry.

2. MORAL AND POLITICAL INCENTIVES

Financial incentives in their various forms have been discussed in great detail in the foregoing. But material interests are far from being the only induce-ments animating top managements and the technical staffs of enterprises. Other factors, which I will summarily label as 'moral-political incentives' for the purposes of the present discussion, do also play a part in our economic life.

Many things come under this head. The most important are these:

(i)   the self-respect of top managements, the stimulating effect of a con-sciousness of work well done;
(ii) the controlling influence of social and political organizations;
(iii) publicity, and the strength of public opinion, which may manifest themselves in several ways ranging from newspaper articles to criti-cisms and proposals voiced at production conferences;
(iv) public praise, appreciation, and the receipt of awards.

The strength of moral and political factors is frequently overrated. There are, in fact, limitations on their effectiveness, which need to be clearly recognized.

Let us look at one or two examples. For some years now, countless newspa-per articles have pointed to the fact that enterprises are reluctant to produce articles having a high labour content, that they neglect quality and try to restrict variety. These matters are also repeatedly brought up in the course of production campaigns—but these ills continue to exist just the same. Political propaganda work cannot fully offset the harmful effects which result inescapably from our present methods of providing incentives and administering the economy. If top managements are pushed in *one* direction by the system of instructions, plans, and material incentives, it is unwise to hope that they will nevertheless go in *another* direction under the influence of propaganda efforts. For example, the one-sided character of the system of premiums provides incentives for top managements to constrict variety, to neglect the improvement of quality, and to avoid the production of articles which require relatively large labour inputs, because this eases their tasks of raising production values and of securing the fulfilment of their indices of adherence to plans as well as accelerating cost reductions. But arguments of a political nature are nevertheless also used, asking top management to improve quality, broaden variety, &c.

In such cases, managers find themselves faced with a conflict between their economic interests as individuals and their sense of responsibility to the national economy. It is possible that the latter prevails in many cases. But it is also very understandable, since it is only human, if individual economic interest proves to be the stronger, and the fact that this often is the case is not to be wondered at. Indeed, a manager faced with a dilemma of this kind is always in a position to salve his conscience by reflecting that the main interests of the national economy must, after all, require the fulfilment of the plan index numbers to which premium payments attach. For, he can reflect, what else could account for the fact that it is just these, and not other indices, that carry financial incentives?

In any case, the main lesson to be derived from all this is that top managements should not be confronted with situations in which such conflicts of interest arise. Exhortation will, at best, only act as a brake on harmful tendencies in such cases. There may be a need for brakes. But we should not allow ourselves to be content with this! If exhortation, agitation, and political propaganda are to exercise powerful influences on top managements, they must be made to serve, not as brakes, but as second engines alongside the other engine of financial incentives. In other words, exhortation and material incentives ought both to be pulling top managements in the right direction, and they should act in a mutually reinforcing fashion.

I would like, here, to repeat the point that the interests of individuals and of enterprises cannot be expected to be in complete harmony with those of the community as a whole at all times. But it is possible for conflicts between them to be both much fewer and less pronounced than they are today—and this would at the same time be associated with a state of closer harmony between agitation and the system of financial incentives.

A different conception of what is required is also to be met with. According to this, the intention is perhaps not so much to employ political agitation to counteract the harmful tendencies evoked by the faulty character of the system of financial incentives. The idea is rather that agitation should go some way at least to complement material incentives, in the sense that top managements should be stimulated, by means of exhortation, to perform tasks which they are not induced to carry out by the system of financial incentives, owing to the gaps which exist in the latter.

It would naturally be a very useful thing if agitation did, in fact, have this effect. But this conception of its mode of operation is hardly borne out by experience. For this shows that where agitation bears on production, it is, in most places, wholly given over to campaigns designed to further the fulfilment of the very same two or three indices which are in any case already singled out for attention in the system of financial incentives by way of premium payments being attached to them. For example, it is customary for directors and chief engineers of enterprises to be repeatedly questioned in the course of production check-ups carried out by party and trade union organizations. What is demanded of them on these occasions is that they account for how they stand in the matter of the fulfilment of the very same two or three indices (e.g. production value, costs) upon which the authorities already place the most emphasis. Moreover, as this controlling activity is sometimes performed in a manner which is, from an economic point of view, amateurish, and fails to have regard to the complex economic activity of enterprises, an extraordinary degree of rigidity is often manifested in the course of it.

It should be noted that the source of the trouble here does not lie in the fact that agitation relating to production works in a way which concentrates attention on the most important tasks. It is rather that—as I have partly already explained in the foregoing, and will partly also show in what follows—the two or more indices upon which so much stress is placed do not characterize the work of enterprises adequately. Hence, uncompromising demands that they be fulfilled frequently do more harm than good.

Agitation is thus as one-sided as is the system of premiums. In some respects it is more one-sided. For example, the system of premiums now in force places a good deal more emphasis on cost reductions than it did a few years ago. Much is also heard about it in the course of agitation and in the press. Yet, when, at the year-end, the newspapers carried daily reports listing enterprises and branches of industry which 'fulfilled their annual plans', they once again identified this exclusively with fulfilment of production plans, or, more precisely, with fulfilment of target figures for the value of production.

Thus, the issue of *Szabad Nép* for 18 December 1955 carried a news report with the headline: 'Numerous enterprises have fulfilled their annual plans.' It stated, among other things, that 'according to reports of the Ministry of Light Industry, more than fifty enterprises have completed their annual plans'. And, to remove all doubt as to what the paper means by fulfilment of plans, the following appears a few lines farther on: 'Of the factories attached to the Ministry for Metallurgy and Machinery manufacture, more than 70 enterprises—almost a third of the factories—have so far fulfilled their 1955 plans in respect to finished production, total production, and exports.' Similar notices appeared in the issues of *Szabad Nép* for 4, 7, 14, 20, 21, 24, and 25 December.

During the weeks of the production campaigns which take place at the end of each year the public praise attaching to newspaper articles of this kind has an undoubted effect. In the instances quoted above, the newspapers relapsed into bad old ways and urged enterprises to fulfil their target figures of production value in a one-sided manner.

Agitation in the field of production has very largely the character of a campaign. As and when improvements in particular fields become the order of the day—they may be the fight against waste, or technical development, &c.—all attention will be concentrated on this, while other tasks will be relegated to the background. This also frequently has a distorting influence on the work done in managing enterprises.

Some of these faults can be got rid of by improving the standard of political work in this field. But that in itself is no cure for the one-sidedness of the structure of incentives and of the shortcomings of the methods we use for administering the economy. It is not a substitute for remedying the latter.

3. THE ROLE OF SUPERVISION BY THE STATE AND OF PUNISHMENTS

The coercive force of the law, the knowledge that individuals will be taken to task for neglecting their duties, and can be punished in various ways, are among the factors which spur top managements on. There is no point in preserving silence on this point, even if the literature dealing with incentives often does so.

The first chapter of this study has dealt with the system of instructions, which includes plan index numbers, decrees, and regulations. Whether they are paid for or not, these instructions have to be carried out unconditionally. The principle is that anyone who fails to execute an instruction handed down by higher authorities has offended against State discipline and must therefore be made to answer for it.

In controlling the execution of their instructions, the authorities employ a number of methods, including various statistics and reports. Enterprises are frequently inspected on the spot. The managements of enterprises are, from time to time, made to give accounts of the work they have done at meetings and conferences.

A number of bodies are concerned with the operation of such controls. These naturally include, in the first place, the industrial directorates and the Ministry, which directly govern enterprises. Regular supervision has also been exercised by the Ministry of State Control; and, in the more important enterprises, by representatives of the Ministerial Council, the National Planning Office, the Central Statistical Office, &c. In suspicious cases, the police or the State prosecutor's office will pursue inquiries.

During the month of June and the first half of July 1956 the sequence of inspections shown in the list on p. 111 took place in the Magyar Gyapjufonó factory. (Inspections carried out on behalf of local district and Budapest city party committees are not included in the list.)

What are the possible consequences of infringements of instructions? There are, in this, a number of gradations: e.g. sharp criticism at the hands of the higher authority concerned; reprimands published in the official gazette; the levying of compensation; dismissal from posts held; in serious cases, the initiation of judicial proceedings.

The process of safeguarding the administration of planning in so far as it involves recourse to law is regulated in accordance with a special decree having the force of law, namely, decree No. 4 (1950) of the Presidential Council of the People's Republic.

According to 5, § (1) 2 of this, for example, 'except in cases of compelling necessity, it is an offence to pursue activities which are substantially at variance with the detail of plans, and thus endanger the execution of the detail of plans'. Persons committing such an offence may be sentenced to jail for up to two years. Acts involving 'serious danger or damage to the national economic plan or some detailed part of it' are classed as criminal acts punishable by sentences to jail for periods ranging up to five years. The superiors of persons who have committed offences or criminal acts of the kind defined in the above decree must also be tried in court if 'it is ascertained that they are guilty of either deliberate or thoughtless omissions in their exercise of their duties of supervision or control'.

	Control authority	Subject-matter of inspection
1.	Woollen Trades' Directorate	Annual control of documents.
2.	Ministry of Light Industry	Economy in the use of materials.
3.	Woollen Trades' Directorate	Balance sheet for 2nd quarter.
4.	Woollen Trades' Directorate	Plan fulfilment for 2nd and 3rd quarters.
5.	Ministry of Light Industry	Composition of list of names of Stakhanovite workers.
6.	Woollen Trades' Directorate Ministry of Light Industry Ministry of Finance	Simplification of wage and salary accounting.
7.	Ministry of Light Industry	Premium regulations for 3rd quarter.
8.	Woollen Trades' Directorate	Dyeing services undertaken and yarn supplied for other enterprises.
9.	Local Branch of Hungarian National Bank	Request for credit.
10.	District Office of Hungarian National Bank	Request for credit.
11.	Woollen Trades' Directorate	Investment problems.
12.	Woollen Trades' Directorate	Execution of collective contract.
13.	City Directorate of Central Statistical Office	Statistical report.
14.	Central Trade Union Social Insurance Authority	Accounts.
15.	Woollen Trades' Directorate	Materials position.
16.	Woollen Trades' Directorate	Plan fulfilment for 2nd quarter.

Naturally, no State can function without discipline and powers to punish those who offend against discipline. In a system, moreover, in which the role of the State in the economy has become very great indeed, the use of disciplinary measures in economic affairs is necessarily enhanced. The question is: to what extent are disciplinary regulations actually invoked in practice?

A very close connexion exists between the effectiveness of material incentives (and moral–political incentives), on the one hand, and the extent to which it is necessary to invoke disciplinary measures, on the other hand. The less the reliance placed by the system on material incentives (and the less it is able to count on the enthusiasm of people), the more it will be driven to employ methods involving coercion.

The experience of recent years is instructive in this connexion. It is a familiar fact that between 1949 and 1953 arbitrary methods of leadership had become widespread in the public life of the country; in many fields persuasion was replaced by bullying. One of the accompaniments of this, during these years, among others, was the beginning of an excessive use of administrative measures in economic affairs, as well as elsewhere.

My colleagues and I have prepared a summary of decrees of a disciplinary character which appeared in the *Light Industrial Gazette*, the official newspaper of the Ministry, in 1952. It appeared that, in the course of a single year, the number of occasions on which directors were subjected to punishments totalled 76, chief engineers 23, chief accountants 45, other technical or administrative employees 36. Punishment took the form of loss of post in 9 cases, and that of a fine in 163 cases. (Incidentally, not all instances in which disciplinary measures were taken were published in the *Gazette*.)

It is worth listing some examples of the grounds for disciplinary punishment during this period. (I refer, in brackets, to the relevant issues of the *Light Industrial Gazette*):

(i) A director was penalized for negligent warehouse management. (6 March.)

(ii) Top managerial staff was penalized for failing to make use of an idle steam-engine. (22 April.)

(iii) A director was penalized for not having visited the Ministry in person (!) about a payment of wages in excess of their planned amount. (15 July.)

(iv) A director was penalized because of 'failure to reduce technical personnel by 1 man, as instructed, thus giving rise to excess payments of wages'. (2 September.)

(v) A director was penalized because his enterprise failed to observe the prescribed norm of raw material utilization. (9 September.)

(vi) A chief engineer was taken to task because 'he failed to make the technical dispositions necessary for eliminating the influence of factors

causing a deterioration in the quality of production at his enterprise'
in connexion with a particular article. (30 September.)

(vii) A director was fined 1,600 forints and the chief technician of the same
enterprise was dismissed from his post because planned holiday periods were not adhered to, and this gave rise to excess wage payments.
(28 October.)

A large proportion of the acts of omission which were penalized by the employment of disciplinary measures in 1952 were of such a nature that they would
probably never have arisen at all if a properly functioning system of financial
incentives had been in force. In a well-organized economic set-up, directors,
chief engineers, and chief accountants act against their own financial interests
if they leave steam-engines unutilized, tolerate disorder in warehouses, turn
out products of low quality, spend excessively on wages, employ too many
men, waste materials, fail to arrange holidays in a rational manner, &c. If top
managements do not solve such problems of their own volition, but have,
instead, to be forced to do so by directives and disciplinary penalties, then
this is evidence of the faulty character of the organizational forms of an economy. In any case, such measures are not really effective. The fact that one or
two directors who have exceeded norms in their use of materials have been
punished, hardly diminishes waste in the use of materials significantly.

There were also occasional instances of court actions during this period.
(The proliferation of punishments and penalties was, incidentally, much more
characteristic of heavy industry than of light industry.)

The case which arose over the plan fulfilment of the Fehérnemü Factory in
the third quarter of 1952 was very characteristic of this period. The factory
had lagged behind in the matter of fulfilling its target of production value. So,
on the very last day of the currency of the plan, they produced quite enormous
quantities of foot cloths (even though more than enough had already been
produced previously). In this way, they eliminated their deficiency—and won
their premium.

The tale of this chicanery has been told in the issue of *Szabad Nép* for 30
January 1953. Shortly afterwards two of the executives of the factory were
brought before the courts. They were given prison sentences. (Cf. *Szabad Nép*,
26 March 1953.)

It would be difficult to reconstruct the case at this stage. It is clear that
the true interests of the national economy were damaged in this factory for
the sake of the premium. But it is also clear that the abuses of which the top
management of the Fehérnemü Factory were guilty are regular occurrences in

hundreds of places (even if they take less noticeable and crude forms)—and are, moreover, committed in response to temptations and inducements held out by the plan index number and premium systems themselves, which, moreover, also provide ample opportunities for committing such abuses.

Naturally, their fear of public ostracism, of losing their jobs or their reputations with the personnel departments of higher authorities, and also certain rather frightening court cases, have deterred many executives from actually making use of the opportunities for abuse provided by the system of plans and of premiums. To this extent disciplinary regulations are capable of counterbalancing the harmful features of the system of financial incentives.

But disciplinary measures are incapable of eliminating these harmful effects. Moreover, court cases of this kind have undeniably reduced the enthusiasm which top managements and the technical intelligentsia feel for their work. A system of financial incentives must therefore be constructed which will at least avoid producing temptations of the kind which produce such cases.

It is no accident that the large-scale proliferation of the administrative apparatus should have coincided, in point of time, with the period under consideration here. The more instructions there are—particularly if they are of such a kind that there are no financial incentives providing inducements towards their being carried out—the greater the need for reports, memoranda, local inspections, spot checks, and conferences. This in turn is inevitably accompanied by a growth of the bureaucratic apparatus at higher levels as well as within enterprises.

The experiences of the years 1953–4 are also instructive. The strict measures mentioned above were much less used by the authorities for strengthening discipline during this period. But this relaxation was inaugurated at a time when a better and more comprehensive system of material incentives, replacing earlier measures, was not yet in existence. The previous economic mechanism continued in operation without modification. Yet this was a piece of machinery which could not work smoothly without the benefit of the type of 'lubrication' provided by a widespread application of administrative measures. In the absence of these, the gears of the mechanism failed to work satisfactorily. This mixed situation was one of the basic causes of the manifold troubles of that period.[12]

---

[12] An example taken from the machinery industry may be mentioned. Every industrial directorate and each enterprise in this industry found that the switch to articles of general consumption involved 'deteriorations in their indices', because the production of these is more troublesome, 'brings in less forints', &c. These, in turn, are notoriously serious disadvantages within the present set-up of planning

The democratization of economic life certainly requires that the exaggerated use of 'extra-economic force' and of legal coercion, as well as the proliferation of punitive measures be brought to an end. But this can be attained in two different ways. One is to preserve the previous forms of the economy while dealing more leniently with breaches of instructions. This is a bad method, for it gives rise to disturbances in the running of the economic machine without removing the root causes of the trouble.

The other method is to change the mechanism of the economy in such a way as to make it much less necessary to employ instructions, replacing these by a wider use of other driving forces, particularly in the shape of financial incentives. The need for making use of disciplinary measures will arise much less often if instructions become much fewer in number, and if those few that remain are as far as possible in harmony with the personal economic interests of managements, instead of clashing with them.

Within an economic mechanism of this kind it would be possible to insist the more strongly that a relatively small number of important State instructions and laws be adhered to. Such a course would have a much greater chance of obtaining the agreement and support of top managements and of the technical intelligentsia.

One other question needs to be raised in connexion with the disciplinary activities of the State. How comprehensive is the system of State control? How far is there, in practice, a demand for the fulfilment of every directive? How far does this type of incentive furnish a complement to financial incentives in the sense that it also promotes the execution of tasks the performance of which is not directly encouraged by prospects of material gains?

It is difficult to give an unambiguous answer to this question. A certain degree of control is exercised over the execution of every instruction contained in plans, if not otherwise, then by way of the requirement that statistics of the degree of fulfilment of each plan index number be furnished regularly to the authorities. An attempt is noticeable to press managements by administrative means to perform just those tasks which do not attract financial rewards, and this was even more noticeable during 1950–3. The examples given above

and administering the economy. Coercive measures were no longer employed on a sufficient scale—but there was not yet a system of financial incentives in operation which would have been capable of furnishing enterprises with an interest in satisfying the real needs of society in a flexible manner, instead of merely fulfilling index numbers.

When a start was eventually made with the production of such articles, this was again merely the outcome of political and administrative pressures, and not the result of financial incentives and of economic motives acting on enterprises. These pressures led, in turn, to 'switching over' even where this was, in fact, uneconomic.

in respect of 1952 bear this out. To this extent, administrative methods play a certain complementary role in 'filling the gaps' left by the system of financial incentives. But, as I have already stressed, we must not overrate the effectiveness of these methods. They were, quite obviously, incapable of putting an end to waste in the use of materials or to the neglect of quality, &c. Moreover, the accent in State control activities is not placed on these tasks. The 3–4 plan indices on the fulfilment of which higher authorities insist most strongly are those which are regarded as having the greatest importance, and these already appear among the conditions for receiving premiums. The problems which arise here are similar to the ones I have already discussed earlier in the section dealing with moral–political incentives. What visiting controllers coming down from the Ministry are primarily interested in checking on is 'plan fulfilment'—i.e. the target of production value—and, in addition, cost reduction as well as observance of the limit set on permitted outlays on wages and salaries. These are the things concerning which directors are liable to get telephone calls and about which they are likely to be cross-questioned at meetings of expert advisory bodies at the Ministry, &c. The occasions on which the Ministry or the directorates will intervene forcibly in what goes on at enterprises will, in the main, be when there is trouble over these figures.

Here also, as in political work, there is a tendency to resort to campaigns: for a time, every control official studied wastefulness in the factories; later on, there followed a host of inquiries into the question of raising standards of technique, and so on.

It follows from all this that the disciplinary powers of the State fall far short of succeeding in evening out the harmfully one-sided effects of the system of financial incentives.

III

SOME USEFUL AND HARMFUL TENDENCIES WHICH RESULT FROM THE JOINT EFFECTS OF PLAN INSTRUCTIONS AND INCENTIVES

IN the first part of this study I surveyed the system of instructions, devoting particular attention to plan index numbers. Next, I examined incentives, giving detailed consideration to financial incentives. Naturally, all of these factors act jointly and in a closely interconnected manner in the economy, rather than singly.

However, the essential element in this complex is the *instruction*. The dominating role played by instructions is one of the most characteristic features of this mechanism, which serves to distinguish it from others. It is customary to controvert this view by saying that a large part is also played by reliance on economic motives. This is true, as the previous chapter served to show. The part played by economic incentives is great—but they do not act in an independent fashion on a significant scale.

For what characterizes the connexion between these factors is that the most effective incentives serve to underpin the instructions and provide stimuli for fulfilling these. This is particularly true of the regular premiums of persons in top managerial positions, but it applies also to a considerable extent, as we have seen, to the mode of operation of political agitation and of State control activities. This is not universally the case; some incentives encourage the performance of measures and processes which are unrelated to instructions. Thus, for example, penalties serve, in a direct way, to promote the satisfaction of the wishes of customers rather than the execution of some instruction coming from the centre. Similarly, there is agitation in favour of the solution of tasks, the fulfilment of which is not separately prescribed by instructions. But surveying the system of incentives as a whole, it is clear that its dominant characteristic and ruling principle is to serve to prop up the instructions.

Overcentralization in Economic Administration. János Kornai translated by John Knapp, Oxford University Press.
© Oxford University Press (2023). DOI: 10.1093/oso/9780192894427.003.0003

Our survey has shown that, to a certain extent, the various incentives complement each other, but it has also shown that they frequently conflict. (For example, financial incentives have a tendency, say, to induce managements to lower quality, while agitation is used in an attempt to dissuade them from this, and, indeed, those who lower quality may even be arraigned before the courts.)

In the end these various factors have a certain joint effect. The system of plan index numbers, together with other instructions, and with the system of premiums, of other material and moral incentives, and of administrative regulations, releases a number of influences of a kind which mutually reinforce each other. As the final outcome of these, a number of characteristic and persistent economic processes and dominant tendencies appear. Our present task is to subject these effects—both the healthy and the harmful tendencies—to closer examination.

1. THE UPSURGE OF THE QUANTITY OF PRODUCTION

The systems of instructions and incentives jointly result in a very powerful effect in leading to production increases. This has been their strongest effect in the last few years, and, in spite of the undoubtedly one-sided character of the resulting drives, they have yielded substantial results.

Let us examine a few data reflecting the large increases in production which have taken place:

The rapid rise of production continued into 1955, even though, for reasons which have already been mentioned, the government was trying, towards the end of the year, to put a brake on this. The total production of light industry in 1955 was 8·4 per cent, above its 1954 volume.

Table XVIII Growth of production in light industry, by trades

Branch of industry	1950	1951	1952	1953	1954
Timber	137.8	222.7	283.5	281.8	262.1
Paper	122.8	148.4	162.0	165.8	178.3
Textiles	120.4	145.5	157.6	154.4	167.0
Leather and fur	133.5	133.9	140.2	151.5	153.1
Clothing	215.7	371.7	461.6	451.3	455.4
Total, light industry	130.0	167.1	188.2	188.5	200.2

Source: Data of the Central Statistical Office. The index has been calculated in terms of total production at constant prices, on a base 1949 = 100.

The tendency for production to rise is revealingly shown by an examination of the course of production by individual commodities. In 1955, which is the year primarily under examination in this study, changes in the production of certain important commodities was as follows:

Table XIX Growth of production in light industry, by principal products

Product	Percentage increase over 1954	Percentage decrease in relation to 1954
Finished cotton goods	4.4	
Linen and hemp cloths	5.2	
Cloth for sacks	7.9	
Finished worsted cloths	22.5	
Finished cloth made of tape yarn	30.6	
Finished silk	22.5	
Worsted cloth made of spun rayon	1,111.6	
Carded cloth made of spun rayon		20.9
Cotton stockings	91	
Synthetic stockings	102.4	
Artificial silk stockings	27.0	
Knitwear	23.2	
Men's shirts	8.9	
Children's underwear	56.0	
Men's coats		1.5
Men's suits	5.7	
Women's coats	24.0	
Women's dresses	15.2	
Boys' suits	5.9	
Men's shoes	21.0	
Women's shoes	5.6	
Children's shoes	26.1	
Paper	1.0	
Polished bedroom suite	51.0	
Polished wardrobe	34.0	
Combination wardrobe	13.6	
Painted bedroom suite	399.3	
Bent-wood chairs		8.3
Utility furniture		0.5

Source: Extract from a Report of the Chief Planning Division of the Ministry of Light Industry. The indices were calculated from data on production expressed in natural units (square metres, pieces, pairs, &c.)

The rise in production enabled increases to take place in the volumes of clothing and of other light industrial products made available to domestic commerce for home consumption. At the same time, light industrial enterprises also made increasing contributions to the export trade of the country.

The question of how far the exporting activities of the textile industry have been economically sound from a national point of view has been much debated. Whatever the truth in this matter, we must certainly count it an achievement of light industry that it was able to accomplish a very rapid rate of increase in the quantity of goods exported. This may be brought out here with reference to two products, cotton and woollen cloths:

The significance of the results attained by light industry is increased by the fact that they were achieved in very difficult circumstances. It is a familiar fact that there was very little investment in this branch of industry during the first five-year plan. The share of light industry in the total of gross fixed investment during the five years was no more than 1·8 per cent.[1] Hence the extent to which the increase in production had been secured by way of new installations and major extensions of plant had been very small: there were few plants in which antiquated machinery was modernized. The chief method of raising production was that of utilizing capacity more fully.

For one thing, in many plants which worked single, or double shifts, respectively, under capitalism, a transition has been made to two-or three-shift working. There has also been an increase in production per worker, i.e. in productivity. In 1955 alone, total production value (at constant prices) per worker per working day grew by 5·2 per cent.[2]

Table XX Growth of exports of certain light industrial products

	Cotton cloth	Woollen cloth
1954 exports as a percentage of 1949	196.5	117.2
1955 exports as a percentage of 1949	204.2	130.4
1954 exports as a percentage of 1938	1,123.0	544.7
1955 exports as a percentage of 1938	1,163.1	619.5

Source: Data of the Central Statistical Office. The indices were based on output data expressed in square metres. This naturally fails to express variations in the commodity composition of production. It does, nevertheless, provide a picture of the orders of magnitude of growth.

[1] According to the *Hungarian Statistical Handbook,* 1956, p. 56, light industry contributed 22·2 per cent, of total production value produced in all factory establishments.
[2] According to data of the Ministry of Light Industry.

The fact that there were frequent hold ups in raw material supplies, stocks being low, was yet another source of difficulties, apart from the meagre allocation of investment to this sector.

A number of factors have played a part in the achievement of these results in the face of difficulties. There is, however, no doubt that we must count the systems of plan index numbers and of premiums among the most important of these factors. They exert a large and powerful stimulus in the direction of raising output. This study discusses many unfavourable aspects of our economic mechanism. But we must not forget that planning has made it possible to ensure full employment and the rapid increase in the quantity of production which has been described above. Hence, improvements in administering the economy must be brought about in such a way as to ensure that any changes made will develop these advantageous aspects of our economic mechanism further, rather than endangering them.

2. THE FALSE 'ORDER OF IMPORTANCE' OF TASKS

We have seen that enterprises, and particularly factory managements, are very greatly stimulated by the systems of planning and of incentives to increase the quantity of production. The question of how far these systems serve to promote the other requirements of. economic performance must also be examined, however.

The six most important *desiderata* are that production be carried on so that:

1. current and embodied labour inputs should be as small as possible;
2. with the minimum practicable use of fixed equipment and circulating capital;
3. in producing articles of the highest possible quality;
4. in as large quantities as possible;
5. these products being those that are most needed by society;
6. all this being done in such a way as not to endanger future production, but rather to promote it, and so furthering the satisfaction of the future needs of society.

It is the intention of the present system of planning to issue separate instructions in respect of each one of these six requirements. Indeed, the procedure is characterized by an attempt to go beyond this in using instructions to say what means and specific methods are to be used in meeting these requirements. Let us, for example, glance at the first requirement. This is prescribed, primarily, by way of the plan of cost reductions, although not unambiguously, and with many distortions. But, at the same time, the methods to be used are also prescribed by innumerable instructions: raw material utilization is prescribed by means of the plan of raw material supplies by the 'index of output co-efficient of materials' and by raw material norms (i.e. in three different ways!), the utilization of labour by detailed personnel plans and plans of permitted outlays on wages and salaries, &c. Indeed, in connexion with the last of these, there is a separate plan saying how much overtime may be worked in enterprises.

The position in regard to the other five requirements listed above is similar. Instructions, particularly plan index numbers, are used to spell out both requirements and the means of fulfilling them.

However, the degree to which the system of incentives lends support to the instructions issued is not uniform. According to what their consequences are, some instructions have much 'authority' and 'weight', and are very effective, while others are of more or less formal importance only, having their existence only on paper. Thus, a definite order of importance of the tasks which arise in the course of the economic process is formed. What is 'most important' is the fulfilment of those indices to which the premiums of persons in top posts and of staffs paid on the basis of the aggregate results of enterprises are attached. The control of production, as carried out by the State and the party, is also primarily concerned with the observance of these indices. Every other index and instruction is 'less important', and those indices whose fulfilment or non-fulfilment does not lead to further consequences are completely ignored in practice. It is sheer illusion and self-deception to think of these latter prescriptions as 'instructions'. (It may be noted that there is a widespread tendency to indulge in such self-deception in our economic literature and in practical economic affairs.)

Let us take an example or two. One is the profits plan. The size of profits is very important from a budgetary point of view. Yet we saw in Table XV[3] that the degree of fulfilment of this plan varies between 87 per cent, and 400 per cent. In these circumstances, prescribed levels of profits can hardly be regarded as real authoritative instructions. Yet profits do not even belong to the group of indices to which no further consequences attach, for the directors' funds and development funds of enterprises are related to it. The variations observed merely reflect the fact that this index is unrelated to the premiums of top managements.

---

[3] p. 104 above.

Another example is the plan of so-called priority technical measures. The fulfilment of these contributes greatly to technical development in industry, but no direct material incentives have so far attached to the fulfilment of this part of plans.[4]

Like profit, these measures are also difficult to plan. But the fact that their degree of execution varies as much as appears from Table XXI, below, cannot be fully explained merely by planning difficulties or by unforeseen obstacles of an objective nature. Evidently, top managements acquiesce more easily in the non-fulfilment of the plan of technical measures than in any shortfalls in regard to the plan of production value, e.g. because their premiums are generally quite independent of the former. An exception to this only occurs where the results expected from planned measures have already been incorporated in production plans or in plans of cost reduction in respect of a current quarter. In such cases fulfilment of the latter indices and, with this, the receipt of premiums will, in part, depend on execution of the technical measures planned.

To give an exact list here of all priority technical measures proposed for light industry would be a very lengthy undertaking. It is, however, sufficient in the present context to look at the degree of fulfilment of the individual priority measures planned for 1955, as shown in Table XXI (p. 124).

It can be seen that, in many instances, no part of plans was fulfilled, and in cases where something was accomplished the degree of fulfilment varied between 4 per cent, and 321 per cent.! In the circumstances, to regard this part of plans as instructions is also illusory—at least if one goes by our present-day notions, according to which plans consist of unconditionally binding commands of a kind which must be translated into reality with 100 per cent, precision.

Then, consider plans for overtime. We have here a characteristic example of a plan the fulfilment of which (or otherwise) entails no further consequences. Let us survey the degree of fulfilment of plans for overtime in individual branches of light industry during the fourth quarter of 1955, as shown in Table XXII (p. 125).

In a number of branches of industry the amounts of overtime planned and actually worked are fairly close to each other—but in others (e.g. in the silk, shoe, leather and fur, and paper industries) the divergence is so great that plan and reality bear no relation to one another. Thus, in practice, we cannot regard

---

[4] It has only come to rank among the tasks to which premium payments attach in the new system of premium payments, which is due to come into force in the second half of 1956. But, as I have already said, I am not concerned with the evaluation of this new system in the present study.

the plan for overtime as a genuine instruction either (even though it is that in point of law). It is, in fact, only a forecast, which gets realized to a greater extent in some branches of industry than in others.[5]

After these examples, let us revert to the question of 'orders of importance'. Is there, in fact, any justification for such an ordering? Consider the six desired characteristics of production (quantity, quality, &c.) listed earlier. When a decision needs to be made at a particular moment in a given place, it is, of course, necessary to weigh up what is of most importance. It may evidently be a matter for judgement in an enterprise whether, at some given moment, it is preferable to produce a cheaper article of lower quality, or a more expensive one of higher quality, &c. But persistent neglect of some of these requirements for the sake of others in the national economy as a whole is undesirable, because, sooner or later, this will lead to adverse reactions of one kind or another. Yet, attention to 'orders of importance' leads to just such an outcome.

One other point requires mention. Earlier, I made a sharp distinction between six *desiderata* of production (e.g. economy in total labour inputs), on the one hand, and methods of promoting their achievement in practice (e.g. economy in the use of materials)—and I pointed out that both ends and means are subject to instructions. Well, the fact is that among the instructions stressed and made especially 'important' by the system of incentives there are some which do not even relate to a basic economic *desideratum*, but merely to one of the methods of their achievement. The planning of outlays on wages and salaries and the very strict enforcement of these plans is a case in point.

We may thus conclude that there is no economic justification for this 'order of importance' of tasks in the production process. It is an unhealthy phenomenon, which has many harmful consequences. It diverts top managements from striving to accomplish each of our basic *desiderata* simultaneously. That involves constant efforts to find optimum solutions to the problem of

---

[5] To avoid misunderstanding I would like to stress that it is not my view at all that stricter plan instructions, better buttressed by financial consequences, are desirable in the interests of securing limitations on overtime. There are two considerations which tell in favour of placing limitations on overtime. One is that overtime costs enterprises more than does work performed during regular working hours. But if top managements are furnished with a sufficient interest in cheaper production, they will find it to their advantage to make sparing use of overtime even though there is no special plan for limiting it. And if, in certain cases, it should appear to them that it is cheaper to pay for overtime than, say, to be late in fulfilling an important order, then it is, indeed, desirable from the point of view of economy that resort be had to overtime.

The other consideration in favour of limiting overtime is that the health and leisure time of workers needs to be safeguarded. The chief instrument required in this connexion, however, is a trade union movement capable of defending workers against exaggerated demands made upon them by managements. Besides, the State can legislate so as to generally set an upper limit to the daily or weekly working hours of individual workers once and for all.

Table XXI Degrees of fulfilment of plans of priority technical measures in light industry

Branch of industry	Degree of fulfilment of individual priority measures in relation to plans	Branch of industry	Degree of fulfilment of individual priority measures in relation to plans
Cotton Industry	92.7	Silk Industry	0
	83.3		105.2
	42.3		104.8
	100.0		102.0
	160.2	Hosiery Trade	117.9
	23.3		78.3
	40		112.5
	78.8		14.3
	0	Clothing Trade	197.0
	0		234.1
	0		163.5
	0		61.4
	220.6	Leather and Shoe Trades	156.8
Flax and Hemp Industry	0		121.2
	0		100.0
	321.5		88.8
	50.0	Paper Industry	0
	0		0
	0	Furniture Industry	50.0
Woollen Industry	114.5		0
	168.0		0
	60.8	Timber Trade	100

Source: Data of the Ministry of Light Industry for the fourth quarter of 1955. The statistics of each technical measure are reckoned in units peculiar to themselves: e.g. new installations—in pieces; production of a new experimental product—in tons, &c.

reconciling opposed and conflicting requirements in a flexible manner in the face of changing circumstances. As things are, managements are taught to wear blinkers and to see nothing but 2–3 'basic plan index numbers'.

Thus a tendency naturally and inevitably arises for other important tasks to be neglected for the sake of the 'basic index numbers' to which premium payments attach. Indeed, the latter may be realized at the expense of the former.

TableXXII Degrees of fulfilment of production plans and of overtime plans in light industry, by trades

Branch of industry	Percentage fulfilment of production plan	Actual overtime as a percentage of planned overtime
Cotton Industry	101.6	109.79
Flax and Hemp Industry	101.1	103.34
Hard Fibre Industry	117.8*	96.37
Woollen Industry	101.2	92.46
Silk Industry	103.2	269.56
Dry Goods Industry	102.4*	114.42
Knitwear Industry	101.7*	139.33
Clothing Industry	99.8*	117.24
Shoe Industry	101.4*	189.44
Leather and Fur Industry	101.0†	303.80
Paper Industry	101.7	101.49
Furniture Industry	103.8†	337.76

Source: Report of the Ministry of Light Industry for fourth quarter of 1955. Data shown refer to that quarter.
Figures marked * in the column showing fulfilment of the production plan refer to targets of total production value; those marked † to finished production; and the remainder to corrected production value. Thus the figures shown are, in each case, those to which premium payments generally attached in 1955.

An example of the tasks which tend to be neglected is the regular renewal of the stock of fixed equipment. The performance of this is one of the means of securing adequate production in the future, which was listed sixth among the desired characteristics of production enumerated earlier. It is of first-class importance from the point of view of securing the smooth functioning of enterprises. Yet there are no premiums attached to this—nor does its performance evoke any marked signs of moral approval. Let us now compare the degree of execution of this plan with the degree of fulfilment of the target of production value, as shown in Table XXIII (p. 127).

It can be seen that the plan of renewals was left unfulfilled everywhere; indeed, in some branches of industry—e.g. in the furniture and silk industries—the contrast between overfulfilment of production plans and the neglect of renewals is most striking.

This harmful tendency towards a one-sided concentration on 3–4 index numbers naturally also evokes measures designed to offset it.

One 'defence' against it is the attempt to employ the system of financial incentives, particularly premiums, for the solution of much-neglected problems. The conditions for receiving premiums change very frequently,

TableXXIII Degrees of fulfilment of production plans and of plans of renewals in light industry, by trades

Directorate	Percentage degree of fulfilment of target of production value	Percentage degree of fulfilment of plan of renewals
Cotton Industry	102.0	97.2
Flax and Hemp Industry	101.6	99.1
Woollen Industry	98.4	96.3
Silk Industry	100.8	81.5
Dry Goods Industry	100.7*	89.0
Hosiery Industry	102.8*	96.2
Clothing Industry	101.0*	96.7
Shoe Industry	101.0*	96.5
Leather and Fur Industry	104.2†	98.7
Paper Industry	99.6	96.2
Furniture Industry	106.3†	88.7

Source: Reports of the Ministry of Light Industry for the fourth quarter of 1955. The table shows data in respect of the entire year 1955. Figures marked * in the column relating to production value refer to total production value; those marked † to the value of finished production; and the remainder to corrected production value.

according as the head of a directorate happens to be extolling the exceptional importance of this or that index, or because note is taken of the latest grounds for sharp criticisms laid at the door of the Ministry, or because some task or other happens to be in the limelight of attention as a result of a fresh governmental decree, &c. It is clear that these changes do not, for the most part, arise in a random manner. They are, rather, connected with a very widespread prevalence of some fault, so that some problem begins to present itself in very pressing form and must therefore be remedied as a matter of urgency. The trouble is therefore not that these matters are brought to the forefront of attention, but that the process of remedying them is normally begun at the expense of pushing some previous 'campaign' into the background. One task now comes to be included among the factors upon which premium payments depend—another is dropped. But this starts off the 'preparation' of some other general shortcoming, which, in due course, is bound to give rise to yet another campaign.

Another form taken by 'defence' against one-sidedness is to provide incentives in respect of as many tasks as possible. Some real improvements have undoubtedly come about in this way. We have passed beyond the stage when the index of production value was almost solely and exclusively dominant, so that a single-minded pursuit of quantity was characteristic of the whole economy. From the point of view of financial rewards, the plan of cost reductions has, by now, been given an almost as great a role. There are, however, limits to the practicability of this kind of extension of the provision of financial incentives. A strong drive in the direction of linking premiums to ever more numerous conditions was, at one time, noticeable; and this trend has not yet come to a halt.[6] The fact that the sources from which it is possible to derive moneys for directors' funds and funds for enterprise developments are so variegated also reflects this intention on the part of the authorities; evidently this set-up was meant to provide separate incentives for the utilization of waste materials, for economy in the use of circulating capital, and for sales of idle items of equipment. This, however, is not a practicable path of advance, for it would render the system of financial incentives—which is, in any case, too complicated already—even more involved, and thus would, in fact, diminish the effectiveness of the incentives.

Thus we are here faced with a harmful tendency rooted in internal contradictions present in our systems of providing incentives and of administering the economy. The larger the number of separate financial incentives employed to secure the execution of a plethora of plan instructions, the more complicated, and, beyond a certain point, the worse the system of incentives will be. If, on the other hand, the number of tasks to which incentives are attached is made small, then important objectives will tend, repeatedly, to be neglected.

3. TURNING '100 PER CENT.' INTO A FETISH

Apart from certain exceptional fields of activity (e.g. coal-mining) premiums are not paid until the degree of fulfilment of the relevant plan index numbers reaches 100 per cent. This is also the point at which moral approval begins to be bestowed on enterprises: public opinion regards them as 'good' or 'bad' according as they do or do not attain 100 per cent.

A certain *mystique* has grown up around '100 per cent'. It has been turned into a fetish. One meets with the view that the figures contained in plans are adequate expressions of what is required by real economic laws; so that whoever fails to keep to the figures with 100 per cent, precision is offending against

---

[6] I would remind the reader of the account I gave on pp. 38–39 of the manner in which attempts have recently been made to halt the production of unwanted articles. A new condition of premium payments in the woollen industry is that there must be no finished cloth in stock that is not held against delivery contracts.

these laws themselves.[7] In fact, the extent to which the figures contained in plans reflect real economic laws, and the interests of society, depends on a number of circumstances. It depends on whether economic policy itself is well conceived or not; on the extent to which the overall national economic plan has been well founded, realistic, and adequately balanced; on how reliably the plan has been broken down and translated into detail in terms of objectives for individual branches of industry and for individual enterprises; on what unforeseeable changes have occurred since plans were determined; on whether the indices contained in plans unambiguously express the actual wishes of the central authorities and the true objectives of economic policy, &c.

The system of plan index numbers aims to do more than merely inducing enterprises to move in the right direction by producing abundant supplies of good quality products as cheaply as possible so far as circumstances permit. It also tries to lay down exactly how far enterprises should move in these directions. But it is impossible to lay this down in advance with great exactitude. For example, I would bid the reader to recall here what I said in the section dealing with indices of costs: one cannot prescribe how the costs of an enterprise should develop to the nearest tenth of 1 per cent.

It is, thus, senseless to make a fetish of 100 per cent. And yet the process of adopting this fetish is not some sort of an accidental phenomenon, traceable, perhaps, to the superficial thinking, or insufficient training, of individuals engaged in top management. The tendency to adopt this fetish is a necessary consequence of the present economic mechanism which wishes to rely primarily on minutely detailed instructions in guiding the activities of enterprises. (It must, however, be observed that this harmful tendency towards fetishism is sharpened and made more widespread by the amateurishness in economic matters which is widely prevalent in economic administration and in campaigns for higher production.)

All this has many harmful effects. One of them is the 'rigidity' of our present methods of managing the economy, a characteristic which is frequently commented upon. Adjustments of the course of the economy to changing circumstances can only be made with difficulty, and consideration of the various alternative ways of meeting problems which arise in the course of executing plans is made difficult by the fact that 'it is necessary to make the 100 per cent.'

A characteristic effect of the fetish mentality, which frequently gets hold of top managements, can suitably be called 'the psychology of losing hope.'

[7] The question of the extent to which the indices of detailed plans provide exact as opposed to distorted expressions of the requirements of real economic laws is discussed in the article by Péter Erdős: 'Some theoretical problems of planned economy', *Közgazdasági Szemle*, June 1956.

Enterprises will try hard to fulfil the plan index numbers to which premium payments attach, to the extent of 100 per cent.; they will make use of a variety of tricks in trying to do so if driven to it. However, if it appears that even this is of no avail, then they will give up the struggle at a certain point. From a financial point of view (though not, of course, from a moral one) it is a matter of complete indifference to top managements whether the degree to which they fulfil their indices amounts to 99 or 91 per cent.

This last effect used to operate with special force, so long as the receipt of any part of premium payments depended on fulfilling each one of 3–5 plan index numbers to the extent of at least 100 per cent.

Under that régime it was sufficient for the fulfilment of a single plan index number to have appeared to be hopeless for the whole premium to lose its incentive force. The position was somewhat improved in this respect by the system which was inaugurated in 1955 according to which top managements may earn two premium payments which are independent of each other. It is possible to earn the premium attached to the production plan even if the premium in respect of cost reductions has been forfeited. Yet, this problem is still very much with us. For the 'psychology of losing hope' continues to have its effect with respect to the two premiums taken separately. Thus, if, for example, the fulfilment of the index of adherence to plans appears to have become hopeless, then the struggle to fulfil the production plan to the extent of 100 per cent, will cease together with efforts to make as good a showing as possible in regard to adherence to plans.

It is difficult to substantiate the presence of a way of looking at things by means of statistics. The evidence furnished by the table which follows is nevertheless worth pondering over. It presents data relating to the degree of fulfilment of plans by enterprises in the leather trade in respect of the first half of 1955. In the course of six months there were altogether ten instances in which the degree of fulfilment of the monthly production plans of the fifteen enterprises in the trade fell short of 100 per cent, (so that there were ten cases of shortfalls in a total of ninety cases). The detail of the distribution of these ten cases was as follows:

Only three of the ten cases in which results fell short of 100 per cent, were followed by another failure to reach the target in the next month. In the other cases, fulfilment or overfulfilment followed.

Thus the figures appear to support the suggestion made above to the effect that when there is not enough hope of reaching 100 per cent., top managements no longer make strenuous efforts to attain at least 99 per cent, or 98 per cent, instead.

Table XXIV Degrees of fulfilment of production plans
in the leather trade

Percentage fulfilment of production plans	Number of cases
(%)	
98–100	—
96–98	—
94–96	2
92–94	2
90–92	2
80–90	1
Under 80	3

Source: Data of the Planning Division of the Leather and Shoe
Trades' Directorate. The degree of plan fulfilment relates to the value
of finished production, as that was the index to which premium
payments were attached in this trade.

In many such cases it is not simply a matter of 'losing hope' but rather, perhaps, of 'building up reserves'. For top managements reason as follows: 'things will not work out this month in any case—let us then at least earmark a part of finished or semi-finished production for next month, so that we can forge ahead then, and earn praise as well as our premium.' (It must be borne in mind that there still existed, in 1955, a régime of monthly premium payments!) This last conclusion appears to be warranted by the fact that the preceding set of data frequently show large shortfalls to be followed by even larger overfulfilments of targets.

Incidentally, analysis of the results attained in the shoe trade in the second half of 1955 yields a picture which is similar to the foregoing. During these six months there were a total of fifteen cases in which the fifteen enterprises in the trade attained results which fell short of 100 per cent, fulfilment of the production values prescribed in their plans. Only two of these fifteen results were in the 98–100 per cent, range, the remainder were under 98 per cent. In fact, eleven of these last thirteen performances fell short of the even lower figure of 96 per cent. It is significant that while seven enterprises failed to reach 100 per cent, in November, all except one of these falling short of 98 per cent., six of these same seven enterprises very greatly overfulfilled their plans by December.[8]

---

[8] Here also, the source of data is the Planning Division of the Leather and Shoe Trades' Directorate. Plan fulfilment relates to the value of finished production, since premium payments were attached to this.

4. 'SPECULATION WITHIN THE FRAMEWORK OF THE PLAN'

When discussing the various index numbers composing the production plan, we saw that none of these indices is unambiguous. Hence it is possible to fulfil the indices to which premium payments attach in a manner which corresponds to the intentions expressed by the form which the index takes, but it is also possible to fulfil them in various other ways which run counter to these intentions. (For example, the index of the degree of plan fulfilment may be met by holding to prescribed programmes of production and of product-mixes in an exact manner, and also by narrowing product-mixes from the outset, or by turning out missing items in a helter-skelter fashion at the end of the planning period, &c.) We may say, more exactly, that results achieved in a proper fashion are 'blown up' by adding 'results' achieved by the employment of undesirable means. Persons who have become veritable 'artists' in devising methods for embellishing results by the employment of undesirable and often harmful means are to be found everywhere among the top managerial personnel of enterprises. These activities amount to a characteristic process of 'speculation within the framework of the plan'. The uses of this are fairly quickly borne in on managerial personnel as they become exposed to everyday realities. I would stress that *I am not thinking of fraudulent activities of a kind which constitute breaches of the law.* It is not a matter of enterprises submitting false statistical returns about their fulfilment of plans. All this 'speculation within the framework of the plan' is entirely legal. It offends against no regulations or laws. The smart economic administrators concerned with it are past masters in the art of juggling with index numbers, and merely exploit the economic ambiguities and contradictions which are contained in the system of indices to which premium payments attach. We have, after all, seen that the index numbers themselves provide incentives in harmful as well as in beneficial directions; we must not be surprised at encountering the fruits of their 'wild' as well as of their deliberately planned effects. It is not, in fact, possible to find a single director or other official concerned with plans who does not know how to conjure up an additional 1 or 2 per cent., when really pushed to do so, in order to secure his premium—and this without any actual infringement of regulations. In favourable cases, such manipulations do neither harm nor good, so far as the national economy is concerned, but they can frequently do fairly considerable harm.

5. BATTLES OVER LOOSENING AND TIGHTENING PLANS

The fulfilment of plans depends primarily on doing good work. But if a plan is loosely drawn up, this naturally eases the task of fulfilling it, of obtaining the premium in respect of it, and of winning moral approval. Top managements of enterprises thus have a direct personal interest in being given a loose plan to fulfil. It is the great merit of the well-known article by Professor E. Libermann[9] that it represents the first attempt ever made in economic literature to discuss this grave problem in a fully articulated, explicit manner. Indeed, the interests of others besides those of top managements are also involved in the same way. All employees of enterprises who are potential recipients of premiums which are linked to the plan index numbers of their enterprises by way of the conditions attaching to the premiums will urge their directors and others in top positions to obtain loose plans.

Let us examine the two phases of planning and of execution separately from this point of view.

At the time when plans are drawn up the phenomenon of finding top managements of enterprises fighting to obtain loose plan figures is encountered again and again; they are seen to protest against the 'excessive tightness' of indices which they merrily proceed to overfulfil subsequently; they withhold information concerning the potentialities and reserves of their enterprises from the authorities. As an example of this we may examine the plans of costs prepared by shoe factories in respect of the first quarter of 1956. Let us compare the production cost quotients proposed by enterprises with those approved by their industrial directorates and with realized results, as shown in Table XXV (p. 134).

A similar state of affairs also prevails in the shoe industry in regard to the targets of cost reduction for standard articles.

Many enterprises collect the most various statistics and records which are of a different nature from those kept at the behest of the central authorities. As the chief of one planning division aptly put it—these serve 'defensive purposes' in that they enable enterprises to present documentation buttressed by a variety of factual data when it comes to protesting against the plans suggested by higher authorities.

It is, of course, not expected of directors and top managements of factories that they should behave like this. Rather, they are asked to try to present realistic but nevertheless ambitious targets for themselves. In demanding this of them, an appeal is made to their self-respect.

[9] E. Libermann, 'Autonomy in accounting and the provision of material incentives for industrial workers', *Voprosy Ekonomiki*, 1955, No. 6.

Table XXV Proposed, approved, and actually attained cost quotients in selected enterprises in the shoe trade

Name of enterprise	Production cost quotients		
	Proposed by enterprise	Approved figure	Actual figure
Duna	95.6	94.9	91.7
Tisza	91.5	89.1	87.2
Bőrtex	100.3	94.7	88.5
Ifjusági	100.9	96.0	94.7
Kecskeméti	96.8	96.1	96.1
Hajdúsági	122.9	93.8	93.8

Source: Data provided by the Planning Division of the Leather and Shoe Trades' Directorate.

But those who respond to what is required of them in this way offend against their own personal economic interests to some extent by doing so.

It should be noted that the law imposes severe legal penalties on failure to disclose information concerning the potentialities of enterprises. Paragraph 5 (1) 1 of Decree No. 4 (1950) of the Presidential Council of the People's Republic, which has the force of law,[10] states the following: 'An offence is committed by persons who, in the course of preparing the detail of plans, fail to disclose the full productive capacity of an enterprise (or plant), with a view to damaging the interests of the national economy.'[11] Offences of this kind are punishable by sentences of up to two years' imprisonment.

However, in practice, even these strict provisions of the law are insufficient to counteract the strong tendency towards activities designed to loosen plans which is produced by our systems of incentives and methods of planning.

The striving of enterprises for loose plans evokes a corresponding reaction on the part of the authorities set above them. The authorities assume from the outset that protesting enterprises are merely bent on loosening their plans. Hence, even legitimate objections are often branded as 'moaning' and as 'bogus difficulties'. The authorities thus become habituated to 'dictating' their plans to enterprises.

Let us now consider the stage at which plans are carried out.

Additional premiums are paid for overfulfilment of those plan index numbers upon which the premium system is based.[12] In spite of this our system of premiums does not provide adequate encouragement of overfulfilment of

[10] I have already had occasion to quote this decree, in part, in the foregoing; cf. pp. 110–11.
[11] Cf. *Major Laws and Governmental Decrees of the Hungarian People's Republic*, p. 61. Office for Publishing Books and Magazines on Law and State Administration, 1952.
[12] I once again ignore the fact that, for the time being, no additional premiums are payable in respect of overfulfilment of production plans in light industry, since this arrangement is undoubtedly of a transitory character.

plans and does not secure an incessant process of striving towards the greatest possible development and improvement of economic accomplishments.

The fact that a 'ceiling' is placed on premiums plays a certain part in this. In light industry, premiums cannot exceed 50 per cent. of basic pay. This does not act as a particularly powerful brake, as this upper limit is very rarely approached by premiums at all closely. Yet from time to time this does happen, and on such occasions a certain retarding influence results.[13]

A much more marked braking effect is exercised by the practice of 'incorporating achieved results into plans'. What are we to understand by this?

Consider an enterprise which has put up a particularly good performance in some field or other during a certain period. This may perhaps have been due to exceptional exertions on its part, or to accidental circumstances, or to the influence of the operation of some purely temporary factor. In any event, this level of achievement, which had led to a sizeable overfulfilment of the plan at the time, is made into a plan requiring 100 per cent, fulfilment by the next, or—if there is not time for this—the next but one planning period. Thus, in subsequent periods, identically exceptional exertions are no longer rewarded by additional premiums; top managements are consequently made to feel that such exertions are now being demanded of them 'for nothing'. Moreover, if the outstanding results of a period reflected the influence of some transitory influence, then, after the sights are raised in the next plan, the basic premium itself will also be lost, as there will be a failure to attain even 100 per cent.

The phenomenon just described is met with in many fields of planning, e.g. in the determination of indices of productivity and of quality. The problem arises in a particularly acute form in the field of planning costs, for here—as has already been mentioned—the incorporation of earlier results in plans is effected before a full quarter has passed. Plans of costs already approved for the current quarter are modified 'in midstream' as soon as reports of the accounts for the previous quarter become available. Indeed, it has frequently been the case that approved plans have subsequently been made tighter not once but twice.

This practice is given a special form where the planning of raw material supplies is concerned. An ordinance of the Ministry prescribes the following: If enterprises keep within their norms of material utilization for two consecutive

---

[13] Whether it is right to set up such a ceiling under present-day circumstances is a very debatable matter. To do so is, in principle, undoubtedly contrary to the principles of socialist wage policy, for, beyond a certain point, it ceases to provide additional wages as payment for additional production. But it is possible to object to this, on the practical ground that our systems of planning are insufficiently exact. A very high degree of overfulfilment of premium conditions very probably indicates an element of looseness somewhere in plans. In such circumstances it would be morally wrong to pay unlimited premiums. It is thus very difficult to settle the issue.

quarters, then, in the subsequent period, the levels newly attained in practice must be prescribed in obligatory form. If, on the other hand, results actually attained during two quarters fall short of the norm laid down for them, then the norm itself must be taken as the basis of the next plan.

As a result of all this, there arises a phenomenon which resembles that of the 'ca'canny' encountered among manual workers before the regulation of their norms was decentralized, i.e. before 1955. Many manual workers had, at that time, reasoned as follows: 'I will not overfulfil my norm by much, because the higher my percentage is, the more will be taken off it.' Similarly, there are large numbers of persons in top managerial posts who reason thus: 'I will not overfulfil my plan by a large margin, for if I do, it will be that much tighter in the coming period.' It is interesting to notice that the chiefs of the planning departments of enterprises become veritably frightened on the approach of the end of a quarter if they see that results will probably 'overshoot by too much.

There are, in fact, ways and means of 'reserving' the fruits of such 'excessive' plan fulfilment for the coming quarter.[14] Smart planning officers know how to lower—as well as to raise—results by 2–3 per cent., while staying within all the rules. For example, output only counts as being finished when it has been checked by the MEO and delivered in the warehouse where finished products are stored. Now, where premium payments attach to finished production, it is sufficient to slow up the process of passing products through the MEO a little for finished output of the present quarter to count as part of the total production of the next, sub-sequent quarter.

In a word, present planning and incentive systems have evoked a spontaneous tendency, the effect of which is to induce managements of enterprises to loosen plans, to hide production potentials, and to hold back outstanding production achievements. This is highly dangerous and harmful. All the interests of society require that the top managements of enterprises, being the persons who are most directly concerned with organizing production and who know local possibilities best, should be the very people most interested in the fullest use being made of local resources and conditions, in the constant improvement of results, and in the formation of ever more ambitious tasks.

---

[14] It is interesting to observe that causes which are diametrical opposites of one another may give rise to the identical phenomenon of 'reserving' production. In the case considered here its cause is the fear that 'excessively large' accomplishments will become 'incorporated in plans'. Earlier, I had shown that production may be 'reserved' also in cases when the fulfilment of current plans has come to appear hopeless—so that it is felt to be preferable to do work in advance in order to obtain the premium in a subsequent period.

6. THE PERIODIC UNEVENNESS OF PRODUCTION

The 'classic' fields for the occurrence of 'work spurts at the month's end' and of 'uneven production' are the machinery industry and coal-mining, but the phenomenon is also encountered in light industry. As in other fields of industry, so here also, it is not so much a matter of a periodic unevenness or fluctuation of the whole of the production process, as, rather, of 'work spurts' in the last stages of production[15] and, associated with this, of 'peaks' in the rate at which finished products are passed out of the production process. Table XXVI (p. 138) is presented as an illustration of this. It indicates the way in which wages cost fluctuates quarterly and month by month. The data refer to the whole of light industry during 1955.

The rhythmic fluctuations of wage costs are partly connected with the fact that there is a tendency to try to concentrate work on goods having a higher content of materials towards the end of each quarter. (As we saw in the course of the discussion of production value, the scope for doing this is, in fact, limited.) Apart from this, the chief explanation of the periodic fluctuations of wage costs lies in the fact that, with a roughly given labour force and given wage outlays, the rate at which finished products pass out of the production

Table XXVI Monthly wages costs in light industry

Month	Fulfilment as a percentage of production plan	Outlay on wages as a percentage of plan	Wages cost per 100 forints of production value (in forints)
January	105.2	103.8	16.23
February	105.4	104.1	15.38
March	108.2	105.1	14.69
April	104.2	105.0	16.37
May	104.5	103.6	15.66
June	105.6	103.2	15.11
July	101.3	101.8	16.59
August	101.8	101.1	15.72
September	102.9	101.2	14.68
October	100.4	101.0	16.44
November	100.5	99.9	16.41
December	104.8	100.2	15.20

Source: Data of the National Bank.

[15] For example, in the textile industry, in. finishing.

process gradually increases as the end of the quarter approaches, and so, with it, does production value. This is, naturally, associated with regular quarterly work spurts at the finishing stages of manufacture. (For example, in the case of textile factories this will take place in sewing repair rooms, in the finishing section, in the packing-room, in the MEO for finished products, &c.)

What, then, is the cause of these periodic fluctuations of production?

The lack of adequate stocks and reserves—which renders the periodicity of peaks in production more intense—undoubtedly plays an important part. The proportions assumed by its work spurts depend on the degree of 'tightness' of the tasks set for an enterprise. The fluctuations are more pronounced, the stiffer the job of accomplishing the tasks set.

Other possible contributory factors in the causation of interruptions and jerks in the production process may be found in bad organization of work, bad planning of the flow of supplies between enterprises, lack of discipline, &c.

But all this still fails to account for the characteristic conformity of the periodicity of fluctuations with calendar dates; of the fact, that is, that the peaks are always found to occur at the end of a month, quarter, or year, and the troughs at the beginning of these time periods. Under capitalism there used to be much instability and unevenness in production—but this kind of work spurt at the end of the month and quarter, followed by a relapse early in the month, was unknown. Periods when production had to be rushed through did exist—e.g. in fulfilling particularly urgent orders, at the peak of the season in seasonal trades, or generally during intense boom periods—but not by monthly and quarterly calendar dates.

The fact which is responsible for repeatedly evoking the unevenness peculiar to our present system of production is simply that the entire process of planning production, as well as the system of material and moral incentives which supports it, is built upon a groundwork of calendar periods. So long as material and moral recognition of services rendered by managements of enterprises depends on the extent to which they meet planned figures laid down in regard to production and labour utilization in respect of given calendar periods, nothing will prevent them from 'going flat out' at the end of each plan period.[16]

---

[16] The problem of the periodic unevenness of production has been studied in detail by two members of the Institute of Economics, András Bródy and Mrs. László Gáspár. Their investigations have covered certain selected parts of light industry. I have made partial use of the results of their researches in the analysis of the text. The first publication to have resulted from this work is the article by András Bródy: 'Our economic mechanism and work spurts at the end of the month', *Közgazdasági Szemle*, July–Aug. 1956.

7. THE CONFLICT BETWEEN 'TODAY' AND 'TOMORROW'

An ever-recurring dilemma facing managements is whether they should risk the future development of their enterprises for the sake of fulfilling or over-fulfilling the quarterly plans of a current period. Alternatively, they may have to sacrifice their current plan for the sake of the future. Experience shows that the majority of economic administrators decide this along the lines of the well-known principle enshrined in the saying 'a bird in the hand is worth two in the bush'.

To some extent this conflict is already reflected in the phenomenon of the fluctuating periodic unevenness of production discussed in the foregoing. When top managements decide to 'go flat out' towards the end of a month or quarter, they must be aware of the fact that this will inevitably give rise to hold ups in production at the beginning of the next plan period. For continuity of work is bound to be hampered by reductions in stocks of semi-finished products; the productivity of workers exhausted by the preceding work spurt is bound to show a relapse, &c.

The extent to which the process of developing enterprises and their products in a continuous fashion is hampered by the conflict we are considering here is even more marked. A number of things are involved.[17]

   (i) Development of production technique; this embraces new manufacturing processes, new working methods, the application of inventions and of innovations.
   (ii) Adoption of up-to-date forms of organization of the labour force.
   (iii) Improvements in the quality of products; the introduction of new products.
   (iv) Careful attention to fixed equipment; continuous maintenance and renewal of machinery.
   (v) Education of personnel, training of apprentices, advanced training of skilled workers, development of the knowledge of technical experts, &c.

All these are tasks the conscientious performance of which promotes the future good work and development of enterprises—while neglect of them must,

---

[17] In what follows I omit all consideration of investment, although it is, of course, of outstanding importance in the development of enterprises. I do so because it raises a series of special problems which are not germane to the present discussion.

sooner or later, exact its own penalty. At the same time, however, these are all tasks, the conscientious performance of which will only infrequently have immediate effects on the outcome of current plans, and then only to a modest extent. They will, on the contrary, generally draw resources away from the performance of everyday tasks. For example, it may be necessary to withdraw skilled workers of high quality from the production process when apprentices require training. Again, work on the design of product-improvements absorbs technological man-power. Indeed, the performance of work of this kind may in certain cases actually lead to set-backs in the execution of the tasks of the moment. For example, timely work on maintenance may require the stopping of machines, the continued working of which could assist very materially with fulfilment of a monthly plan.

The trouble does not arise from the fact of the existence of a conflict between the interests of the present and of the future. That is inevitable, more or less. The same dilemma will face a capitalist producer as well: should he maximize his immediate profits over the next year or two, possibly at the cost of risking the firm's reputation and goodwill, by dealings at the expense of his customers, or perhaps by imposing excessive wear and tear on his machines and other installations—but, in any event, at the risk of forgoing even larger profits in the future? Or should he remain content, for the time being, with more modest, but also more securely based profits, preferring to try building up his enterprise soundly, in a slow but sure manner? The dilemma exists, but it takes a form which entails that, in their extreme forms, either of the two solutions have their own advantages and disadvantages from the point of view of the individual capitalist. In the first case, today's profits are larger, but tomorrow's are uncertain. In the second case, less is pocketed today but future profits will, in all probability, become more and more ample as time goes by. In our conditions, however, it is not a matter of both courses of action having their own advantage and disadvantage. It is, rather, a case of finding that all or practically all advantages lie with one course of action—namely, that which puts the emphasis on the present—while neglect of the future is not associated with any marked disadvantage to particular individuals.

The plans and instructions do, it is true, also contain numerous prescriptions concerning the performance of 'long-term' tasks. Each enterprise has an approved plan of technical development, which contains plans for measures to be taken in technical and organizational fields. There are plans concerning plant renewals, technical instruction, &c. The organization of planned maintenance, the dissemination of the best techniques, &c., are regulated by decree. All this is true—yet at the same time our system of incentives definitely operates in such a way as to impel the top managements of enterprises in the direction of neglecting such work as will only bear fruit in the future while possibly requiring sacrifices of the present. The most powerful material incentive, the premium, is definitely made to depend on fulfilment of the current quarterly plan. But the recognition accorded to managements by higher authorities, as well as their criticism, or other corrective action they may take, is also primarily dependent on this. Party and social organizations, also, look upon quarterly plan-fulfilment as the chief yardstick for judging whether an undertaking is functioning well or badly. Even moral approval is but rarely accorded to directors or chief engineers who dispose of clean, neatly ordered, and well-maintained sets of machines, or have organized the process of training their skilled workers in an efficient manner. Moreover, if levels of production gradually rise as a result of such activities, this is taken into account from the outset in determining plans—future tasks are set on a basis which discounts it. The process of 'incorporating results into plans', a phenomenon I have already discussed,[18] operates also over the long run. Consequently, managements fail to obtain financial rewards in respect of the slowly maturing fruits of their efforts.

Furthermore, top managements must reckon with the possibility that they may be leaving their enterprises sooner or later, so that they may not be in a position to reap the future harvest of their present-day efforts. The greater the frequency of changes of personnel in top managerial positions, the stronger this feeling will be; to the extent that it prevails, it acts as a further damper on top managements' zeal to perform conscientiously tasks which lay foundations for future advances. What is more, they must also reckon with the possibility that the reason for terminating their appointments may be precisely that they had failed to fulfil current plans several times running—so that this consideration in itself makes it worth their while to concentrate all their attention upon the fulfilment of current plans.

By contrast, there is no particular risk attached to the neglect of long-term tasks, so far as top managements are concerned. For such neglect will only show itself slowly and gradually in a matter of several years perhaps. Moreover, when revealed it must be accepted as a fact by the higher authorities when they come to fix plans—even if they do so in a reproachful manner. The process of 'incorporation into plans' applies to back-sliding as well as to progress. If they are to have realistic plans, then the authorities must base themselves on the

---

[18] Cf. pp. 135–6 above.

state enterprises and trades are actually found to be in—and this may be a worn out or antiquated state.[19]

Here again we are faced with a harmful tendency which is unavoidable given our present methods of managing the economy. Three main avenues of escape from it exist. One is the provision of a more complex and comprehensive system of material incentives for economic administrators, the rewards under which would be designed so as to attach a value to all aspects of the entire activity of managements instead of being confined to 3–4 selected indices of current production. This has been dealt with in the foregoing, and there is no need to repeat it here.

The second thing to do is to stabilize the staffing of the top managements of enterprises as much as possible and to prevent constant changes in it. Employees' feelings of attachment to their enterprise must be reinforced by economic rewards. (Practical ways of doing this have also been discussed already.) In this way, all will be beneficiaries of, or sufferers from, the consequences of the good or bad work they themselves had done years before.

Finally, the third thing to do is to provide every worker in an enterprise, its entire collective membership, with a serious stake in the results shown by it—e.g. by means of profit-sharing schemes. A certain minimum turnover of personnel is unavoidable, especially in years of rapid industrialization. Yet there is no tendency whatsoever for the entire personnel of a factory to change from one year to the next or even in a period of 2–3 years. (Indeed, our aim must be to secure that the bulk of workers should stay with their enterprises for years or even decades.) Thus if profit-sharing or some other similar devices were adopted, it would become a clear and unambiguous direct financial interest of all workers that the results shown by their enterprises should improve year by year. Moreover, if and when we come to make institutional arrangements which will enable the workers to exercise an important influence on the process of managing their enterprises, they will then see to it that the robber's tactics involved in neglecting the future interests of their enterprises are halted.

The six undesirable phenomena discussed in this chapter are all well known; a great deal is said about them in the press and at various conferences.

---

[19] All this is much more manifestly the case in coal-mining than in light industry. In the course of several years many of our mines have been allowed to get into a neglected state. Current plans are designed to set stiff tasks for these mines as well. Yet, when plans are formulated, the point of departure must, of course, nevertheless be the present-day condition of a mine and not the condition it would be in if it had not been neglected.

It is, however, frequently the case that these phenomena are regarded as accidental in character, being taken to be due to the subjective shortcomings of individual economic administrators. 'Director X fails to heed the national economic interest sufficiently—and is therefore bent on loosening his plan', or 'Chief engineer Y does not look ahead, and neglects the training of skilled workers', &c. Of course, such statements may well contain an element of truth; it is possible that if there had been some other more conscientious, devoted, or self-sacrificing person in the shoes of X or Y, he would have acted otherwise. Nevertheless, this is an entirely wrong way of looking at the matter.

When some fault or harmful phenomenon is not of exceptional occurrence, but is, rather, very common and indeed general, then it is a requirement of scientific analysis that we do not, in looking for the explanation, confine ourselves merely to the subjective attitudes of individuals, but that we also search for impersonal—and in this sense, objective—precipitating causes of it. In the present instance this means the institutions, forms of organization, and systems of financial and moral incentives which so generally and typically evoke faulty behaviour among most economic administrators.

Some analysts of the phenomena we are discussing admit that they are not accidents, but spring from deeper causes, which they identify as consisting solely of the shortcomings of the system of premiums. They say, for example, that it is our present system of premiums, with their reliance on figures contained in plans, which is responsible for strivings to loosen plans. They maintain that if the system of premiums were altered, the trouble would disappear.

In fact the problem is not as simple as this. At present, premiums are a most powerful source of financial incentive. But, as we have seen, the main influences of many other incentives, not least of moral pressure and of political agitation, act chiefly in the same direction as does that of the premium. Nor does the premium exist independently. It is merely a buttress of certain defined plan index numbers. The premium makes the beneficial and positive effect of plan index numbers more effective—and also accentuates their undesirable, negative, 'wild' effect.

Let us consider the degree of evenness of production, for example. I have discussed this already, and it is only for the purpose of illustrating the present problem that I bring it up again. Some people regard the premium as the chief source of the characteristic periodic fluctuations of production, as the fate of it is finally decided at the end of particular planning periods, in the 'finish'. But experience in light industry shows that the fluctuation of production within

Table XXVII The volume of production of selected light industrial products over ten-day periods

Article	Unit of measure	First ten days	Second ten days	Third ten days
Finished cotton cloth	1,000 sq. metres	4,343	5,825	7,674
Men's shoes	1,000 pairs	40.9	37.2	50.4
Women's shoes	1,000 pairs	75.6	98.2	128.5
Children's shoes	1,000 pairs	103.6	115.2	133.5

Source: Data of the Chief Planning Division of the Ministry of Light Industry.

the month did not cease even in 1956 when a change-over was made to paying premiums to top managements quarterly instead of monthly.

The consequences of changing over to a quarterly system of premium payments ought some time to be studied on the basis of data drawn from longer periods. In any event, the data in respect of May 1956, for example, also show that unevenness of production within the month has not ceased. At the time of writing this, the rate at which finished products emerge from the production process still shows 'forward leaps' at the month's-end.

The reason why the unevenness in production has persisted is that the Ministry, the directorates, or the enterprise or district party committees still check up on how enterprises are doing in regard to their monthly plans—and it 'looks bad' if monthly plans are not fulfilled. In many places directors continue to pay premiums to individual employees of their enterprises on the basis of their monthly plans, for 'safety first' reasons, &c. Thus the origin of the phenomenon of work spurts does not lie simply in the system of premiums but rather in the calendar basis of economic administration and of supervision of production results. The evil has merely been accentuated and exaggerated by the system of premiums. The other phenomena discussed in this chapter have a similar character.

The six phenomena listed in the foregoing may be regarded as necessary tendencies. They are not necessary consequences of a planned economy. But they *are* necessary consequences of present methods of administering the economy, that is, of our present economic mechanism. They are tendencies that cannot be simply wished away; they can only be mitigated, not eradicated, by words designed to enlighten. In order to eliminate these tendencies, it is necessary that our planning and incentive systems, our methods of administering the economy, be themselves made the objects of comprehensive and far-reaching improvements.

IV

RELATIONSHIPS BETWEEN ENTERPRISES

THE ROLE OF ENTERPRISES AS BUYERS AND SELLERS

So far, the main question we have been concerned with in this study has been the manner in which the wishes of the State and of the central authorities are transmitted to enterprises by way of instructions and incentives. We must now examine the relationships which develop between enterprises. These relationships run in two directions. In one of these, enterprises figure as sellers: they dispose of their products. In the other, they act as buyers: they purchase the means of production they require for the manufacturing process.

A whole series of questions arise in connexion with both sets of inter-firm relationships. These cannot all be taken up in the present study; it was necessary to limit the field of inquiry. So far as the role of enterprises as sellers is concerned, I shall confine my description to that part of this theme which is concerned with distribution in the home market. A considerable part of what emerges from study of this sphere is also applicable to the relationship between industry and selling abroad. But study of the special problems peculiar to external trade will have to be taken up on another occasion.

So far as the role of enterprises as buyers is concerned, the position is that enterprises purchase a great many different things: raw materials, power, machines, components and tools, as well as services of various kinds, &c. I can only deal with the *procurement of materials* here; indeed—as will be seen—I shall only be concerned with certain problems which arise in connexion with this.

Overcentralization in Economic Administration. János Kornai translated by John Knapp, Oxford University Press.
© Oxford University Press (2023). DOI: 10.1093/oso/9780192894427.003.0004

1. THE RELATIONSHIP BETWEEN LIGHT INDUSTRY AND DOMESTIC COMMERCE

Stocks of finished goods

The size of stocks of finished goods is one of the most important determinants of the nature of the relationship prevailing between light industry and that part of the distributive trades which caters for the home market. When stocks held by the distributive trades are adequate in size and composition, then distributors are able to exercise pressure on industry in a way which will further the satisfaction of the various requirements of consumers. In those circumstances distribution is really in a strong position to insist on greater variety, better quality and finish, attention to seasonal requirements, &c. Industry will be obliged to take account of the requests of distributors in these respects because the latter, being in possession of sufficient stocks, will refuse to order goods which do not suit them (and customers). In this situation, a whole series of things required of enterprises, which are of the first importance, will be secured by pressure exercised upon them by the distributive trades 'from below'—without enterprises receiving any instructions concerning them 'from above'.

It is true that the pressure exerted by the distributive sector is to some extent weakened by the circumstance that it is obliged to order and to accept industrial manufactures up to the extent indicated by the figures shown in plans—even if it has become clear that customers would prefer other things.[1] Distributors have little choice in deciding on the factory with which to place their orders for goods, as the factories are fairly strongly specialized. In any case, production programmes are laid down by the industrial directorates. Yet, in spite of these limitations, the size of the stocks at the disposal of the distributive trades does play a very large part in the way things go.

Let us take the example of the year 1955. Stocks were a great deal larger in that year than previously. Let us first examine the course of change of wholesale stocks of certain important articles of clothing over time:

The data indicate a sizeable enlargement of stocks of clothing.[2]

---

[1] How this situation leads to the production of unwanted articles has already been discussed. Cf. pp. 38–40 above.

[2] I would point out here that stocks were, at the same time, very low in a series of other articles of consumption in fields other than clothing: e.g. wireless sets, bicycles, motor-cycles, enamel-ware, furniture, &c. Thus the market could not be regarded as being generally saturated—clothing alone

Table XXVIII Wholesale stocks of clothing

Article	30.4.1955	31.12.1955	30.4.1956
Cotton cloth	92	94	86
Woollen cloth	63	112	160
Men's clothing	132	183	169
Women's clothing	166	231	229
Children's clothing	130	169	207
Men's and women's underwear	116	117	127
Leather shoes	126	165	152

Source: Data of the Central Statistical Office. The figures shown in the table express stocks in terms of daily sales equivalents.

Let us consider the position of a single article—shoes—as it developed over a number of years.

The fact that these stocks were available had in 1955 put the distributive trades in a position to insist more effectively on better quality, &c. I witnessed a 'bourse-negotiation' of the shoe trade at which the offerings of the Szombathely Shoe Factory were rejected by the wholesalers of shoes on the ground that this factory had, for some time past, been producing unattractive shoes by the use of inferior techniques. Although the factory has a capacity of many tens of thousands of shoes, orders were simply withheld from it. The factory was requested to prepare fresh models, using new techniques, for submission to distributors, future orders being made conditional on these turning out to be acceptable. And the factory was forced to comply.

Table XXIX Wholesale stocks of shoes

Date	Stocks (1,000 pairs)
1.1.1953	2,172·6
1.1.1954	1,711·1
1.1.1955	2,189·0
1.11.1955	3,887·4
1.1.1956	4,336·1

Source: Calculations based on data provided by the Ministry for Light Industry.

was in sufficient supply. Moreover, as we shall see later on, even in this last field saturation was merely partial and relative.

A similar tendency for distributors to have more success in 'extorting' sat-isfaction of consumer requirements was apparent in the textile and clothing industries. Having 'secured their rear' owing to the availability of stocks, sub-standard shipments of industry could be and were rejected by the distributive trades. For example, the following consignments of goods were rejected:

(i) 16,000 metres of checkered buckram canvas, made by the Győri Pamutszövőgyár, because the goods were husky; also 8,000 metres of coloured woven cotton flannels because their fluffiness was not satisfactory.
(ii) 87,000 metres of deeply scraped printed flannels, because of inade-quate tear-resistance; also 50,000 metres of crease-resistant synthetic cloth for the same reason—both consignments being products of the Kistex Factory.
(iii) 26,000 metres of calico made by Szombathelyi Pamutipar, because of its faulty weave and oiliness.
(iv) 18,000 metres of claret-coloured balloon cloth made by the Hazai Pamutfonó Factory, owing to its not being colour fast.[3]

When the distributive trades do not dispose of sufficient stocks and there is a shortage, the position becomes very different. Industry can afford to ignore the importunities of commerce when there are shortages and when there is a 'hunger for goods'. It can adopt a 'take it, or leave it' attitude. It can choose what-ever course is most comfortable for itself, e.g. by concentrating solely on the production of articles which present few technical difficulties or which are best suited to improve the showing made by an enterprise from the point of view of its various plan indices, by ceasing to bother about offering greater variety in its productions, &c. In such a situation industry is in a position to force commerce to accept even those of its products which are of a poor standard. The 'prin-ciple' which is often repeated is: 'It is the duty of commerce to represent the interests of consumers'—'Commerce must not accept shoddy products from industry', &c. But in the situation we are envisaging this function of commerce is simply incapable of being exercised. For the material conditions of its being able to do so are not present. Commercial executives will be pleased if they can lay their hands on any goods at all, and can thus at least fulfil their global sales plans. This enables them to obtain their premiums, and they are willing

[3] The data given in the text were derived from records prepared by the Central Planning Division of the Ministry of Domestic Commerce.

to forgo their various detailed requirements for the sake of it. The distributive trades treat consumers as industry treats the distributive trades in this situation. Consumers are told, more or less politely: 'Take it, or leave it—you will not get anything different, wherever you go.'

A very close connexion exists between the general relationship of purchasing power to the availability of goods, on the one hand, and the position in regard to stocks, on the other hand. There can, of course, exist shortages, or excessive stocks, of particular commodities even if there exists a satisfactory balance between purchasing power and the volume of goods available. Nevertheless, this latter relationship is the decisive influence upon the overall stock position. If purchasing power is excessively enlarged, so that the growth of the volume of goods available falls significantly behind it, then stocks will sooner or later be used up all round—and there will follow in the wake of this the troubles just described: the 'defencelessness' of commerce, and, in the last analysis, of consumers. Conversely, if the volume of goods available always grows so as to keep somewhat ahead of rises in purchasing power (and if the composition of the output of consumption goods is appropriate)—then adequate stocks of goods will be built up throughout the economy.

This is a matter which is of basic importance in connexion with the relationship between centralized direction of the economy and the autonomy of enterprises. For shortages of goods provide the soil for the growth of excessive centralization. A multitude of instructions are issued from the centre in an attempt to prevent enterprises from concentrating exclusively on their own narrow interests, and to induce them to provide adequate variety, improved quality, &c. If, on the other hand, goods are in ample supply, then enterprises will pay attention to the requirements of consumers even if directives from the centre are much less in evidence, for, in the last resort, consumers themselves will be able to act forcibly to secure this.

As I have said, when goods are in short supply, an attempt is made to replace the 'pressure' of commerce by various directives emanating from the centre and by prescribing a detailed programme for enterprises. But (apart from the disadvantages of this which have already been discussed earlier, like lack of flexibility, &c.) this procedure cannot lead to complete success because the higher authorities involved, and the industrial directorates particularly, are themselves the possessors of an 'industrial outlook'. As they are not directly interested parties so far as premiums are concerned, they may perhaps be able to take a more detached view of the position than enterprises can.

Thus the higher authorities will have somewhat more regard for the national economic interest. Yet, in a situation characterized by shortages of goods, they will prefer to back up industrial enterprises rather than commerce. Indeed, this is very natural, since a good showing of the indices of enterprises serves to improve the indices of their industrial directorates as well—and it is this that causes the authorities still higher up to look with favour upon the directorates. The Ministerial Council alone is 'neutral' where the relationship of industry to commerce is concerned. But it is hardly possible to appeal to the Ministerial Council over every small matter of detail! (Although it will, not infrequently, happen that ministers themselves are obliged to negotiate with one another and decide in trivial disputes of this kind.) For these reasons, the higher authorities, e.g. the Ministry for Light Industry and the Ministry of Domestic Commerce, cannot be expected to overcome these problems in negotiations held among themselves—the crucial question will still continue to be: who has the upper hand—industry or commerce? The question of who has the upper hand becomes increasingly decisive the farther one descends towards the enterprise level. Yet the points of detail which are of such importance to consumers can only be decided at these lower levels. The ministers for Domestic Commerce and for Light Industry may agree in a certain degree of variety of products, in terms of particular commodity groups. But this will be of little use. Even if these ministers are able to rise above their departmental interests, the industrial directorate, and, even more, the producing factory, on the one hand, and the commercial enterprise which does the selling, on the other hand, will continue to cling to their own respective industrial and commercial interests. And it is these latter who will decide on the specific articles to be produced within each commodity group as well as on whether it will be an attractively and carefully turned out product delivered in time for the season or not.

This last consideration is of such central importance that it should cause one to regard the scare which developed towards the end of 1955 over the allegedly 'excessive' size of stocks in domestic commerce as having been unnecessary. The question of what constitutes large or small stocks cannot be settled on the basis of global forint values alone. Total stocks of clothing held by distributors have, it is true, increased recently. In 1955 their average value, reckoned at retail prices, was equivalent to four months' sales. This was a good deal more than in 1954 but not much more than in 1952, for example, and a good deal less than in the first half of 1953. But this, in itself, still tells us very little: the crucial question relates to the composition of stocks. Now this was much less reassuring than the summary figures of the total volume of stocks. Late in 1955 and early in 1956 the position in this respect was as follows.

(i) The composition of stocks by commodity groups was an unbalanced one. Supplies of shoes, clothing, and cotton knitwear were excessive, while stocks of cotton piece-goods and of woollen knitwear were inadequate, the large aggregate size of stocks notwithstanding.

(ii) Nor was composition satisfactory in terms of specific items within commodity groups. It is estimated that, at that time, 15 per cent, of stocks consisted of goods which were unsaleable at original prices. A part of this consisted of articles that had gone out of fashion, another part had been produced in response to orders which it was a mistake to have placed from the outset or which had, for some reason, been unnecessarily produced by industry. In addition much of the available stock was little sought after, even if not unsaleable.

(iii) Articles for which the demand is seasonal are produced all the year round in our productive set-up. Consequently, these articles are stored for considerable periods before their season arrives, and this also augments the volume of stocks.

(iv) At the same time there still exist, at the time of writing this, articles which are very much in demand, stocks of which are too small. In certain cases there may even be an absolute shortage of such goods. In the foregoing[4] I have already cited a report of the Central Planning Division of the Ministry of Domestic Commerce. I had listed articles which are in short supply because light industrial enterprises are reluctant to produce them, owing to their labour requirements being too high, so that they cause 'a deterioration of the productivity index'. But the same report also mentions many other articles in short supply where the factors which deter industry from pushing ahead with production are different (excessive troublesomeness of technique, &c.). Examples of such articles are: white satin for corsets, woollen cloths of the 'Komarom' and 'Oslo' varieties, children's lacquered beds, play-pens with step-up platforms, standard deck-chairs, meatboards, clothes pegs with springs, women's plastic slippers, &c.

---

[4] Cf. p. 34 above.

I would emphasize that the articles I have listed both here and earlier[5] are restricted to goods the shortages of which are not caused primarily by a lack of materials or of capacity. It would be possible to add to this a very long list of articles, the inadequate supply of which is in fact explicable in terms of 'objective causes' (lack of materials, &c.).

Thus the position is that while commerce really does need to divest itself of some part of the stocks it holds, another part requires a gradual process of building up. (This is even more true if we have regard to the position over the whole range of the distributive trades and not merely the trades dealing in clothing.) It would be a serious mistake to reduce commercial stocks excessively, yet some economic administrators are inclined to do just that. The consequences would be that, having felt the favourable and stimulating effect exerted by the accumulations of stocks on both production and distribution in a number of fields during 1955, we would loose these advantages again in subsequent periods.

Relationships between enterprises versus *relationships between directorates*

The question of the extent to which there are direct contacts between industrial and commercial enterprises is also an important one.

The typical state of affairs in light industry at present is for industrial directorates to be in touch with commercial directorates so that the economic contacts which matter have developed primarily between higher authorities. While contacts between industrial and commercial enterprises which are direct do exist as well, their significance is quite subordinate and secondary. I would emphasize that this is the typical situation; but it is not uniformly so, as has already been partly shown in my discussion of the process of planning[6] where I explained that in some branches of industry—e.g. in the shoe trade—direct discussions do take place between industrial and commercial enterprises even before programmes are laid down by higher authorities at the centre. Elsewhere, on the other hand, e.g. in the woollen industry, the industrial directorate will itself agree with commerce upon every single specific product.

[5] Ibid.
[6] Cf. pp. 19–20 above.

Such a degree of centralization in the placing of orders inevitably entails a certain dullness and lack of ideas in the assortment of goods produced and tends to impose uniformity. The top personnel of industrial ministries perceive this clearly—when it is a matter of excessive centralization in the distributive trades. The fact that orders for the entire supply of woollen cloth for the whole country are placed by a single official of the Ministry of Domestic Commerce acting alone, after consulting two or three persons at the most, was mentioned sarcastically several times in the wool trade. This official decides upon the materials to be used in making the clothes of all of us. It is he who decides the range of cloths to be made even in such an enterprise as the Pomáz Budakalászi Factory, whose function is to produce 'exclusive' cloths in small quantities!

Even if the person concerned had an excellent grasp of his business, is it right that a single human being should decide in a matter such as this?[7]

An excellent departure exists in this connexion in the system of 'bourses' which has taken root in the shoe trade. I have discussed the limitations of this in the foregoing:[8] it does not provide as much independence of action for enterprises as one would be inclined to think at a first glance. Even so, it does provide valuable opportunities for factories to acquaint themselves with the views of distributors at first hand, while distributors are given a chance to hear of the problems factories have to contend with, they learn about worries connected with raw material supplies, &c. The outcome of such face-to-face discussions is to ease the reconciliation of the interests of industry with those of consumers.

The need for developing direct contacts between industry and commerce is made the greater by the fact that the present systems of laying down programmes centrally, as well as those of channelling by far the largest part of contacts with the distributive trades through the central authorities, have the effect of more or less divorcing the top experts of light industrial enterprises from contacts with the distributive trades, and, ultimately, from a knowledge of the requirements of consumers. This is one explanation of the fact that enterprises usually have little to say about the programmes prepared by

---

[7] There are seven wholesale enterprises engaged in the distribution of clothing, the largest of which is the one operating in Budapest, 'Bétex'. To all appearances, Bétex places its own orders with industry. In reality, however, orders are placed for them by an official of the central clothing directorate; he may set their requirements aside, negotiates directly with the industrial directorate, &c. He also issues instructions for the transfer of goods from Bétex to other wholesalers. Bétex thus becomes—to some extent, at least—a 'central enterprise' under the immediate direction of the central clothing directorate, and finds itself inserted between industry and the wholesale enterprises of the provinces.

[8] Cf. p. 20 above.

directorates from the angle of whether the contents of programmes correspond to what the consuming public really wants. They have been so conditioned that they have become less prone to take the initiative, for they are no longer sufficiently familiar with consumer requirements. The top personnel of light industrial enterprises stands in need of more of a 'commercial outlook'!

Contracts

Contracts concerning terms of delivery play an important part in the relations which industry has with commerce. They connote a direct contact between factory and commercial enterprise, since their representatives sign the contract. However, this in itself is no more than legal form. Whether the conclusion of a contract really does entail direct contacts of a substantial nature depends on how far the signatories are in a position to decide freely about the matters involved in the contract. Regarded as a separate means to the establishment of direct contacts, contracts are, in many ways, of no more than formal significance at present. For the industrial directorates and the central commercial directorates will already have agreed between themselves on all matters of substance, and, indeed, having agreed on the programme, on numerous questions of detail as well. And enterprises are bound to fulfil their programmes, quite apart from whether they conclude a contract or not. All a director of an enterprise does, beyond appending his signature, is to agree certain matters of quite secondary importance.

It is, in general, difficult to modify a contract once it has been signed. Industrial enterprises will agree to do so only if it 'does not worsen their indices' and if it 'fits into' their plan figures to which premium payments attach. These conditions for a modification will only be waived by enterprises if their plans are also modified by their directorate. There are, however, numerous obstacles to this last actually happening, as was made clear in the foregoing.[9] A flexible process of adaptation to requirements is made very difficult by the rigidity which is consequent upon this.

The opinion is often voiced that the way to diminish the excessive amount of centralization that has developed in planning is to increase the part played in our economic arrangements by delivery contracts. There is some substance in this; even within the present set-up, much of what is now centrally prescribed could be left to be settled within the framework of contracts. And yet

[9] Cf. pp. 24–25 above.

this view is only a half-truth. For what I have said in relation to many other similar conceptions applies to this one also: it does not, in itself, open a door towards substantial improvements unless a whole host of other conditions are realized. To indicate only a few of the more important of these:

1. It must be possible to modify contracts by mutual agreement, in a more flexible manner than has hitherto been the case. The realization of this would entail a reform of our rigid system of planning minute details, with all the overcentralization and fetishization of indices that goes with it. The objective of a more flexible system based on contracts would also require that, whenever circumstances permitted, efforts would have to be made to provide enterprises with a certain amount of reserve capacity. This would permit the placing of repeat orders where necessary.
2. The distributive trades must be able to dispose of adequate stocks of finished goods, the possession of which is a condition for their being in a position to put up a successful fight in the interests of consumers.
3. Besides merely having opportunities for bringing pressure to bear on industry, commerce must also be put in a position where it can provide industrial enterprises with financial incentives to satisfy the requirements of consumer demand to the utmost possible extent.

The provision of such incentives is an insoluble task so long as the crude system of price-fixing which we now operate remains in force and so long as enterprises are left without any serious interest in increasing profits.

As things are at present, the price an industrial enterprise obtains from commerce is the same, irrespectively of whether the latter has placed its order in good time, or whether it requests an exceptional rush consignment. What incentive is there for a factory to fulfil the latter request? Then, the price paid by commerce is the same whether it orders in large lots or, in a hand-to-mouth manner, in small lots. What incentive is there for a factory to accept orders of the latter kind? Again, given that costs are the same, the amount paid by commerce for an article which is easy to produce, as it is technically a straightforward job, will be the same as the amount it pays for an article which poses numerous production problems and is likely to raise the risk of rejects, &c. Again, we may ask: what incentive is there to accept orders of the latter kind?

Where articles which have become established lines are concerned, costs will probably have been reduced as compared with the costing figures used in the process of fixing prices as a result of experience gained in manufacture. Profits will therefore probably exceed the 2 per cent, allowed in the price as originally fixed. But when the price of a newly introduced article is determined, a profit of 2 per cent, is, once again, all that is approved. Thus the new product is less advantageous for enterprises from this point of view. (The only factor 'mitigating' this disadvantage is that factories are not greatly interested in the size of the profits they earn, anyway.) What incentive is there, then, to cause enterprises to keep providing a fresh range of choice of articles?

Generally speaking it is, from a price point of view, a matter of complete indifference for enterprises whether they produce an article which is gladly accepted by commerce, and is, ultimately, eagerly purchased by consumers— or whether they produce articles which please no one. The distributive trades are not in a position to influence the make-up of production in accordance with consumers' demands by varying the prices they offer. In any case, whatever prices may be, industrial enterprises are not particularly interested in raising profits as such.

What is needed, if there are to be really useful direct contacts between factories and commercial enterprises, is that these two parties should really bargain with one another—within limits set by the price policy of the state, of course— and should not confine their discussion to various objective conditions of the consignment such as colour, pattern, latest date of delivery, &c.

That a better balance than now exists is needed between central direction, on the one hand, and the autonomy and initiative of local bodies and local managements, on the other hand, is a view which is, by now, generally accepted as being the chief requirement in the further development of our planned economy. It seems to me that the price system cannot remain exempt from this principle. An optimal adjustment between centralization and local initiative can and must be found in this field also. The present situation cannot be said to represent such an adjustment in any way, for both industrial and commercial enterprises fail to have any serious influence over prices. A flexible system of agreements between enterprises on prices can, and must be, reconciled with the requirement of a unified price policy formulated centrally by the State. Unless this is done, the achievement of a flexible and stimulating relationship between industry and commerce, and between producers and consumers, is out of the question.

Our present crude, undifferentiated, and insensitive price system prevents the distributive trades from making their requirements sufficiently effective— while at the same time industrial enterprises are insufficiently rewarded for any extra trouble they may be put to.

In my opinion a modification of the price system in the directions suggested—together with the provision of additional incentives designed to make the earning of larger profits attractive—is a basic condition for the achievement of a situation in which consumers can notify their wishes to producers in a direct manner by way of the orders placed by commerce. And the more opportunities exist for doing this, the less is the need for the requirements of demand to be conveyed to factories indirectly by way of the system of plan instructions from above. And this would be all to the good for the reason that, instructions from the centre, even when they are incredibly minute, cannot be as finely differentiated and unambiguous as the direct orders of customers. Besides, they require an enormous administrative apparatus, they tie the hands of factories and distributive enterprises, &c. Moreover, the more minutely detailed instructions are, the more the attention of the central authorities is diverted by the work involved in preparing them from the true object of planning, which is the fashioning of plans concerning the main outlines to be assumed by the national economy.

Reverting now to the system of contracts we may say that, in the absence of the fulfilment of the three sets of conditions discussed in the foregoing, contracts merely add a legal stamp to the detailed programmes prescribed at the centre and complete it in some respects. Of course, they play a significant part even so—but they cannot be regarded as independent substantial economic forces in the manner of those experts who are at present looking to an enhanced role of contracts for the solution of our fundamental difficulties.

The period of currency of agreements made between industry and commerce

At present the ministries of Light Industry and of Domestic Commerce conclude agreements in broad terms which run for one year. In addition, enterprises conclude agreements between themselves which have a currency of a quarter of a year. The latter are in exact terms and are of a binding force: a failure to meet them involves enterprises in having to pay penalties.

The annual agreements made in broad terms refer to a lengthy period of time. They are therefore necessarily very general in character. A quarter is, on the other hand, a short-time period. It does not allow industry time to prepare sufficiently for its tasks, especially where production periods are fairly lengthy.

One mistake which is made in this connexion is that the so-called *standard articles* of light industry and fashion goods are treated identically both in the process of planning and in the course of the placing of orders by commerce. Demand is fairly stable in the case of the former goods—examples of which are peasants' high boots, dark blue worsted cloths, and children's brown ankle-boots. For these goods, demand shows practically no change so far as quality is concerned. By contrast, the demand for fashion goods is of a fickle character.

There is no reason why the orders of commerce should not be of a long-term character, say perhaps for one year ahead, so far as the production of at least the bulk of standard articles is concerned. This would provide a solid foundation for the production programmes of factories. At the same time, there is a great need to secure the possibility of placing repeat orders for standard articles too, and fashion goods need to be dealt with in a far more flexible manner than at present.

It is worth taking note of experience in capitalist light industry in this connexion too. In that system the branches of industry concerned with the manufacture of clothing worked on a basis of two seasons, each being of six months' duration: articles sold during the spring and summer were manufactured during the winter and the spring—and those sold during the autumn and winter were made in the summer and autumn. Let us consider the shoe trade, for example. By October or November a shoe factory would have got out its collections of models for the following spring and summer and its salesmen would have been sent out to canvass distributors armed with these. The salesmen would book their orders and would report daily on them at the factory. These reports would include comments on variations in the reception accorded to the various different lines and on the character of the offerings of competing suppliers. Conceivably, this process could lead to immediate modifications being made in the collections offered. Meanwhile, the factory would have been engaged in fulfilling repeat orders until Christmas time. Orders for the spring and summer would be coming in at the same time. A production programme would now be laid down on the basis of these and a start would be made on carrying this out as soon as Christmas was over. The peak period of production for the summer season was reached in April and May; repeat orders were met at this time. The repeat orders of commerce were concentrated on the articles which sold best—and the factory would reckon in advance, to a greater or less extent, with the probability that it would be receiving repeat orders of this kind. The whole cycle would start afresh in May, this time in connexion with the autumn–winter season.

This arrangement (which, incidentally, was very similar to that in use in the textile trades also) had some disadvantages. Production was uneven: there was great pressure of work and much overtime working at the peak of the season, when repeat orders were being fulfilled, while at the beginning of the change-over to a new season, i.e. after Christmas and in early summer, rates of operation were reduced and some workers were sometimes actually dismissed for a time. But—at any rate from the point of view of timing— the arrangement also had considerable advantages. The individual phases of the production process formed 'natural' units which were synchronized with changes in demand arising in the natural course of events, rather than being simply tied to the quarterly divisions of the calendar. Factories received orders six months ahead for the bulk of their production programmes, but opportunities existed for modifying and complementing these and for dealing with repeat orders in the light of real changes in demand.

It is necessary to round out what has been said in this section with one further remark. I have so far pictured commerce as being, by its very nature, the chief repository of knowledge concerning the wishes of consumers and the champion of their interests—but for the fact that from time to time it lacks the necessary economic power for a successful defence of those interests. In reality, however, matters are not quite as rosy as this.

When, as often happens nowadays, it is discovered that actual requirements differ from those that were foreseen in the plans, this is frequently due to commerce having misjudged demand at the time when plans were formulated rather than a reflection of real changes in requirements since then. Excessive centralization has left its mark upon the set-up to be found in the distributive trades as well as in industry. They, too, suffer from serious shortcomings in their system of incentives.

A detailed investigation of the distributive trades is not within the scope of the present study. But this much should be said: if we want to achieve a partial replacement of instructions from the centre by influences emanating from commerce, then it is necessary that the distributive trades be provided with a greater stake than they now have in the swift and flexible satisfaction of demand, and in serving consumers in the best possible way.

2. PROBLEMS IN THE FIELD OF MATERIALS SUPPLIES

I propose to discuss three sets of questions:

(i) The evolution of the position as regards stocks, and the economic consequences of chronic shortages of materials.
(ii) Interrelations between shortages of materials and excessive centralization.
(iii) The fundamental causes of the shortages.

The position as regards stocks. The economic consequences of shortages of materials

Shortages of materials have been an ever-recurring phenomenon in light industry in recent years. Shortages have repeatedly appeared in regard to supplies of basic materials, of numerous ancillary materials, of fuels (particularly of coal), electric power, and also of various semi-finished products.

The size of stocks is one of the surest indicators of the degree to which materials are in ample or in scarce supply. Table XXX shows the evolution of the position in regard to stocks of the most important raw materials used in light industry over the period of the last six years. The official norms of stocks—which are determined on a very bare and modest basis—are taken as equal to 100, and total annual opening stocks throughout light industry are related to this.

It is clear from the table that there is hardly a single material the available stocks of which regularly attained the levels prescribed in present norms. If stocks of some materials did reach this norm from time to time, they soon fell off again.

Table XXX Stocks of materials for use in light industry

Product	1951	1952	1953	1954	1955	1956
Cotton	110	50	58	65	53	47
Cotton-type synthetic fibre.	214	132	76	68	50	40
Merino wool	—	—	105	45	90	110
Coarse wool	—	—	142	341	124	155
Wool tops	63	71	50	44	24	27
Synthetic fibre tops	67	36	81	81	93	112
Artificial silk yarn	84	67	119	98	75	102
Synthetic yarn	—	—	56	59	27	68
Stripped flax	62	17	11	28	43	54
Swingled hemp	33	39	113	79	77	80
Cattle hides	65	21	54	84	56	60
Sulphite cellulose	66	76	98	130	68	72
Natron cellulose	12	78	80	93	182	60
Timber for papermaking	—	97	47	17	20	70
Panel board	—	—	—	—	47	51
Veneer	—	—	—	—	87	129

—Indicates data not available.
Source: Data provided by the Central Planning Division of the Ministry of Light Industry. Norms in this field set the size of necessary supplies in terms of days, not tons (e.g. coarse wool needed for sixty-two days' production, &c.). In constructing the table, the calculations have throughout been based on the norms at present in force, so that the figures are fully comparable.

Early in 1956 stocks of several light industrial materials amounted to no more than 15–30 days' supplies. This is extraordinarily little! Besides, it is, in this case, not really sufficient to focus attention on aggregated data alone, because such data obscure the true nature of the problem in two distinct ways. Firstly, the figures show summary data in respect of groups of raw materials. But there are many kinds and qualities of each raw material, and they have different uses. They are not by any means easily substitutable for one another. If the statistics were to show the volume of stocks by specific kinds of materials, we would often obtain much lower figures still.

Secondly, the data refer to the country as a whole: but stocks are unequally distributed between factories. It is, therefore, worth having a glance at some data for individual factories. It may have appeared from the previous table that the position in the wool trade was more or less satisfactory in 1956.

The following quotations, extracted from a short-term report dated 13 February 1956 and issued by the Woollen Trades' Directorate, should correct this impression:

(i) Győri Gyapjúfonó: only provided for until 16 February.
(ii) Lóden: at a standstill owing to lack of materials.
(iii) Magyar Posztó: a third of the workers in the wool-scouring section on leave owing to shortages of materials.

Table XXXI shows selected data relating to stocks held at cotton-spinning mills operated by some of our textile factories during October 1955. The figures show stocks available at the dates indicated in terms of number of days' supply.

This table needs no comment—the startlingly low figures in it speak for themselves.

Table XXXI Stocks of cotton held by cotton-spinning mills

Enterprise	Middling cotton		Short staple cotton	
	5th Oct.	24th Oct.	5th Oct.	24th Oct.
Budai Pamutfonó.	3	17	5	27
Győri Fonó	3	24	16	16
Szegedi Textilművek	0	15	1	16
Pamuttextilművek.	6	25	6	18
Goldberger	6	15	not required	
Lőrinci Fonó	4	11	7	12

Source: Joint memorandum of the Ministry of Light Industry and the Ministry of Foreign Trade (dated Dec. 1955).

The next thing we need to get clear is: what is the extent of the damage caused by the chronic shortage of materials and the low level of stocks?

1. *It is a persistent cause of stoppages and disturbances in production.* Consider the cotton industry, for example. A few hundred tons of cotton may be acquired by the State-importing organization from Brazil. This will be divided up between plants by the Cotton Trades' Directorate. By the time machines have been reset and knowledge of the quality of the cotton, as well as some experience in working with it, has been acquired, the mills will already find themselves presented with cotton from yet another part of the world. Each time machines need resetting, time and materials are wasted and the earnings of the workers suffer a setback. Calculations have been made to show the number of times it has been necessary to reset machines during 1955 at the Lőrinci Fonó, the largest cotton-spinning mill, in cases when the reason for the change-overs lay in the uneven rate of arrival of consignments of cotton together with the fact that adequate stocks were not available for smoothing out the consequent fluctuations of supply. A total of 440,000 spindles had to be reset, which is equivalent to resetting the whole plant five times within a single year. The addition to wage costs caused was put at 405,000 forints, and the loss of production at 45,650 kilograms of yarn.[10] Conditions were much the same in other cotton-spinning establishments.[11]

The effect of disturbances in supplies of materials is to hamper the optimum utilization of the capacity at the disposal of enterprises. It also militates against steady employment of the labour force. These troubles sometimes manifest themselves in extremely sharp forms. For example, in February 1956 a total of thirty-one factories were either completely or partially at a standstill as a result, primarily, of shortages of coal and also of imported materials.

Thus, throughout the greater part of February, five large textile finishing establishments (Pamutkikészitőgyár, Kistext, Kőbányai Textilművek, Goldberger, and Textilfestőgyár) were out of action owing to shortages of coal.[12]

Shortages of materials and delays in their arrivals lead to nervousness and hasty action on the part of factory managements. For example, a regular process of swapping dyes to and fro goes on between enterprises in the textile trade. It has even been known for an official of a factory to have been got out of bed in the middle of the night on account of another factory happening

---

[10] Equivalent to about four days' wages and two days' output of yarn.
[11] The data referred to were taken from the joint memorandum of the Ministry of Light Industry and the Ministry of Foreign Trade which has already been mentioned in the foregoing.
[12] The source of this statement is a report of the Central Statistical Office.

to want to borrow some dyes. It was necessary to obtain dyes by aeroplane for one woollen cloth factory in 1955 because it was completely out of stocks. The job of securing adequate raw material supplies, which, in normal circumstances, could easily be accomplished by a department of a factory, actually absorbs a sizeable proportion of the time of directors chief engineers, and top technicians.

Thus, in the last analysis, trouble over raw material supplies puts a brake on the performance of light industry from a quantitative point of view, and slows up the rate of increase of productivity. It also puts obstacles in the way of light industry's attempts to meet its commitments towards domestic and foreign customers punctually at all times.

2. Shortages of materials have the effect of accentuating the phenomena of periodic fluctuations of production and of work spurts. If stocks were larger, they could absorb a large part of the shocks administered to factories engaged in working up materials by fluctuations in the rate at which the output of factories making semi-finished products is turned out. Some fluctuations would probably remain, but both the peaks and the troughs would be gentler. For it would be possible to make good from stocks, and without delay, any shortfalls in arrivals of materials or semi-finished products occurring early in a month or a quarter. As, however, stocks are low, any interruption in the flow of arrivals promptly induces a sympathetic setback in factories at later stages in the production process. Incidentally, this problem is not confined to the realm of relations between enterprises. It is also prevalent within enterprises. Stocks of yarn and of grey cloth are too small in many of our vertically integrated textile factories, so that hold ups in particular parts of a factory lead to immediate difficulties in other parts of it.

3. *The lack of adequate stocks leads to serious waste in the use of materials.* Enterprises are frequently driven to substitute the use of expensive materials for cheaper ones in the production of given articles, merely because cheaper materials happen to be out of stock.

A practice which has prevailed with minor alterations since 1951 in the purchasing of cotton has been that—in the event of a foreign trading organization having to supply materials of a better quality than that which had been ordered—the price chargeable to the manufacturing enterprise remains the lower one corresponding to the original order. This procedure is called 'down-grading' the cotton. The sums involved in this procedure provide an approximate idea of the loss which results from the fact that industry is obliged to use better materials than is necessary.

Table XXXII   Sums involved in 'down grading' in the cotton trade

Year	Sum involved in downgrading in million forints	As a percentage of the value of total cotton consumption
1951	41·5	6
1953	6·2	1
1954	18·1	3
1955	40·7	5
1956 1st quarter	5·2	3

Source: Data of the Central Planning Division of the Ministry for Light Industry.

This anomaly is also encountered in other branches of industry. Calculations were made at an important enterprise in the woollen industry, the Kistarcsai Fésűsfonó Factory, concerning the losses caused by the need to use better quality wool than was necessary, owing to the lack of adequate stocks and irregularities in the rate of arrival of raw materials. In 1955 alone this caused additional costs of 160,500 forints. A commission of inquiry composed of eminent experts drawn from the woollen industry carried out a similar investigation in 1954. According to their calculations the phenomena considered here cost the woollen industry additional costs amounting to about 4·5 million forints in 1953.[13]

4. *Shortages of materials often lead to lower standards of quality.* We have just discussed cases in which enterprises had been driven to substitute more expensive materials for cheaper ones. The reverse also occurs frequently: enterprises are forced to use worse materials than those which are really required, because better materials are not available. This, of course, leads to deterioration in the quality of the finished product.

I have already mentioned that repeated changes in production runs are frequently necessitated by the halting and unsystematic character of the materials supply set-up. This, too, harms quality. I mentioned the Lőrinci Fonó Factory as an example of the foregoing. In that factory a total of 36,000 spindles had to be reset on nine occasions in September. The proportion of substandard yarns was at that time 6·2 per cent. By October, when the resetting of 84,000 spindles on twenty-one occasions had become necessary as a result of difficulties over

---

[13] Cf. Report by István Szávai, Ferenc Tobisch, and Egon Burkus: *Possibilities of Lowering Costs by Way of Economizing in Costs of Materials in the Woollen Industry*. The additional costs referred to in the test were the equivalent of $1\frac{1}{2}$ days' production costs.

materials supplies, the share of substandard yarns in the total had jumped up to 12 per cent., i.e. to double its previous value.[14]

5. *The lack of adequate stocks handicaps the organizations engaged in importing materials.* This is because these organizations are prevented, by the perennial urgency of procuring supplies, from biding their time until the most favourable buying opportunities and offers materialize. The main disadvantage in this concerns the price factor, but it also contributes to the emergence of failures to meet the specific requirements of industry in point of type and quality.

6. An 'intangible' source of economic loss must, finally, be added to the foregoing tangible ones. This is that *user enterprises are made incapable of insisting upon the strict observance of their requirements* whether their suppliers are factories, warehouses, or importing enterprises. This problem is entirely analogous to the one I discussed in a previous section in connexion with the relationship of industry to domestic commerce: there also, when there is a shortage of goods, the distributive trades are obliged to close their eyes to the misdeeds of the factories because they count themselves lucky to be provided with any goods at all. The hungry man is not choosey. Nor does an enterprise which 'hungers' after materials spend much time thinking over the suitability of the qualities and types of materials it is offered. The *absence of pressure from the side of users deprives the process of production of one of the most important stimuli that can be brought to bear upon it.* This is one of the most serious consequences of difficulties over materials supplies.

Interrelations between shortages of materials and excessive centralization

Centralized administrative forms of direction of the economy are the inevitable consequence of chronic shortages of raw materials.

This is so even under capitalist conditions in spite of the fact that the independent autonomous character of enterprises owned by individual capitalists or groups of capitalists is an essential feature of that system. However, in certain special circumstances—most notably during periods of accelerated rearmament and in war-time—when chronic shortages of particular materials and products appear, various centralized forms of administering the

---

[14] The data referred to were taken from the joint memorandum of the Ministry of Light Industry and the Ministry of Foreign Trade which has already been mentioned in the foregoing.

economy emerge in that system also: e.g. centralized State control over the distribution of raw materials, price regulation of various articles in short supply, &c.

The Office of Price and Materials Control was an example of this in Hungary during the days of capitalism. It was called into existence by the requirements of the armaments drive and by war-time conditions. A centralized government authority, it was engaged in operating rationing schemes for the most important raw materials as well as for semi-finished and finished products. In addition, it performed certain functions connected with regulation of prices.

To pass now to the present system of production: central direction of the economy is undoubtedly an essential feature of a planned economy. However, its tendency towards centralization is greatly strengthened and intensified by shortages of materials.

In our field of inquiry, in light industry, the effect of the chronic, and not infrequently severe, shortage of materials upon the authorities responsible for the direction of the economy has been to induce them to attempt the solution of the whole range of problems resulting from the shortages by the use of administrative measures emanating from the centre. Specifically, this attempt assumes the following forms:

(i) The authorities hope to force enterprises to exercise economy in their use of materials by means of a number of prescriptions concerning their use. (This is quite generally characteristic of our methods of administering the economy: the authorities are wont to 'over-insure'; they seek to induce the performance of a single task by several parallel instructions, orders, and plan indices.) On the one hand, there are *norms for materials*. On the other hand, each enterprise is provided with a *planned bill of supply of materials*. There are, in addition, in certain trades, a variety of indices concerning the utilization of detailed types of materials among the so-called techno-economic indicators. For example, in the woollen industry there is a prescribed *output coefficient for materials*, as it is called, which lays down the quantity of finished output that has to result from the use of a given amount of material. It should, incidentally, be noted that these three prescriptions, all of which concern the use of materials, will, at best, only correspond with one another as a matter of accident.[15]

---

[15] The explanation of this is as follows: the real situation corresponds, roughly, to what is in the planned bill of supply of materials. However, as I have already said (cf. p. 136 above), this need not

(ii) The exact times, methods, and conditions under which enterprises are to order materials are all regulated by means of decrees from the centre. A significant part of orders is, in several fields, aggregated, modified, and then placed with the supplier (whether it be a manu-facturing or importing enterprise) by the industrial directorates rather than by user enterprises.

(iii) In several branches of industry, only the industrial directorates are entitled to negotiate on matters of substance with importing enter-prises.

(iv) The industrial directorates dispose of all basic raw materials and semi-finished products, and are in sole charge of allocating these, down to the last gramme.[16] (Enterprises may only buy auxiliary materials with comparative freedom from restrictions.)

(v) The planning of raw material allocation is carried out at the centre in closest possible connexion with the elaboration of detailed quar-terly production programmes. Indeed, this constitutes one of the chief arguments in favour of the central determination of programmes in the eyes of light industrial directorates, for they maintain that, in order to be able to allocate materials with exactitude, it is necessary for them to have detailed knowledge of what specific products are to be produced.

(vi) A sizeable part of the output of individual enterprises is destined to be worked up further in other enterprises also belonging to the Ministry for Light Industry: some of the yarn goes to the weaving mills of other factories, some of the finished cloth goes to clothing

correspond with the norms for materials; for if, in one period, an enterprise achieves economies in the use of materials beyond what is envisaged in the norm, this achievement will be 'incorporated in its plans', and future supplies of materials to this enterprise will be diminished accordingly. So far as the 'output-coefficient of materials' is concerned, this, like most techno-economic indicators, results from a mechanical process of passing on a figure laid down at the centre. In the course of fitting materials supplies to production plans the Central Planning Office adopts a formula for use in its calculations: x tons of wool can, on average, be made into y square metres of woollen cloth. This formula, being an average figure derived from experience, is capable of being of use in planning for the country as a whole, and it may well represent a piece of information which it is appropriate that the Ministry of Light Industry and the Woollen Trades' Directorate should possess. However, our practice is to pass these figures on, promptly, to enterprises, with the instruction that they be observed. However realistic the national average figure may have been, it may be outside the range of possibilities open to an individual enterprise which is confronted with a mechanically uniform, rigidly determined version of the same figure. For it is clear that the materials output coefficient of an enterprise will assume a value which will be very greatly dependent upon the specific composition and quality of the cloths it produces. These last will be much more nearly reflected in the norms for materials and in the planned bill of supply of materials.

[16] 1 oz. = 28·352 grammes.

manufacturers, leather to the shoe trade, &c. As there are very often shortages of each one of these semi-finished products the central authorities try to use the instructions contained in programmes to secure the production of the specific variety of leather most needed by the shoe trade or the production of the kind of yarn most wanted by the weaving mills, &c. This provides administrators in light industry with another argument in favour of detailed centrally elaborated programmes: thus alone, they maintain, are they able to ensure that scarce raw materials will be made up into the most needed semifinished products.

(vii) It should be noted that similar considerations are also put forward in justification of the central determination of programmes of finished consumer goods: this, it is said, is the most effective way of securing that scarce raw materials and semi-finished products will really be used in the production of those consumer goods which are most needed for domestic consumption or export.

It can be seen from the foregoing how very closely shortages of materials are bound up with the extraordinarily high degree of centralization which prevails in the direction of production. The trend towards centralization—which is, in any case, inherent in our present economic mechanism—is, here again, pushed to its ultimate consequences by the authorities in charge of light industry. It all seems very logical: when once the policy of allocating materials in short supply centrally, and by purely administrative methods, has come to be accepted as being desirable, then the most precise way of doing the job is also to prescribe centrally the quality and variety of products to be made out of these materials. Furthermore, a centrally elaborated, detailed production programme will appear as the logical complement of a very strictly centralized system of allocating materials and semi-finished products for the additional reason that—according to the proponents of this view, at any rate—the central authorities are in the best position to see what it is that is most worth producing given that supplies of materials are as short as they are.

However, this apparently very logical train of thought is contradicted by practical experience owing, not least, to the action of the very shortage of materials which is the point of departure for this train of thought. For the effect of irregularities in the supply of materials is repeatedly to play havoc with minutely planned production programmes as well as with plans of raw-material supplies and with those for the disposal of products.

I have already discussed this problem in the foregoing[17] in connexion with my discussion of the degree to which annual and quarterly production plans are well founded—but it is necessary to revert to these matters briefly here. It is a regular occurrence for the quality of imported materials to turn out to be different from the quality industry has been counting on; more often still, deliveries are delayed, and their timing is out of phase with what had been intended. As we have seen, stocks of numerous materials are extremely low; thus it is not always possible to make up for irregularities in the flow of circulating capital by drawing on reserves of materials. As a result, the fulfilment of the detailed programmes prescribed in quarterly plans is very often found to run into difficulties: sometimes enterprises are instructed to depart from their programmes by their industrial directorates, at other times they are forced to deviate from their plans on their own initiative. Being placed as they are, enterprises might, perhaps, be capable of holding to production programmes defined in a broad, as distinct from a finely broken down, manner: for example, they may be capable of producing x pairs of men's shoes or x square metres of worsted cloth. But it is beyond their power to hold themselves exactly to plans which prescribe in detail what individual lines they should produce down to the last pair or square metre.

It is clear, then, that a peculiar situation has developed. It contains contradictory features within it. On the one hand, the shortage of materials is one of the factors which has led the authorities to go in for minutely detailed planning. On the other hand, this very same shortage of materials is one among a number of factors which renders the exact observance of these plans impossible.

Let us examine this situation as it manifests itself in two branches of industry.

A peculiarity of the leather industry consists in this feature of it, that every single piece of raw hide has individual characteristics calling for individual evaluation. A separate decision is required in respect of every individual piece of leather in order that the best use to which it can be put may be decided: it might, for example, be made into expensive box-calf, or into oiled leather uppers, which are less valuable, or even into soles.

In principle, there are two possible ways of securing economical operation in the leather industry. One is to lay down the qualities and varieties of finished leather products each factory is to deliver in exact detail, while leaving factories with a completely free hand in choosing the raw hides which are most suitable for what they have been asked to make. The factories themselves would thus be enabled to acquire the hides they need in good time, or, if adequate stocks

---

[17] Cf. Chapter I, pp. 11–14 above.

of raw hides existed, the factories could be allowed to pick and choose from among the contents of the warehouses, &c.

The other possibility would be to leave factories no choice in regard to the raw hides they were given: they would have to work up what they were presented with, while being left entirely free to decide on what to produce. Factories would merely be provided with incentives to be as economical as possible in their use of materials, thus ensuring that raw hides suitable to be made into high-priced leathers really were turned into high-quality products, &c. On this procedure, the output of factories would be channelled into warehouses, and the shoe trade would be free to make its choices there.

Either of the above alternatives could work economically in practice. Unfortunately, however, neither of them corresponds to what actually happens. Leather factories are subject to constraints on two sides simultaneously. On the one hand, they cannot pick and choose between raw hides; stocks are too small for that. Their orders go to the Leather and Shoe Trades' Directorate; and that body will negotiate with Tannimpex, modifying the original orders placed by enterprises more than once in the process. After this, Tannimpex sees to the import-transaction, the actual outcome of which will again differ, as a rule, from the terms of the agreement concluded on paper with the industrial directorate. The main thing that goes wrong at this stage is that there are considerable departures from the timing of supplies as originally envisaged. In the end, the factories are faced with a fait accompli: they will be supplied with raw hides, but these will differ considerably from what they had been hoping to get.

On the other hand, in spite of the existence of a situation such as has just been described, the full detail of the exact composition of the finished leathers factories are expected to deliver during the same quarter is prescribed for them. They will already have contracted to deliver the finished leathers they are to produce through having signed delivery contracts—involving the assumption of responsibility for meeting specified standards of quality—at a time when they do not yet know what raw hides they will have to work on.

This double set of constraints puts the leather factories into a very difficult position. They are frequently unable to keep to the programmes prescribed for them. They are often forced to use the hides available to them for purposes other than those which correspond to the individual characteristics of each piece. Thus they might not make as valuable a product as the raw material would warrant (e.g. they may, let us say, turn out less valuable oiled leather uppers instead of box-calf) because their production programmes happen to be calling for other types of leather. Or, conversely, factories may be unable to avoid using inferior raw materials in the production of an article which makes great demands on the quality of the materials it is made of. In such cases the finished product will turn out to be rather poor, and will be graded as third-or fourth-class leather.

I will also deal briefly with the woollen industry, where a situation highly peculiar to the trade prevails. The guiding principle here is that the directorate is wedded to a policy of economy and therefore wishes to prevent factories from ordering anything at all unnecessarily. But this is something that can only be checked upon if there is some 'objective basis' for orders given. A practice has therefore developed whereby the orders of enterprises for basic materials are related to their production programmes of finished goods in the immediately subsequent quarter. But this leads to the development of an absurd situation. For example: when materials are ordered for a fourth quarter, this will consist of an order for wool which is, in principle, to be made into cloth due to leave the factory in a finished state in October, the first month of the quarter. However, the process of spinning that cloth would already have started in August! And when the material that entered the spinning mill in August was originally ordered in May or June, there was as yet no way of knowing what finished cloths would be required to be produced in October, so that this order was placed at that time 'as if' the material concerned were to have been turned into finished cloth as early as the third quarter. The order would have been 'based' on the third quarter, even though those placing it were fully aware of the fact that this would not yet be turned into finished goods during the third quarter.

It may be held that to provide an 'objective basis' for orders of materials in such a way as the foregoing is simply senseless, and should be stopped.

Indeed, there is a case for a change of policy here. Yet, a question worth asking is this: what are the factors which drive administrators in light industry to adopt such 'solutions'? One factor is the shortage of materials, which forces enterprises to order materials very sparingly. Another is the mechanism of the economy, which, instead of relying on the independent action of enterprises and their managements, circumscribes their freedom of action in a hundred different ways.

The examples of these two branches of industry provide clear indications of the extent to which the troubles caused by inadequate stocks are accentuated by rigid planning and materials supply policies associated with excessive centralization.

What, then, is the solution?

First: it is necessary to make far more determined attempts to alleviate the shortage of materials. This needs emphasis, even though it is so obvious. For, so long as the materials supply position remains as it is, disturbances and losses in the production process are inevitable no matter what the mechanism of the economy is like.[18]

We have seen that shortages of materials lead to excessive centralization in spite of the fact that the troubles to which these shortages give rise cannot be overcome even by such means. It follows that the authorities must liquidate the state of chronic and widespread shortages of materials if they wish to get rid of all traces of the excesses to which centralization has given rise and if they really want to grant more autonomy to enterprises. Otherwise the disease of over-centralization will recur whether the authorities like it or not.

That this is so is shown in a telling fashion by the example of materials balance sheets. Before the rationalization drive of 1954, materials were classified into three categories: there were (i) materials subject to O.T.[19] balance sheets (these were allocated on the basis of balance sheets drawn up in the National Planning Office); (ii) materials subject to ministry balance sheets (allocated on the basis of balance sheets drawn up at the responsible ministry); and (iii) materials not subject to the process of planned central allocation. The second of these categories was abolished in the course of rationalization and this group of materials ceased to be subject to the process of central allocation. However, several of these materials continued to be in short supply. The result has been that demands for a resumption of allocation on the basis of ministry balance sheets are being voiced in a number of quarters. Similarly, certain articles have been withdrawn from the scope of the O.T. balance-sheet system. Some of these, however, continue to be in short supply, and in connexion with them also it is being urged by some that a resumption of allocation on the basis of O.T. balance sheets is what is required.

Thus shortages give rise to demands for central allocation.

Secondly: an economic mechanism based on a greater measure of independence of action for enterprises could cope fairly well with shortages of materials provided that the shortages were not excessively acute. Given this last proviso—which needs to be stipulated, since very pronounced shortages must, in any case, give rise to serious harm—a mechanism such as is suggested here would be superior to the one we have. For it would allow factories and

---

[18] It is only fair to add that if the materials supply position were better, if stocks and reserves in the economy were larger, the *present* highly centralized economic mechanism would, itself, also be capable of functioning much better than it does at present. Small mistakes and inaccuracies in central planning are much more easily offset when stocks are larger. Therefore, if large stocks existed, it would be much easier to fulfil the minutely detailed programmes elaborated at the centre, &c. But, of course, if the situation as regards stocks did improve as drastically as that, then the authorities would feel far less conscious of a need for a high degree of centralization.

[19] O.T.—Országos Tervhivatal = National Planning Office.

commercial enterprises to engage in a constant search for rapid and flexible optimal adjustments between consumer requirements and the materials supply position. As these are always changing, decisions directly arrived at by the mutual agreement of producer and distributor are likely to be superior in this field to those of a higher authority. The latter must deal simultaneously with hundreds of problems of this nature, and is, of course, somewhat remote from both producers and consumers.

This is not to deny that centralized allocation of materials may be inevitable from time to time in some fields. This, however, can assume much simpler and more flexible forms than at present.

Thirdly: in addition to a greater degree of independence for enterprises we need forms of economic organization which will make enterprises feel that they have an interest in economizing in materials. The prices of raw materials are at present generally independent of the relationship between supply and demand. Economy in the use of materials would be greatly stimulated if the system of prices itself also exerted an influence in this direction. This would entail relatively high prices for materials in particularly short supply, so that enterprises which wished to lower their costs and raise their profits would be forced to economize increasingly in their use of just these materials, possibly by substituting others for them.

3. THE ACHIEVEMENT OF A PROPER BALANCE BETWEEN PRODUCTION AND CONSUMPTION. THE FUNDAMENTAL CAUSES OF SHORTAGES

The lack of adequate stocks is often mentioned as being one of the main factors responsible for our economic troubles. All textbooks on economic planning emphasize that adequate reserves and stocks are an indispensable element in the smooth functioning of a planned economy. But most of these books merely voice this proposition in a general way. They fail to provide detailed discussions of what they really mean by reserves, of how these are to be established, of what their size should be, of the current situation in planned economies in regard to reserves, &c. It seems to me that the unsatisfactory state of the theory of reserves has been a contributory factor in producing the difficulties which have arisen in connexion with them.

The facts are well known. The complaints voiced by the distributive trades from time to time have to do with the low level of stocks of consumer goods. The factories say that they do not have sufficient reserves of raw materials and of semi-finished products. There is repeated criticism of delays and hold-ups in raw material supplies, &c. Ultimately, all this relates to a single set of interdependent problems: it is a matter of balance between the volume of production and of consumption (consumption being taken to refer to industrial purchases as well as to personal consumption).

Just before the onset of a crisis under capitalism, production used to exceed actual consumption all round by such a large margin that a restoration of the necessary proportionality between them could only be brought about to the accompaniment of profound upheavals. Socialism is capable of eliminating harmful over-production of this kind. It can end devastating cyclical crises and the waste of goods and of man-power that goes with them. (This is not, unfortunately, inconsistent with the prevalence of several other types of waste in our economy.)

Having eliminated large-scale over-production of the type which used to lead to crises, economic policy in our country has gone on to create a situation which (in contrast to over-production) could rather be characterized as widespread 'under-production'. The fact that our socialist economy produces less than society feels it wants in absolute terms is not what I have in mind, for that is natural: in all forms of society the constant growth of new wants is the force which propels production along. The notion I have in mind concerns certain relative shortages. On the one hand, there are shortages of some means of production, primarily raw materials and semi-finished products, relatively to plant capacity and to production objectives. On the other hand, there are from time to time shortages of consumer goods relatively to effective demand.

In my opinion, the achievement of a suitable balance in these matters requires the replacement of our present 'under-production' by a certain degree of relative over-production. This should not be very large, but it should be general and permanent.[20] (I will revert, in what follows, to a detailed discussion of what I mean by desirable relative over-production.)

---

[20] Marx discussed the question of what would be the part played by reserves 'after the capitalist form of reproduction has been eliminated'. For example, he refers to the fact that the amount of worn out fixed capital requiring to be scrapped varies from year to year. In order to replace it, 'the aggregate output of the means of production would have to increase in some years and diminish in others. The only possible solution of the problem thus presented lies in persistent relative overproduction. It is necessary, on the one hand, to produce somewhat more fixed capital than is immediately needed. On the other hand, it is essential to establish stocks of raw materials, &c. on a scale in excess of annual requirements. (This holds especially with respect to essential goods.) Relative overproduction of this kind is a sign of society having assumed control over the material means of its own reproduction'. (*Capital*, vol. ii, pp. 476–7, Szikra, 1953.) The fact that Marx speaks **of** *persistent relative over-production*, rather than simply of reserves and stocks, is significant.

What causes the under-production of which I have spoken?

In part it is an unpleasant but necessary accompaniment of rapid progress. But this is by no means the whole story. A number of mistakes have been made. These have accentuated the difficulties naturally associated with the rapid pace of development of our productive resources.

The chief causes of under-production are the following:

1. First and foremost: *serious mistakes were made in connexion with industrialization policy.* As a result of the authorities' decision to step up the first five-year plan, the country was faced with objectives which were over-ambitious and unrealistic. The investment programme did not correspond to the real possibilities and requirements of the situation. Owing to this, the results attributable to these investments fell far short of what would have been in keeping with the sacrifices made.

The effects of this policy on the materials supply position were as follows:

(*a*) While the national economy strained to fulfil plans which were both over-ambitious and, in part, misconceived, several tasks of basic importance for the economy were necessarily neglected. The due replenishment and expansion of stocks of materials as production expanded was one of them. (Others included provision for regular increases in living standards, the systematic introduction of up-to-date machinery, &c.)

The use made of funds available for investment was one-sided. Balanced growth requires that the process of investment should serve to increase both *fixed* equipment (machines, buildings, &c.) and *circulating* capital (stocks of raw materials and semi-finished products, work in progress, &c.) in appropriate proportions. In our country, however, investment has been concentrated on the enlargement of fixed capital in a one-sided manner, and the objective of proportionate enlargements of circulating capital has fallen very much into the background. It is no accident that investment and investment in fixed equipment are spoken of in everyday usage as if they were identical; it is as if the process of augmenting stocks of producer goods did not really count as investment. Somehow, the authorities do not seem to find it in their hearts to devote a significant part of that proportion of the national income which is allocated to investment to stock formation. Those who prepare national economic plans have come to adopt the habit of regarding sums allotted to the augmentation of stocks as 'hidden reserves' of some sort, which they simply consider to be expendable in case of need (e.g. for the sake of economizing in foreign exchange or for stepping up fixed investment).

Every year since 1951, the need to increase stocks has been repeatedly insisted upon by the Ministry of Light Industry at the time when plans are prepared towards the end of the year. Thereafter, however, it is either the case that this objective is already lost sight of by the time the plan's index numbers are approved, or else—if the annual plan does provide for an increase in stocks—the bulk of them nevertheless fails to materialize in practice.[21]

(*b*) Although this whole set of problems is often discussed as if it all boiled down to nothing more than a question of stocks, I have already emphasized that there is more to it than this. Let us suppose that adequate provision has been made for stock formation up to a particular moment of time. Even so, these stocks would be rapidly run down if production were to fall behind consumption. Hence, one reason why it is important that a correct balance should exist between the various interrelated phases of the production process is that this is necessary if supplies of materials are to be adequate. The fact that the first five-year plan failed to promote the creation of such a balance was one of its most serious shortcomings. Indeed, in some fields, the plan actually led to an accentuation of disproportions.

What is the nature of the balance required in this connexion? A rule which could serve as a first approximation would be that the output of materials should be somewhat in excess of their rate of consumption, as determined by the requirements of industries at later stages of the production process. This same principle also needs to be observed within individual sectors of industry: the production of leather needs to exceed its rate of utilization by the shoe trade, the output of yarn from spinning mills should be greater than the amount required for weaving, &c.

Actually, what is required is somewhat more complicated than the foregoing formula suggests. There is, in fact, no need for the output of leather to exceed the requirements of the shoe trade continuously.[22] When once an adequate stock of leather in excess of the current requirements of the shoe trade has been established, then all that is necessary thereafter is to ensure that stocks are stabilized at this level, or alternatively expanded in step with any growth in the consumption of leather as the output of shoes expands. A further thing that needs to be secured is that capacity to produce leather should at all times be greater than corresponds to normal rates of consumption of it on the part of the shoe trade. This would enable the leather industry to take on repeat orders arising from unforeseen requirements of the shoe trade. This will only be possible if capacity in the leather trade is not, as a general rule, fully pre-empted. In other words, in order to ensure a smooth

---

[21] I would, at this point, remind the reader of the testimony of Table XXX, p. 163 above.
[22] The leather trade is, of course, only cited as an example in what follows.

flow of production, it is necessary to develop a balance between industrial sectors such that, in addition to securing the availability, at all times, of adequate stocks of raw materials, of semi-finished products, and of finished goods, there are also adequate reserves of capacity at the disposal of the economy.

One reason why capitalist industry shows such considerable flexibility in meeting unforeseen demands upon it is that it disposes of surplus capacity. (Indeed, it often has too much of it.) By contrast, the much-discussed 'rigidity' of our own industry—while partly due to faults in our methods of planning and administration which have already been discussed—is also closely connected with the fact that it lacks reserves of capacity in many lines of industry. This weakness has been perpetuated and enhanced by the fact that there has been a persistent attempt to represent this fault as a source of strength. The 'maximum utilization of capacity' is often regarded as something that is enormously advantageous. As I have already explained in an earlier chapter, the fact that we do make much better use of our machinery and other installations than capitalist economies do is a truly considerable advantage. (In capitalist economies, surplus capacity can result from imperfect competition, from monopolistic restrictions, or from fluctuations of the trade cycle.) But an excessively high degree of utilization of capacity ceases to be an advantage, and becomes a source of weakness which is responsible for much damage.

To sum up: what we need to achieve is that the rate of growth of the production potentials of the leather trade, the spinning mills, &c., should outstrip the rate of growth of the raw-material requirements of the shoe trade, the weaving mills, &c. Stocks must also grow, *pari passu*, at the same time. The simultaneous fulfilment of these two interrelated requirements is what I mean by a correct balance between production and the rate of consumption of materials. It is this, also, that I have in mind when I call for a certain degree of 'relative overproduction'.

Let us now revert to the question of balance in the actual structure of Hungarian industry, and to consideration of the first five-year plan. In a number of fields, relative rates of growth have been the reverse of what would have been required for balance. The rate of growth of machine manufacturing has outstripped that of iron and steel production; manufacturing industry as a whole has grown faster than the industries supplying power—coal, electricity, & c.

This has been partly due to the balance of the industrial structure we had inherited. It has also been due to the fact that while it is for technical reasons generally relatively easy to expand the production of manufacturing industry, we had additional opportunities for doing so (e.g. by the introduction of additional work shifts, &c). Apart from these factors, however, the shortcomings of planning and of investment policy have been a major cause of unbalance. Investment plans failed to aim consciously enough and consistently enough at the fullest possible degree of realization of the principles outlined in the foregoing. In order to secure early increases in the volume of output of finished products on as large a scale as possible, their production was expanded disproportionately faster than that of earlier stages of the production process, i.e. faster than capacity for the production of materials, power, semi-finished products, and components. New installations were being brought into operation at breakneck speed—but provision was not made for providing necessary support for these advances. That would have required planning ahead for the satisfaction of the enhanced demands for materials entailed by newly created capacities.

This shows up a basic weakness of our past methods of planning. The main object of planning is to secure that the evolution of the general structure of the economy corresponds to the social interest. It is just this that Hungarian planning has, in practice, failed to secure. It has been unable to shape a sound general structure for the economy, while being bogged down in concerning itself with thousands of minute questions of detail.

2. Along with the mistakes made in industrialization policies, the state of agriculture has been an important additional factor in the production of shortages. Detailed analysis of this is not within the scope of the present study. All I wish to do here is to refer to the fact that our agriculture has not kept up with growing national requirements. This lagging behind of agriculture has been a major cause of the appearance, from time to time, of shortages of foodstuffs and of industrial materials derived from agriculture.

3. A very close connexion exists between our problems in the field of materials supplies and the difficulties we experience in regard to foreign trade. An important part of the raw materials used by our industry comes from abroad. However, our capacity to import has been very disadvantageously affected by the well-known fact that we have become debtors on foreign account in recent years.

Credits from abroad can of course be of considerable assistance in the process of industrialization. The trouble has been that we have made use of credits on too large a scale. Their burden is excessive, and the process by which we have come to be increasingly indebted was, in general, insufficiently thought out. Incidentally, the difficulties resulting from this are not to be regarded as a separate phenomenon which lends itself to isolated analysis. It is, rather, a consequence of mistakes made in the direction of industrial and agricultural development and in economic policy matters generally.

It is customary to dwell upon one point only in connexion with difficulties over foreign trade. This is that it is very hard to raise stocks to adequate levels in the face of such difficulties. Other relevant considerations also exist, however. For one thing, as has already been explained, the halting character of the supply of raw materials and shortages of stocks lead to serious waste in the use made of foreign exchange resources, particularly by way of inducing irresponsible prodigality in the utilization of imported materials.[23] In addition, fulfilment of export orders is frequently hampered by hold ups in raw material supplies. Thus there is an adverse feed-back effect of inadequate raw material supplies and stocks upon our foreign trading position. This constitutes a 'vicious circle', but this much is certain: there is no way of breaking out of it by turning stock shortages into a permanent state of affairs.

4. The fact that insufficiently good use is made of such materials supplies as are available is one of the causes of shortages in them. Our economic mechanism contains insufficient incentives of a kind designed to encourage economy: indeed, some parts of it amount to a veritable invitation to indulge in waste.

I will confine myself to pointing to no more than a selection of factors in this connexion, including some already mentioned elsewhere in this study in other contexts.

(a) Their plans of cost-reduction cause enterprises to be economical. At the same time, however, the rigid limitations imposed upon them by the *modus operandi* of permitted wage and salary bills work in such a way as to induce enterprises to be particularly tight-fisted in the matter of expenditure on wages—at the cost, if necessary, of waste in raw-material utilization.

(b) Industry is driven, by the action of the index of production value, to turn out articles which make heavy demands upon raw-material supplies.

(c) For the most part, interest cost incurred in carrying stocks is small relatively to additions to costs which result from production difficulties or from stoppages due to shortages of materials. Enterprises therefore do their best to amass as large an amount of stocks as they can possibly lay their hands on. This passion to gather stocks together would very probably diminish if the build-up of stocks and the supply of materials

---

[23] Cf. pp. 166–7, where this was discussed in detail.

proceeded in a smooth way and according to a plan. If stocks were ampler and of better, more varied, composition, then less superfluous stocks would be held. Higher interest charges might also be used to provide stronger deterrents against unnecessary holding on to stocks by enterprises.

(d) While unnecessary holdings of stocks of some materials and semi-finished products exist, in the case of others, stocks have been unduly reduced to artificially low levels by excessive zeal over what is called 'saving of circulating capital'. There is, of course, a need to speed up the turnover of circulating capital, but this must be done in conformity with general economic requirements. With us it frequently becomes an end in itself. (Incidentally, points (c) and (d) both suggest that the composition of stocks is determined in a largely unregulated manner in our economy. While production programmes are worked out centrally in minute detail, no conscious designs and plans are, in general, prepared with a view to influencing the composition of stocks. These come to be made up of whatever does not happen to be needed.)

(e) In the last analysis, the fact that materials are used in the production of articles which are not those that are most needed, also entails that they are wasted. Materials are worked up for the sake of augmenting 'production value'—irrespectively of what the actual composition of demand may be. The great variety of ways in which more or less completely unwanted articles can come to be produced was discussed in an earlier chapter.

We are faced with a peculiar contradiction here. On the one hand, it is a characteristic feature of the economic mechanism which goes with excessive centralization that it is capable of achieving high levels of output while tying up relatively small quantities of circulating capital in throughputs and stocks. On the other hand, the same mechanism permits and, in part, actually causes waste in the use of raw materials and induces unnecessary holding of stocks. Elements of economy and of waste are mingled with one another here. For a long time, however, the former of these elements was alone regarded as being truly characteristic of the mechanism, while the latter element was regarded as merely reflecting the personal shortcomings of individual economic administrators. In fact, this second element of waste is not accidental either; there are a number of ways in which our economic mechanism itself necessarily induces waste.

5. It is desirable to arrange for some degree of 'relative over-production' of consumer goods as well as of raw materials and semifinished products. So far, however, there have been shortages of these. It is necessary to consider the question of prices in their relation to purchasing power in this connexion.

We must distinguish between general shortages and shortages in specific fields. During the years in which we have had a planned economy, there have been several periods during which shortages of goods have appeared in a fairly widespread and sharp form as a result of a general lack of balance between purchasing power and the volume of goods available. The period preceding the measures taken in December 1951 and the situation which was developing in 1954 are examples of such conditions. Equilibrium was restored by repressing purchasing power in the first of these situations, while in the second the imbalance was righted by the vigorous growth of the volume of goods made available during 1954–5.

Such an imbalance is actually considered to be desirable in some quarters. Those who profess such views often quote a statement of Stalin's in their support: '... with us, in the Soviet Union, the consumption (purchasing power) of the masses grows all the time. It outstrips the increase of production, and stimulates its growth.' In the same work, Stalin identifies the following state of affairs as being helpful in economic development: '... the growth of the internal market will outstrip the growth of industry and will ceaselessly stimulate industry to expand its production.'[24]

In my opinion this view is merely another characteristic instance of trying to make out that some fault is really a virtue. A lack of balance of this kind between demand and supply, resulting from the latter lagging behind the former, will, at the most, only serve as a stimulating influence upon the planners themselves; for the various kinds of unpleasantness which flow from shortages (queuing, complaining customers, &c.) do have the effect of inducing the planners to search for measures which will restore the balance of the economy as soon as possible. However, the performance of producers is not improved in any way by such a state of affairs. On the contrary, we have seen that it is conducive to slackness, to a comfortable way of going about things, and to a lack of regard for the wants of consumers.

6. In addition to periodic shortages of a generalized kind, it is also possible to distinguish shortages in specific fields. These assume two principal forms. (They can also take shape in a variety of admixtures of these, which are

[24] Report of the Central Committee to the XVIth Congress of the Communist Party of the U.S.S.R. (Bolsheviks), *Collected Works of Stalin*, vol. xii, pp. 345 and 312 respectively, Szikra, Budapest, 1950.

intermediate between the two.) First, industry often simply fails to produce certain consumer goods. (The so-called 'goods in short supply' of the period before June 1953 were an example of this. It will be remembered that our industry entirely neglected the production of a whole series of articles in common demand for household and technical use.)

Secondly, it often happens that shortages of certain goods exist even though they are being produced, given that their prices to consumers are what they are. The prices set for our consumer goods do not help to promote equilibrium between supply and demand. For example, a problem arises from the fact that these prices are insufficiently sensitive to changes in supply and demand which occur after prices have been fixed.

Sales of 'unsaleable' unwanted goods do take place at reduced prices from time to time in our system as well. In most cases, however, a number of years must elapse before the responsible authorities bring themselves to reduce prices. Meanwhile the goods lie in store at the warehouses, unnecessarily taking up their capacity, and a part of the circulating capital of the national economy. Thus, the Szombathely and the Szeged shoe factories produced so-called 'normal flexible' women's shoes with pigskin uppers as long ago as 1953–4. Something like 500,000 pairs of these were left to lie in warehouses over a period of several years. They are only just beginning to be sold now that their price has been reduced from 126 forints to 68 forints. If the price had been reduced earlier it is possible that demand could have been activated by a price reduction of smaller proportions, so that the losses of the State would have been less.

I have listed six factors which may be regarded as being the proximate causes of the shortages we experience. All these can; however, be shown, in the last analysis, to derive from two fundamental sets of causes. One of these consists of *mistakes in economic policy*, foremost among which are the unrealistic, over-ambitious objectives set for the rate of development of the national economy. These have led to haste and exhaustion in the execution of policy.[25] The other set of causes is made up of *harmful aspects of our economic mechanism*.[26] It should straightaway be added that it is not possible to separate these two sets of problems from one another in a rigid fashion.

The point can be illustrated by glancing over the debates of recent years which have been concerned with these questions. After June 1953 our attention in this country was focused on industrial development policy questions relating to the speed and direction of industrialization; problems concerning

[25] What has been said under points 1, 2, 3, and, partly, 5, can be related to this.
[26] The phenomena listed under points 4 and 6 are mainly consequences of these.

the economic mechanism were hardly discussed as yet at that time. Later, in 1955 especially, our methods of administering the economy became the most-debated subject, and problems of economic policy relating to industrialization practically disappeared from the agenda of public discussions. Yet, in reality, these two questions are most intimately connected with one another. In its simplest terms, the nature of the connexion is this: the more adamantly a very rapid pace of industrialization is insisted upon, the more inevitable the adoption of a high degree of centralization will be. Conversely, if the pace of industrialization has a more deliberate and calm character, it is then possible for an economic mechanism to develop in which enterprises have much more independence, and in which direct relationships between enterprises play a greater part.

The foregoing has been confined to analysing those consequences of the serious mistakes made in industrialization policy which lead to shortages of materials. However, there are other ways as well in which excessively ambitious policies of industrialization have a tendency to lead to bureaucratic centralism. To mention only a few of the numerous and complex ways in which this connexion arises:

(i) Enterprises have had the greatest difficulty in coping with very ambitious plans; actual performances have repeatedly fallen short of plans over a very wide range of productive activity. In their attempts to master these difficulties, the central authorities proceeded to interfere with the work done by enterprises on an ever-growing scale, and sent more and more of their own representatives from the centre to 'help' in the factories.

(ii) The massive programme of investment and building was associated with large expenditures on wages which were not immediately matched by corresponding supplies of food and other articles of general consumption, so that there was a constant danger of disequilibrium between purchasing power and the volume of goods available. In these circumstances the central authorities made use of the most forceful administrative measures in an effort to limit increases in the aggregate wage and salary bill. As is well known, mistaken policies of industrialization were associated with a temporary period of reduced living standards. In that situation, pressure in favour of easing norms and loosening up on wage payments grew by leaps and bounds. The desire of the authorities to counteract this was a contributory factor in strengthening the centralization of control over wages.

(iii) The over-expanded investment programme produced an acute shortage of labour. Strict centralization of controls over personnel was
introduced in order to counter tendencies to hoard man-power.

It is sheer illusion to suppose that a novel economic mechanism, based upon
a more independent role for enterprises, can be made compatible with an
over-ambitious policy of economic development of a kind which preserves,
and, indeed, accentuates the chronic character of shortages of materials, continues to demand an overly rapid rate of growth of production at any price,
and continues to persist over long periods in pushing the degree of utilization
of capacity well beyond its optimum point in the mines, power stations, and
plants of several important branches of industry. Yet there can be no doubt
that the tendency to pursue such a policy is still with us.

I had stressed, earlier on, that it is desirable to have, permanently, a certain
degree of relative over-production. What should be the magnitude of this?

Let us first make one or two comparisons with the state of affairs under
capitalism.

We may first take an example drawn from an individual factory. In capitalist times, the Magyar Gyapjumosó Factory regularly disposed of stocks
of raw materials equivalent to 6–12 months' requirements. Generally speaking, orders for raw materials were placed for the purpose of replenishing
stocks rather than to satisfy requirements arising from current production.
Against this, stocks held by this factory during June–July 1956 normally ranged
between 5–15 days' supply.

Yet another relevant picture of the situation is provided by Table XXXIII,
in which a comparison is made between the stocks of cotton held by certain
capitalist countries and our own stocks. I have deliberately chosen countries
which—like ourselves—are importers of cotton. Thus, the size of these stocks
is free from the influence of over-production in agriculture, which is a factor
in the swollen stocks of cotton held by the U.S.A., for example.

The original table from which the figures shown in the above table were
calculated give data for stocks held on 1 Aug. of each year, together with figures
for consumption of cotton during the subsequent economic year, from August
to August. Therefore, the table here shown indicates the number of days actual
requirements during the year 1952/3 covered by the stocks held on 1 Aug.
1952. The aggregated figures for capitalist countries include data for India and
Japan, as well as data for the countries separately listed.

The source of the Hungarian data is a report of the Central Planning Division of the Ministry of Light Industry. The data in that source relate to stocks

Table XXXIII Stocks of cotton in major capitalist
importing countries and in Hungary

Country	1952	1953	1954
England	264	178	160
France	70	80	78
Italy	154	130	120
West Germany	63	60	70
Belgium	103	79	93
World total of main cotton-importing capitalist countries	140·3	103·6	107·9
Hungary	31	36	40

Notes and sources: The figures contained in this table show the
number of days' production requirements covered by the stocks of
each country. The source of data relating to capitalist countries is the
issue of *Bulletin Innosztranoj Kommereseszkij Informacij* (*BIKI*) for
27 Mar. 1956. The BIKI data were taken from the Cotton *Quarterly
Statistical Bulletin* for Oct. 1955.

held on 1 Jan. instead of 1 Aug. It is, however, clear from quarterly reports that
the size of stocks does not vary substantially in the course of the year. One
can, therefore, have confidence in the comparative orders of magnitude of the
capitalist and Hungarian figures.

We may now answer the question which was raised in the foregoing as to
the desirable magnitude of 'relative' over-production, in approximate terms,
by saying that this should be less than it was, say, in 1952 in England, but a
good deal greater than it is at present in our country.

It seems clear that no prescriptions for the optimum degree of relative over-
production and the optimum size of stocks can be valid for all times and all
places. These things evidently depend on factors related to specific conditions
obtaining in particular areas, the degree of dependability of sources of supply,
considerations of economy, &c. Economists engaged in the investigation of
practical aspects of this question need to use mathematical methods on an
extensive scale in attempting to determine these magnitudes.

This whole line of reasoning will be opposed by some people on the ground
that the sacrifices involved in satisfying the requirement of 'relative over-
production' are too great. They would hold that great losses would result
if we permanently maintained unused capacities in our factories, and tied
down a larger volume of circulating capital and more stocks in the course of
production than we do today.

It is, of course, undeniable that meeting this requirement entails that some material sacrifices would, in fact, have to be made. It would be naïve to suppose that a 'deal' of some kind is feasible by virtue of which it would be possible for the national economy to reap nothing but gain, at no cost whatsoever to itself, in the course of achieving the establishment of an economic mechanism which depended increasingly on transactions between enterprises and did away with some part of the constraints on the economy which now exist. No: at least to begin with, the fashioning of such a mechanism would probably involve a need to tie up more fixed equipment and circulating capital in securing a given volume of output than hitherto. However, this increase in inputs would be amply repaid in enhanced results. There are two main considerations in support of this last view.

First: we have to pay a heavy price, at present, for the economies in fixed equipment and circulating capital which we secure by keeping ourselves short of reserve capacity and stocks and by operating an excessively centralized economic mechanism. This price includes various kinds of disturbances in the production process, waste in the use of materials, lack of improvement or deterioration of quality, dullness of the available assortment of goods, a retarded pace of technical development. There is also the damping influence exercised upon the initiative of the workers by the present mechanism, the brake it puts on the activity of the masses—a factor, this, which cannot be measured in economic terms.

Secondly: an end to the régime of shortages of goods and of materials would entail that one of the major factors which now drives our entire system of economic administration in the direction of excessive centralization would cease to operate. More than this, if we succeeded in creating reserves of raw materials, of semi-finished products and also of capacity, we would find a new and extremely important driving force appearing in the production process: the pressure of the customer, the user, the consumer.

This has, in fact, already been touched upon in the course of our earlier analyses of the relationships which exist between industry and commerce and between suppliers and users of semi-finished products.[27] These relationships are merely two different manifestations of what is essentially the same, single, coherent problem. The problem itself is this: should there be competition between users, buyers, and consumers for the favours of producers, or should the converse be the case, so that producers will find it a bit of a problem to find

---

[27] Cf. pp. 148 and 167–8.

buyers and consumers for their products and to obtain orders which will take up the bulk of their productive capacities? The issue has been well put in an article by György Péter. He pointed out that competition inevitably occurs in our economy. The question that needs to be decided is what is more advantageous: 'buyers' competition' or 'sellers' competition'?[28] The first of these phenomena is bound to emerge if stocks are low and the productive capacities of enterprises are overloaded. On the other hand, the second of these phenomena will appear automatically if stocks are plentiful, if factories dispose of a certain amount of spare capacity, and if, at the same time, the managements and workers of enterprises have an incentive to utilize their capacities as fully as possible.

The first phenomenon—which entails that buyers are powerless—has the effect of putting a brake on improvements in production. It accustoms producers to a comfortable laziness and to a neglect of their customers' requirements. By contrast, the converse state of affairs stimulates enterprises to try to win the favour of their customers by satisfying their requirements in regard to quality and variety, and by producing well made, up-to-date articles as cheaply as possible.

This effect will be particularly powerful where the situation just described is coupled with a state of affairs in which other circumstances are also such as to facilitate the emergence of competition. A competitive struggle among enterprises for customers can exert such 'pressures' and economic compulsions on enterprises as will make it unnecessary to elicit the performance of at least a part of the foregoing requirements by the employment of administrative methods and detailed instructions from the centre. The effect of these 'pressures' is exceedingly multifarious and complex. It forces enterprises to satisfy the most varied requirements simultaneously. If a factory should neglect any one of them—whether it be quality, type of product required, or the punctual observance of delivery dates, &c.—it will find itself at a disadvantage in competing and will risk losing orders to other enterprises.

This, incidentally, also explains why there was a need for a detailed discussion of the various problems of balance between production and consumption, of shortages of goods and materials, and the role of stocks, in a study such as this, which set out to deal with the phenomenon of excessive centralization. The reason is that the former set of problems is very intimately connected with excessive centralization. The essence of this connexion can be briefly summarized as follows.

---

[28] 'The role of economy and of profitability in a planned economy,' *Közgazdasági Szemle*, June 1956.

The lack of stocks and the helpless position of consumers both gives rise to and strengthens excessive centralization. Conversely, the creation of adequate reserves promotes the emergence of competition between producers. In suitable conditions, competition for the orders of customers can develop into a powerful driving force. This force is capable of replacing a considerable part of the system of centralized instructions which now regulate production together with the incentives relating to them—and it can do so with a net gain in effectiveness.

4. A 'MODEL' OF OUR ECONOMIC MECHANISM

The system of centralized instructions and incentives which regulates the productive activity of enterprises from day to day was surveyed in the first two chapters of this study. The three previous sections of the present chapter examined the character of the relationships which exist between enterprises in light industry. Our next step should be to study the overall result of the various influences to which enterprises are subject, by surveying and weighing their relative importance and effects.

Let me therefore try to sketch the 'model' of our present-day economic mechanism. I propose to do so in a somewhat abstract manner by indicating no more than the main outlines.

'Horizontal' connexions

We may choose the enterprise as our point of departure. It is the basic unit, the 'cell' of the economy. The influences to which it is subject emanate from two different 'planes', as it were.

One of these 'planes' is horizontal. An enterprise will have economic relations of a commercial nature with other enterprises. It will receive materials, power supplies, machinery, tools, and a variety of services from them. It will also give things to them, handling its own products over to them. These connexions involve contacts with other enterprises which can be of the most various kinds: they may be industrial, foreign trading, domestic trading, assembling, agricultural, or transport undertakings. An enterprise will, in any event, confront any one of the above either as a buyer or as a seller. It will either be making payments to them for some product or service or it will be receiving payments from them. I refer to these as 'horizontal' connexions because our concern is here with enterprises having equal legal rights and standing. The forces which influence enterprises in this context arise at their own level, as it were.

The other 'plane' is vertical. Enterprises are subject to influences which emanate from the central directing organs of economic administration. (Naturally, the most common source of such influences is the directly superior authority, i.e. the Ministry's industrial directorate, but other authorities also come into the picture.) Here we are no longer dealing with connexions between equals. Rather, it is a matter of authority and subordination; these are relationships of power between the leaders and the led. That is why I call these 'vertical' connexions.

The sketch we have is still excessively abstract at this point. To make it more concrete and lifelike it is necessary to look at the two 'planes' in relation to each other.

What is characteristic of our present economic mechanism is that the 'horizontal connexion' arising from transactions between enterprises exerts a relatively small influence on their activities. Direct agreements between enterprises and their customers have a sub-ordinate part to play in determining what enterprises should produce in point of the type, variety, and quality of the articles they are to make. All this is decided by programmes drawn up at the centre, agreements between the makers and their customers being confined to fine shades of detail. There is no scope at all for decisions at enterprise level in the matter of who should receive the products they make; this is determined for them by sales plans. As for the prices at which products are to be delivered—this is decided by central pricefixing authorities.

Looking at things from the other end, we again find the central authorities deciding how much of materials can be bought, at least so far as the most important basic materials are concerned. Prices are, likewise, the province of the central price-fixing authorities. The sources from which materials are to be obtained are also laid down centrally, rather than being the outcome of competition for orders among producers.[29]

We can see, therefore, that the manner in which products are passed on among State-owned enterprises is subject to a far-reaching system of central regulation. There is, moreover, no substantial difference in this respect

---

[29] Exceptions to this do also exist, of course. Instructions issued centrally, e.g. detailed production programmes, are from time to time found to be in outright conflict with the requirements directly expressed by customers. The latter are occasionally allowed to prevail in such circumstances. Whenever this happens, the part played by 'horizontal connexions' is suddenly much enlarged. Naturally, however, the opposite of this also takes place. Instructions will then be fulfilled in the face of their divergences from real social requirements as expressed in orders placed.

between producers' goods and consumer goods. The influence of central regulation is no less great in the course of the passage, say, of a piece of woollen cloth from a factory to the Betex wholesaleing enterprise, than it is in the course of the passage of woollen yarn from the enterprise that makes it to the one that works it up into cloth. Indeed, the degree of centralization of production programmes and sales is, in light industry, even higher in respect of finished products than it is in respect of purchases of raw materials and semi-finished products, the latter being relatively freer, and more 'commercial' in character.

There is practically no trace of dealings of a 'market', 'business', or 'commercial' character along the path followed by goods in the course of their passage towards a retail shop. Production and distribution are entirely (or almost entirely) subject to instructions from the centre. What happens in regard to the quantity, composition, and variety of goods produced, as well as in regard to the channels of trade and prices, is hardly at all affected directly by the influences of demand. Such effects as it has in these respects are all transmitted indirectly, by way of plan index numbers and State instructions.

'Vertical' connexions

Let us now consider the other 'plane', that of vertical connexions, which involves the relationships of enterprises with the centre.

The fact that these vertical connexions are the dominant ones has already been made clear in the course of our examination of the character of 'horizontal' connexions. The influences which result from direct contacts between enterprises are dwarfed by those which reach them from the centre.

This, however, does not tell us enough about the working of the 'model'. We need to make a more detailed survey of the nature of the connexions between enterprises and the centre. We must ask what means of transmission are employed by the centre in influencing the activities of enterprises.

I would like to pick out eight of these means of transmission here. They may be likened to a set of 'levers' or 'gears'. Let us take them in turn.

1. *Centralized operative direction of current production.* The central authorities tell enterprises how much they should produce in each quarter, exactly what types and qualities of articles they should produce, and also what costs they are permitted to incur during each period. They are informed of all this by way of plan index numbers and instructions, and it is chiefly to the fulfilment of these last that both financial and moral incentives are attached.[30]

---

[30] The first two chapters of the present study were primarily concerned with the description of the *modus operandi* of this particular 'lever'. The treatment of the second of these chapters, which dealt with the system of incentives, was unavoidably of a broader character, as it was necessary to touch

This system of centralized operative direction employs an administrative machine of its own. It consists primarily of the planning departments of the ministries, the industrial directorates, and of enterprises. It also includes the so-called 'production-divisions'—where these exist. The part played in this connexion by the ministries and directorates may be likened to that of a national 'dispatch office'.

2. *Investment.* The system of planning, allocating, authorizing, and financing investment is one of the most important levers operated by the central authorities. Its function is to secure an appropriate balance in the development of industry and of the national economy. The administrative machine concerned with this is both large and extensive in its ramifications.

3. *The monetary system.* The central monetary authorities have a variety of means at their disposal which can be used in checking up on the performance of enterprises. Indeed, it is also possible to use these in such a way as to exert a positive influence on what enterprises do. These means include supervision of the accounts rendered by enterprises, furnishing them with credits, the recording and regulation of profits and turnover taxes due to be paid over by enterprises, &c.

These are the possibilities. In practice, the monetary system is only used to control the activities of enterprises. The extent to which it is used as an indirect method of directing and influencing production is negligible.

4. *The price system,* or more precisely, in present circumstances, the system of producers' prices employed in the measurement of the performances of productive enterprises. All prices require central authorization at the present time. This also involves the maintenance of a separate administrative machine. There are separate sections or divisions concerned with prices in the central accounts departments of ministries and of industrial directorates.

The influence of conscious State price-fixing policies on the course of production in enterprises is very small, within the framework of the mode of operation of our present economic mechanism.

This question has two sides to it. First, there is the question of how far enterprises are influenced by producers' prices *in their capacity as consumers.* To what extent are they influenced by these prices in their choice of materials or in the degree to which they are inclined to exercise economy in using them, for example? Under present conditions the answer is—very little. The part played in such decisions by other factors (like the system of central allocation of materials, &c.) is much more important.

upon matters relating to incentives of a wider character, the influence of which is not confined to the current production process. However, those two chapters do, I think, provide a broad picture of the interrelated system of centralized operative direction of production from day to day.

Secondly, there is the question of the extent of the influence exercised by prices on enterprises *in their capacity as producers*. That is, to what extent are they influenced by these prices in deciding on product-mixes, in introducing new lines, and in adapting themselves to the course of demand in a flexible manner? The answer, as before, is that this influence is very slight too. The price system does, to some extent, provide a stimulus to efforts to improve quality, but, as we have seen,[31] it does so in an extremely lopsided fashion. And this is just about all. This could hardly be otherwise seeing that top managements have no interest in increasing their profits. As a consequence of this, they feel more or less indifferent about the prices fetched by their products.

5. *The system of materials supplies.* The bulk of basic materials is, at present, subject to central allocation. There is a separate administrative machine concerned with budgeting for supplies of materials (supplies offices, &c.), but planning and production departments are also concerned with this.

We have seen that this set-up has an extremely powerful influence on what enterprises do; it constitutes the most powerfully effective link between enterprises and the central authorities.

6. *State regulation of foreign trade.* All export and import transactions had, until recently, to pass through foreign trading enterprises, direct dealing on the part of industrial enterprises having been prohibited altogether in this field. (Quite recently a few enterprises in the machinery industry have acquired the right to do business abroad on their own account. There are no enterprises in a position to do this in light industry.)

The activities of foreign trading enterprises are also directed by means of a separate, strictly centralized administrative machine. In indirect ways, this set-up exerts an important influence on the functioning of industrial enterprises as well.

7. *The system of permitted wages funds and of man-power budgeting.* This also employs a separate administrative machine of its own, consisting primarily of the departments concerned with labour matters. The wage and salary budgets and the labour forces of enterprises are regulated by means of instructions and plans, some of which are very strict in character, being strongly buttressed by both financial and moral sanctions. Their influence upon the actions of enterprises is very strong. The forms that may be taken by systems of

---

[31] Cf. p. 51 above.

wage and salary payments, as well as decisions as to which of these forms is to be used in particular instances, are laid down centrally over much of the field. Wage rates are entirely a matter for determination at the centre, and norms partly so.

8. *The system of central appointment and allocation of managerial personnel.* The character of this 'lever' is, at first sight, very different from the purely economic levers listed in the foregoing. Yet there is every justification for including it here. The fate of an enterprise depends upon who directs it to a marked degree. Consequently, as the ministries and other central authorities possess full powers to appoint and transfer or dismiss managerial personnel, this constitutes another channel through which they exert influences of very great economic importance upon the activities of enterprises. Again, a separate bureaucracy is involved in running this—the personnel departments.

Naturally, the eight 'levers' listed in the foregoing are closely interconnected. This is evident, among other things, from the form taken by plans; for example, the annual plans of enterprises include sections dealing with production, labour and related matters, materials supplies, investment and maintenance, finance, &c. The fact that these appear as distinct sections in the plans has a justification, in that one is here dealing with what are, to some extent, chains of administrative command. Let us, for example, consider the seventh lever listed: the system of permitted wages funds and of man-power budgeting. The administrative machine involved consists of the labour division of the Secretariat of the Ministerial Council, the central labour division of the National Planning Office, the central labour divisions of individual ministries, the labour divisions of industrial directorates, and the labour divisions of enterprises. All these divisions are, of course, subordinated to the responsible heads of the larger units of which they are parts; e.g. the labour division of an industrial directorate is subordinated to the head of the directorate, and so on. Yet at the same time this division will also receive instructions from a higher authority in its own field of operation, the central labour division of the Ministry, and it will also have a certain amount of power to influence the activities of the labour divisions of enterprises in a direct manner.

The above is known as the 'functional system' of industrial administration.[32]

The fact that the size of these administrative machines is as large as it is does not result, as of necessity, from the nature of the tasks needing to be performed.

[32] I will be reverting to this later, cf. p. 209 below.

This is, rather, a result of the forms assumed by the economic mechanism of the present day. It would be open to the central authorities to make use of the extremely important 'levers' of wage and price-policy, &c., while employing a much smaller administrative apparatus in doing so!

Having analysed the various levers at the disposal of the central authorities, we may now turn to sum up the most characteristic features of the present economic mechanism, as it affects the process of managing enterprises.

(i) The first lever, 'centralized operative direction of current production', has the greatest influence on enterprises. It has a dominating role, and may be likened to a camshaft linking enterprises with the centre. The centralized systems of materials supplies (fifth lever) and those of permitted wages funds and man-power budgeting (seventh lever) also exert very powerful influences on enterprises, as they are ultimately connected with the process of operative direction of current production from the centre.

(ii) Levers of the sort that could be used by the central authorities to exert indirect influences on production (e.g. the monetary and price-systems, these being the third and fourth levers referred to above) are, in fact, hardly employed for this purpose at present.

(iii) The central authorities rely primarily on instructions in directing the activities of enterprises. Financial incentives generally serve merely to buttress instructions.

(iv) The system of central operative direction of current production is so minutely detailed that direct connexions between enterprises exert practically no independent influence on their activities.

V

EXCESSIVE CENTRALIZATION AS A SOCIO POLITICAL PROBLEM

I *HAVE* so far discussed excessive centralization as an economic issue and have tried to analyse its influence on the working of the economy. In fact, however, a close connexion exists between the phenomenon of excessive centralization and various problems in the field of political administration. These in turn are ultimately bound up with our social arrangements as a whole. It is clear that factors of a political nature are partly responsible for the phenomenon of excessive centralization.

Although the primary object of this study is to examine the economic aspects of this matter, it is also necessary to digress to the extent of considering at least some of the broader sociological issues which are involved.

In what follows I shall try to bring out what are the principles which lie at the root of excessive centralization. I shall also attempt to illustrate the way in which the emergence of defective methods of economic administration has been associated with a retreat from democratic practices in recent years. At this point the discussion will not, of course, continue to be confined to specifically light industrial problems. It will, rather, have a more general character.

The discussion which follows does not pursue a systematic and unified train of thought: I shall merely select five topics for consideration from among a wide range of problems.

1. THE THEORETICAL ORIGINS AND SOCIAL CONSEQUENCES OF THE PROLIFERATION OF INSTRUCTIONS

A well-known statement of Stalin's lays it down that: 'Our plans are not forecasts, nor guesses. They are instructions.'[1]

---

[1] Report of the Central Committee to the XVth Congress of the Communist Party of the Soviet Union (Bolsheviks), *Collected Works of Stalin,* vol. x, p. 350, Szikra, Budapest, 1952.

Overcentralization in Economic Administration. János Kornai translated by John Knapp, Oxford University Press.
© Oxford University Press (2023). DOI: 10.1093/oso/9780192894427.003.0005

Stalin used these words in a specific context. His emphasis at the time when his speech was made[2] was on contrasting the plans of the Soviet Union, which have binding force, with the attempts at economic planning then being made in capitalist countries.

However, this statement, like many other dicta of Stalin's, was fastened on later and turned into a dogma. It became practically impossible to find a text-book or pamphlet dealing with economic planning in which this quotation did not appear as a basic proposition, and the few words it contains have been used in a multitude of articles and speeches a million times over. Yet, taken by itself, the sentence in question is over-simplified and one-sided—and this makes it misleading.

Those who are wedded to administrative methods of a kind which seek to make use of nothing beyond instructions, and who wish to base the direction of economic life entirely on a comprehensive and minutely detailed system of binding instructions, were furnished with an 'ideology' by the thesis I have quoted. It provides a 'theoretical formulation' which overrates the value of instructions and lends support to an excessive use of them. It also expresses profound contempt for other methods of operating the process of economic administration. This sentence, or, more precisely, the dogmatic edifices of economic thought which have been erected upon it, were, in fact, a reflection of an undesirable state of affairs. They served, at the same time, to maintain the existence of that state of affairs by virtue of the authority of theory and the force of propaganda, and this in turn led to an intensification of undesirable practices.

Is this view, which is widely held—not least on the strength of Stalin's quoted words—that instructions are the essence of planning, really valid? The essence of planning lies in shaping the main outlines of the national economy in accordance with the provisions of a consistent, centrally formulated plan the object of which is the promotion of the interests of society as a whole. Instructions are indispensable as one set of means for achieving this end. But it is both possible and necessary to make use of other means as well.

There can be no doubt that instructions have an important part to play in a planned economy. In particular, the government must consider itself bound to regard national economic plans as instructions, the execution of which they are obliged to take steps to organize, when such plans have been discussed and approved by competent authorities.

---

[2] On 3 Dec. 1927.

Moreover, the government must itself also make use of instructions in giving effect to policy. I will only refer briefly, in this connexion, to what I regard as the main weapon at the disposal of the government in shaping the planned outlines of the national economy, namely, the central allocation of the bulk of the funds set aside for capital accumulation. The central organs of State administration must plan the allocation of the bulk of the funds available for investment for use in the main branches of the national economy and the individual industries composing them. They must also decide upon the parts of these sums to be earmarked for the establishment of new factories and for large-scale extensions of existing factories respectively. The government must also decide which branches of industry most require technical reconstruction, &c. These are all things that need to be laid down in the form of binding instructions.

The foregoing should perhaps be regarded as the main spheres in which instructions should be employed, although there are, of course, many other fields in which their use is indispensable.

However, it is one thing to recognize the great importance of instructions in a well-defined but limited field, and quite another thing to overrate instructions and to proclaim them to be the only desirable means of giving effect to planning.

The excessive proliferation of instructions which we observe nowadays is pointless from an economic point of view, as has already been pointed out in the various parts of this study. It is, however, necessary to add a number of social and political considerations to the economic arguments.

One consequence of the excessive use of instructions is the *tendency for economic administrators to develop into bureaucrats.*

A socialist society must be based on the activity and initiative of the workers. It must promote the development of the personalities of people; it must educate persons in top positions to be capable of independent creative action, of shouldering responsibilities, and of courageous thought. But the development of people in these directions is hampered by the excessive use of instructions. If instructions were confined to a few important matters, this would exert a useful educational influence: it would accustom people to discipline and to respect for the common good. But a proliferation of instructions inevitably throttles independent action and initiative on the part of individuals. It threatens to transform economic administrators from being active agents of progress into being mere passive tools governed by instructions. An instruction is a command which brooks no argument. Plainly, the readiness of the managements of enterprises to criticize is diminished by the inordinate proliferation of instructions.

A characteristic social type has emerged in this situation—the top manager who is reluctant to make decisions independently, that is, in the absence of instructions or the approval of central authorities. It is not that he is a cowardly type, as it were, from the outset. Rather, he has become accustomed to doing everything in accordance with instructions.

All this had been associated with the incipient spread of an extremely limited standard for judging the performances of people: one would be counted as a 'good managerial executive' if one carried out all instructions without any reservations or objections and at any price. Now discipline, and the observance of State laws, are greatly to be desired. But this is only one requirement: society must also want managers to be talented, expert at their jobs, capable of independent thought, the possessors of powers of quick decision, and of initiative. They should also be expected to dare to criticize and to speak up if they find some instruction or other to be faulty. It must be frankly admitted that the latter set of requirements has frequently tended to drop out of view. And this has not been simply the fault of heads of personnel divisions. The emergence of such limited criteria for judging people has been the result of the mode of operation of the economic mechanism.

Tendencies towards bureaucracy are often put down to the personal shortcomings of individuals. A bureaucrat is a person much inclined to transact business on paper, a file-pusher, a soulless type of worker lacking in zest, passion, and enthusiasm for work. What can be said about this? Of course, people differ from one another. Some managers are, by nature, much more prone to adopt a bureaucratic style of working than are others. At the other extreme, one finds people whose temperament is such that bureaucracy is utterly alien to their characters. The trouble is that bureaucratic tendencies are strengthened in people by excessive centralization, by the proliferation of instructions, and by the degree to which the independence of top managements working at local levels is curbed. All this inevitably leads individuals in managerial positions to form an outlook which may be roughly paraphrased thus: 'The main thing, really, is not so much to see that all is well in our factory, but to make sure that my superiors are satisfied. That is, I must fulfil the indices which are most insisted upon; and I must not make too many difficulties by arguing about plans.'

I am not concerned to argue that we have reached the stage where the foregoing provides an apt general characterization of our managerial personnel. Far from it. Luckily, we have, to this day, industrial managers of talent and creativeness by the hundred, even by the thousand, who are capable of independent action and critical judgement. All I am saying is that the characteristics I sketched earlier are those which are inculcated by an economic mechanism which relies on instructions to an exaggerated extent and in a one-sided manner.

Another social consequence of the excessive use of instructions is the growing tendency to *order people about in the course of work.*

Organization and discipline are both indispensable in modern conditions of factory production. It is necessary that those who are in charge of individual units of production should possess authority to command—whether they be supervisors of labour, plant managers, or directors of enterprises. The central authorities must evidently also possess the right to issue commands in planned economies, for their functioning requires co-ordination of the work of thousands of enterprises.

To this extent, the situation resembles that of an army. And yet, production is not war, and the people active in economic life are not soldiers. The part played by unprompted individual initiative in the productive process is enormous. Moreover, in a socialist economy special significance should attach to the process of persuading people of the significance of instructions and to inspiring them with an enthusiastic desire to carry them out.

So long as the number of instructions issued from the centre is kept small, it remains possible to explain them to the personnels of top managements who are responsible for their execution. But when instructions sprout like mushrooms all over the place it becomes quite simply impossible to go on explaining every one of them. A phrase often to be heard is: 'I have no time to agitate you, go and do it!' The more instructions are given, the greater the tendency of ministries and other highly placed authorities to 'dictate' and to rely on ordering people about. And this is like a contagious disease: when a director is not persuaded, but merely ordered about, he will tend to deal with his subordinates in the same way.

It is, therefore, impossible to fail to perceive a connexion between the facts that excessive centralization inevitably leads to an undue proliferation of instructions—and the coincidence, in point of time, between the period at which (in the years 1951–2) excessive centralization was at its peak, with the beginning, throughout our public life, of the spread of arbitrary bullying.

This is not to suggest that everyone should always be fully persuaded of the propriety of every single instruction. All I am concerned to say is that if we had fewer instructions, and if these were confined to matters of decisive importance, we would then be able to attain a significantly better balance between instructions and persuasion. This would also ease the task of repressing the style of working which relies on arbitrariness and bullying, and is alien to the spirit of democracy.

Next, I want to discuss a third problem: that of *harmful uncontrolled processes* which emerge as a result of the use of instructions on an excessive scale. One of the causes of our 'over-production' of instructions, commands, prescriptions, and restrictions emanating from the centre lies in our policy of striving to eliminate all manifestations of uncontrolled behaviour at all costs. The result, however, is, in many ways, the reverse of what is intended. The economic mechanism of excessive centralization itself gives rise to processes of an uncontrolled, spontaneous, and, what is more, frequently very harmful character. These have already been discussed in various preceding chapters of this study; I wish only to summarize them briefly at this point.

(i) New and unforeseen circumstances inevitably arise in the course of the execution of plans. This repeatedly plays havoc with the details of plans, the figures in respect of which, being laid down in minutely elaborate form at the centre, are necessarily upset. This in turn frequently leads to trouble which may take irregular forms at points other than those first affected (cf. the discussions of pp. 12–16 and 22–24 above).

(ii) Individual plan index numbers (like those of production value or of cost reduction) have undesired so-called 'wild' effects as well as effects which work in desired directions. The former do not correspond to the intentions of the central authorities in any way (cf. pp. 30–42 and 54–64).

(iii) Our present methods of planning and systems of incentives lead to several tendencies which are harmful. In the circumstances, such tendencies manifest themselves in uncontrolled forms with elemental force. Examples are: strivings to loosen plans; deliberate policies to prevent the overfulfilment of plans; the periodic unevenness of production; the unbalanced fulfilment of economic objectives requiring simultaneous attention—some being pressed forward while others are neglected. (These were described on pp. 121–46.)

(iv) The development of 'speculation within the plan', which cleverly exploits contradictions that exist between the restrictions, instructions, and incentives (cf. pp. 132–3).

All this goes to show that it is an illusion to suppose that socially harmful uncontrolled processes can be eliminated by the device of multiplying instructions and prohibitions indefinitely.

The fourth and last problem which emerges as a consequence of the excessive use of instructions is the *effect of the types of punishments used on society.*

I have already touched on this question in the course of my discussion of incentives, but it is necessary to revert to it here.

Everybody frequently makes mistakes. The work of economic administrators is extremely complex, so that they may be expected to make mistakes more frequently than most people. This is regrettable, but it is natural and obvious. Yet it does not follow that it has to be accepted without anything being done about it. If society wishes to have its economic administrators make fewer mistakes, it must see to it that mistakes are attended by consequential sanctions. The question is: *what sort of sanctions?*

Suppose that economic administrators are prompted to pursue the satisfaction of some economic requirement (e.g. the improvement of quality) by some personal economic incentive and, possibly, some 'compulsion' of an economic nature (e.g. competition for customers). In such a case economic administrators who fail to meet the requirement in question (say they allow quality to slip) will automatically find themselves losing by it: their products will fetch lower prices, they will lose their customers, have to pay penalties, find their share of profits reduced, &c. They will be made to pay a financial penalty without any special steps being taken, simply because this will follow from the workings of the economy.

If, however, economic administrators are prompted to pursue economic requirements by nothing but instructions, the position will be very different. Administrators who offend against instructions must be punished. For if this were not done it would mean putting up with instructions being ignored. This would tend to have a disintegrating effect on the normal functioning of an economic system of such a kind. The rest follows by simple arithmetic, as it were: the more instructions there are, the more frequent their infringement, and so the frequency of punishments goes up.

It is clear that no State can shirk taking disciplinary measures where it is absolutely necessary to have recourse to them. But society should be so organized as to restrict the area over which, and the frequency with which, such measures need to be used. Let those who are genuinely anxious to labour for the good of their country have nothing to fear. That this should be so is an important pre-condition of reaping the full benefits of the enterprise and initiative of which the technical intelligentsia, the workers, and the population generally are capable.

2. THE EXPANSION OF THE ADMINISTRATIVE MACHINE

The growth of the number of persons engaged in economic administration is one of the most significant social consequences of excessive centralization. It has a measurable impact on the composition of the labour force and thus on the social structure. The man-power withdrawn from the productive process by the growth of administration is excessive. This applies both to technical personnel and to other workers who ought either to be engaged in supervising production on the spot or should be working on construction projects or doing manual work, &c.

To illustrate the orders of magnitude involved, let us make a comparison with the state of affairs under capitalism. (The comparisons relating salaried staffs to manual workers in Table XXXIV are confined to persons working in enterprises, so that salaried staffs of central authorities are not included.)

What explains the magnitude of the increase in the importance of salaried staffs? As technology advances, the proportionate importance of technical personnel tends to grow. But the bulk of the increase registered in the table is not accounted for by this. It is a reflection of the extraordinary growth of the size of administrative staffs.

There is an 'iron law' relating the growth of the administrative machine to excessive centralization.

Some people attribute the phenomenon of bureaucracy, and other evils too, to the expansion of the administrative machine, and they deduce from this that if administrative establishments were cut these problems would solve themselves.

But the expansion of the administrative machine is not a cause but an effect: it is a consequence of a specific type of economic mechanism. It does,

TABLE XXXIV Number of salaried persons engaged per 100 manual workers in Hungarian light industry under capitalism and today

Year	Number of salaried staff per 100 manual workers in light industry
1938	14·7
1954	26·5

Sources: Data for 1938 were obtained from the Central Planning Division of the Ministry of Light Industry. The source of the figure for 1954 is the Central Statistical Office. Salaried staff includes technical personnel and all administrative employees.

of course, react back upon its cause: for when once an inflated administrative establishment has come into existence this will itself almost automatically produce ever-recurring attempts to promote centralization.

The framing of any instruction entails a need for staff. The execution of instructions must be controlled, it is necessary to report on their fulfilment, to summarize reports, &c. This is not a matter of the minister's or departmental chief's liking for paper documents. It is a requirement which flows from a system of administration overwhelmingly based on instructions.

I would now like to proceed to illustrate the inevitability of the emergence of a large central administrative machine in the circumstances of our present set-up, using the administration of technical progress as an example.

Social ownership of the means of production and planned central direction of the national economy have several advantages where technical development is concerned. Secrecy no longer surrounds manufacturing processes in industrial enterprises. There is greater scope for the planned extension to other enterprises of experience gained in pioneering establishments.

Unfortunately, our present systems of financial incentives do not provide a sufficient stimulus towards the exploitation of these advantages. Until quite recently there were no financial incentives directly attached to the fulfilment of tasks of technical development in light industry. Competition for the orders of customers could be a highly effective force in inducing a ceaselsss search for improvements of both products and production processes, but such competition does not exist.

Unavoidably, in these circumstances, the central authorities attempt to promote technical progress by addressing detailed instructions on the subject to enterprises. Minutely detailed technical development plans for individual enterprises are not merely subject to central approval but are also largely *prescribed* by the central authorities in the first instance. Enterprises do not try to develop new products, because continuing with their existing ones is, in many ways, more advantageous for them.[3] They must therefore be instructed to do this by means of plans for new products. Similarly, enterprises do not show themselves to be avid to exploit technical inventions or to adopt new processes introduced by other enterprises. They do not do these things, because they derive no benefits from doing them owing to the fact that any improvements in their performances are quickly incorporated into their plans. The adoption of new techniques must frequently therefore be made the subject of orders from the centre. The drafting and supervision of the multifarious instructions

---

[3] I revert to this on pp. 231–2 below.

and orders which this gives rise to evidently necessitates the establishment of central staffs and so a large administrative machine concerned with technical development is born. Technical divisions exist in the Central Planning Office and in each individual department of that office, as well as in the Ministry and in every industrial directorate.

It is not my purpose to argue that no part of the work concerned with technical development should be carried out centrally. On the contrary, it is expedient that the following matters should be centrally dealt with: marking out the main lines of technical development, elaboration of measures needed for technical development which affect entire branches of industry or several branches of industry simultaneously, and consideration of the implications of various aspects of technical development in the course of drawing up national economic plans. In addition, a measure of central direction is also needed in connexion with technical propaganda, exchanges of technical experience, and the dissemination of new inventions and processes and of advanced working methods.

An important part of the foregoing functions could be discharged otherwise than through a paid central administrative machine. The only possible method of working out technical development plans on a national scale is, in any case, that of arranging gatherings of the best of the experts working in factories, design offices, and research institutes, and allowing the plans to emerge from their debates. The material of these debates can be assembled and analysed by a small staff; the main requirement is the creative collaboration of engineers, scientists, and inventors. As for technical propaganda and exchanges of experience—this is a field in which the part played by organizations of the technical intelligentsia—notably by the Association of Technical and Scientific Societies—could be much enlarged.

As things are at present, the bulk of the work done by the State administrative machine which is concerned with technical development is not in fact concerned with functions that are best discharged centrally. It is mostly engaged in urging enterprises to attend to tasks which enterprises would see to themselves, without any prompting, if the necessary incentives existed.

The case of technical development is merely one example of the process which leads to the expansion of the administrative machine. In a similar way, large separate central administrative machines have grown up for dealing with each of the major tasks facing economic administration: labour utilization, the utilization of materials, investment policy, &c. Excessive centralization automatically breeds bureaucracy. It does this constantly, from day to day and from hour to hour, and on a massive scale.

Moreover, the foregoing relates only to central administration. The story continues with the fact that each of these 'functional organs' builds an organization of its own at the enterprise level as well.[4] This is natural, since otherwise they could not do their work. The expansion of the central organs of administration is thus associated with a growth of the salaried staffs of enterprises. The figures shown in Table XXXIV reflect this last result.

Of course, some of the workers classed among the salaried staffs of enterprises in Table XXXIV do work which would be necessary and useful in any conceivable set-up. We should recall that technical personnel in operative charge of production (plant managers, chief engineers, &c.) are classified to this group in the statistics, together with those engaged in indispensable accounting and administrative work. At the same time, many people in this category are engaged in work which could, in the last analysis, be dispensed with.

But only eventually—not now. For it is excessively naïve to think that the inordinate numbers of people engaged in administration are a reflection either of slackness at work or of the existence of stupid and patently unnecessary posts, which could be abolished, at the stroke of a pen. Such things may, of course, exist, but they are not typical features of the situation.

What is characteristic of it is that all these people are doing work which is, at present, necessary, so that simply cutting it out would, indeed, give rise to upheavals in present circumstances. In order to make the work of these people really superfluous it is necessary to alter our methods of administering the economy.

3. THE ISSUE OF CONFIDENCE IN THE MANAGEMENTS OF ENTERPRISES

An atmosphere of distrust had developed during the years 1949–53. Increasingly, people became wont to regard each other with suspicion. The theory of the ceaseless sharpening of the class struggle created a mood in which people were inclined to detect a conscious enemy in anyone who had been found to make a mistake. This harmful spirit of distrust was most noticeable in relation to intellectuals in general and the technical intelligentsia in particular.

Here was yet another breeding ground for excessive centralization. The less subordinates are trusted, the greater the desire to take decisions for them. The

---

[4] Cf. also p. 197 above.

more it is suspected that mistakes reflect conscious sabotage, the greater will be the emphasis laid upon the apparatus of control.

Many observers oversimplify this question by regarding the prevalence of distrust exclusively as a cause of excessive centralization. It is, in fact, a consequence of it as well, for the nature of the contacts produced between people by this method of administration is such as to lead to ever-recurring distrust.

I have attempted to show in this study how present methods of administering the economy lead to a series of harmful tendencies. Given these, it is not hard to see why the representatives of higher authorities should, to some extent, distrust their subordinates. For they will feel that unless they interfere a series of important things will be either neglected or badly done by the managements of enterprises. In the absence of instructions, they will neglect quality; in the absence of centrally prescribed assortments, attempts will be made to avoid widening the range of choice available, &c. Moreover, so long as enterprises are not induced to satisfy these requirements by other factors in the situation without external prompting, suspicions of this kind are entirely justified.

Again, higher authorities rightly feel that enterprises attempt to maintain hidden reserves of capacity, and try to obtain loose plans which they can fulfil comfortably. The authorities therefore conclude that they cannot take the word of enterprises at face value. Thus, if the latter say that their plans are too tight—that is regarded as mere 'moaning'. A mutual lack of frankness in dealings between enterprises and higher authorities results.

We have seen that our present forms of administering the economy are also themselves a cause of the distrust in which the managements of enterprises are held by higher authorities. Conversely, too, this mechanism produces a lack of confidence in higher authorities among managements. There is a tendency for the personnels of enterprises to see a bureaucrat in every administrator working at a ministry. The latter are thought of as people who take decisions about the affairs of enterprises in a manner which is superficial, who act slowly after much shilly-shallying, are prone to 'dictate' to enterprises, will not listen to views expressed by the latter, &c. There may be substance in such criticisms in individual instances, depending on the persons involved. But we must ask what circumstances lead the personnel of a ministry to adopt such ways of going about their work? As they have to deal with millions of questions of detail, administrators at a ministry are quite simply incapable of always reaching quick and practically applicable decisions based both on a thorough study of the matter in hand and on full consideration of the views of local managements! At the same time our present system of administering the economy forces them to make decisions by themselves. They cannot leave things to be decided by the managements of enterprises.

The tendency to blame the higher authorities at the centre for all failures and troubles will tend to be more pronounced the greater the degree of centralization. (This is one of the great political disadvantages of excessive centralization.) And when this happens, it is no use for people at the centre to say: 'You should not look to higher authorities for everything'—in the nature of the case, that is just what the managements of enterprises will do.

It follows that to demand, in this situation, that more trust be placed in directors and in other managerial personnel at the enterprise level is not sufficient. It is true that they should be trusted more, but the financial, economic, and organizational conditions which would justify such trust need, at the same time, to be created as well. This involves reforming the economic mechanism in such a way as to channel the activities of the managements of enterprises into directions favourable to the interests of socialist economic development, *even in the absence of minutely detailed intervention from the centre.*

4. DEMOCRACY AT THE FACTORY LEVEL

The fact that control from below has not been sufficiently developed in our economy is closely connected with the excessive lengths to which centralization of control has been carried. Arrangements designed to facilitate control from below have, of course, existed. These have included conferences for explaining plans, production conferences, &c. They have yielded a very great deal of valid criticism and many useful proposals, which have proved helpful to industrial production. Yet the results reaped have not been great enough. This may be attributed to the fact that factory workers have not possessed an institutionally guaranteed right to have a say in the affairs of their enterprises. If a director thought fit to do so, he could take up the criticisms and proposals which had been voiced, but there was not a single aspect of production or development policy over which the workers had actual rights of decision. There is also this to be said: while the workers could at least meet their directors face to face, directors themselves had very little effective power in practice even though they had many rights on paper. Consequently, when confronted with issues of any seriousness, the replies of directors were wont to take some such form as: 'this must be discussed with the industrial directorate (or the Ministry)'; 'we need permission for this'; 'I will put that up to the authorities', &c.

In these circumstances the main body of the workers in enterprises have regarded their own part in the direction and control of production as being of no more than formal significance: they have not been able to feel that they really owned their enterprises. And the fact that the central authorities have not relied on the workers in these connexions has contributed to the need of the former to depend on an ever-expanding administrative machine.

What we must do in the future is to seek out the methods and forms of associating the workers with the process of decision-making in enterprises which are best suited to our own conditions in this country. The workers should have rights in this connexion, and these should be given appropriate institutional form.

There are very weighty arguments in favour of developing democratic institutions at the factory level. I will only try to list some of them.

1. Serious attempts are now being made to secure greater independence for enterprises, which would place more power in the hands of their directors. This will no doubt promote a rise in standards of management. But, on a realistic view, the possibility must be considered that this development may also, up to a point, facilitate abuses of their new-found powers on the part of directors. This factor alone makes it necessary that more control should be exercised over the activities of directors by the general body of workers.

2. It is desirable that the general body of workers in each factory should have a far greater interest than they now have in the success of their enterprises. It is, by now, a widely accepted view that the best method of achieving this is some form of profit-sharing. But if all workers in an enterprise are to have a stake in the profits which are made, they will then have every right to demand to be provided with a say in decisions concerning those basic questions upon which the profitability of their factories depends. They should, furthermore, also have a say in the matter of how that portion of profits which is retained by their enterprises is to be disposed of.

3. The imperative need to diminish the size of the central administrative machine makes the development of factory democracy into an urgent matter. This is because social control *from below* would be capable of replacing the State system of administrative control exercised from above to a considerable extent; it is both cheaper and more effective. It is, therefore, an important method of overcoming excessive centralization.

4. Political considerations reinforce the need for an early introduction of factory democracy. A general adoption of institutions securing the rights of the general body of workers in these matters would strengthen their sense of proprietorship of their factories.

The objection most frequently voiced against these considerations is that the principle of *sole responsibility in leadership* would be undermined by interference on the part of the general body of workers in the affairs of their factories. It remains true that it is undesirable to fritter the operative direction of the production process away in endless debates. That process requires rapid and definite decisions and the assumption of far-reaching personal responsibility, both of which are unthinkable if those in charge of production do not have wide powers of independent decision. The position encountered in the current production process is somewhat akin to the military manœuvres of armed forces: it calls for commands and unconditional execution.

However, there are certain matters in respect to which the position is different. Examples are: the directions in which production should be developed, the use to be made of funds available for investment, the filling of top managerial posts, the determination of wage and salary differentials, questions of technical development, &c. Unfettered individual leadership can easily lead to biased and consequently wrong decisions in these matters, so that the comprehensive debating of pros and cons, and the clash of opinions arising from the experience of all concerned, can only be beneficial in these fields.

It follows from all this that it is necessary to find the most fruitful combination of individual and collective forms of leadership in such a way as to unite the advantages of individual leadership in the daily management of the production process with the advantages of collective guidance through far-reaching discussion of fundamental questions.

VI

ATTEMPTS TO DEVELOP LOCAL INITIATIVE AND AUTONOMY FOR ENTERPRISES

1. EXCESSIVE CENTRALIZATION IS A COHERENT, UNIFIED MECHANISM

WE have now surveyed the various phenomena which arise from excessive centralization. These phenomena do not make their appearance together by chance. They are not independent of one another. They form a coherent, unified whole.

We need not go over these phenomena again in detail here. We have seen that instructions play a dominating role in economic administration; incentives serve mainly to buttress these; the other motive forces operating in the economy are also merely secondary to instructions, which are the direct regulators of current production. We have seen how excessive centralization is related to the phenomena of shortages of materials and of goods. Finally, I have made an attempt to indicate briefly the nature of the connexion between methods of economic and political administration—that is, between excessive centralization of economic administration, on the one hand, and the relegation to the background of democratic procedures, on the other.

We are therefore justified in saying that excessive centralization is a coherent, unified mechanism, which has its own inner logic and several tendencies and regularities peculiar to itself.

The statement that we are here concerned with a logically complete system by no means implies that we must regard it as harmonious and free of contradictions. On the contrary, this economic mechanism harbours deep contradictions within itself.

(i) The fact that it is a basic objective, and inner tendency, of this mechanism to regulate everything by means of instructions, conflicts with the fact that there are elements and processes in the economy which it is very difficult, or impossible, to control by means of instructions.

Overcentralization in Economic Administration. János Kornai translated by John Knapp, Oxford University Press.
© Oxford University Press (2023). DOI: 10.1093/oso/9780192894427.003.0006

(ii) The fact that it is a basic objective, and inner tendency, of this mechanism to decide everything at the centre, conflicts with the fact that it is impossible to weigh every question of detail properly from the centre. Moreover, the better developed and the more powerful productive forces become, the more complicated they come to be, which makes it the more difficult to regulate details from the centre.

The very presence of these contradictions has given rise to a continuous stream of attempts to alter the mechanism we are examining so as to make it more harmonious. Two trends have been of importance.

The first of these has been in evidence in attempts to overcome the contradictions just mentioned by curbing the proliferation of instructions and other excesses arising from centralization and by proposing that more autonomy be given to the men on the spot. It must not be thought that this is a newly fashionable idea. Demands of this sort have been voiced ever since the very beginnings of centralized administration of the State-controlled sector of industry.[1]

The second trend is reflected in attempts to overcome the inner contradictions of our economic mechanism by trying to make centralization even more complete. This involves an intensification of the use of instructions and an extension of their scope. It is, in its way, a cogent policy to pursue, for it is based on the idea that if we are to go in for centralization we might as well be consistent about it and leave as few gaps as possible.

If an attempt is made to regulate the details of current production in individual enterprises by means of centrally prescribed plan index numbers, and if this is buttressed by offering premiums for 100 per cent, fulfilment of these figures, then it is logical to try to make the figures as exact as possible. Now, in principle at least, the degree of exactness of planning will be the greater the more detailed the advance planning of the exact composition of production. Thus, for example, the planning of materials supplies has undoubtedly been made more reliable by prescribing production programmes for individual articles centrally, because it has resulted in the planning divisions of industrial directorates having simultaneous responsibility for programmes and for the allocation of materials. The plans of cost reductions and of labour utilization have also become better based in this way. While it follows that so long as we operate a system based on excessive centralization this is the more consistent solution, it is nevertheless impossible to impose it in a consistent manner owing to the contradictions already mentioned. This is why even the more

---

[1] i.e. ever since 1947–50.

detailed production programmes and plans of materials supplies are repeatedly upset in real life, and why even the most soundly based plans of cost reduction often turn out either to be very loose or too tight, &c.

It is often said in economic circles that planning must be made more 'refined', or that the system of plan index numbers must be made 'more complete'. It is undeniable that, within the framework of our present economic mechanism, it is easiest to plug the gaps left by instructions by yet other instructions. For example, if the central authorities confine themselves to laying down production plans in terms of broad commodity categories, and if enterprises proceed to exploit this by arbitrarily pushing the production of articles of high unit value, which 'bring in more forints', then the most logical defence is to lay down central programmes in much more detail. One of the most important features distinguishing the work of planning at the Ministry of Light Industry from the corresponding process at other ministries lies in the fact that the plans prepared are, in the sense here discussed, a great deal 'finer' and 'more complete'.

We must not, therefore, suppose that what we are concerned with here is perhaps no more than the reflection of a mania for centralization on the part of individuals. The trend we are examining is necessitated by the workings of the inner logic of our present economic mechanism!

It is a characteristic feature of the situation that economic administrators who have themselves had to endure the paralysing effects of excessive centralization and, indeed, complain about them, can nevertheless be heard to demand more detailed instructions, prescriptions, and restrictions for others—that is, for the economic organizations with whom they have contacts. For example, a number of top executives in the distributive trades, having spoken to me about the way in which excessive centralization hampers distributive enterprises in satisfying demand in a flexible manner, then went on to applaud what appeared to them to be great achievements, namely, that (i) the Ministry of Light Industry and its directorates have lately been giving much more detailed information than previously, in respect of a period as far ahead as a full year, about just what products will be made available for domestic distribution, and (ii) that the proportion of total production which is not so specified for a year in advance is now less than it was, &c. All this 'refinement' eases the task of planning at the Ministry of Domestic Commerce, but it greatly restricts the freedom of manœuvre of the Ministry of Light Industry, of its directorates, and, ultimately, of its enterprises. Conversely, if executives in light industry begin to demand that the distributive trades should place their orders in greater detail of specification for a full year ahead, and also that they should do this in a binding form, this will ease the work of planning in light industry at the cost of intensifying the restrictions to which domestic commerce is subject.

2. THE RATIONALIZATION MEASURES OF 1954

Let us now revert to the first trend distinguished in the previous section. The widespread and far-reaching rationalization measures of 1954 represented a very important manifestation of this in action. It was the first comprehensive large-scale step designed to do away with excessive centralization. Several expert committees appointed by the government were entrusted with drafting the orders needed. Dozens of experts were involved in the preparation of proposals. On the basis of these, several important decrees of the Ministerial Council were issued, dealing with the simplification of planning, of the utilization of materials, of man-power, and of permitted outlays on wages and salaries, as well as of investment, accountancy, statistics, &c.[2]

From the outset, the rationalization measures had objects more far-reaching than the mere simplification of official work at the centre and the achievement of corresponding reductions in personnel required in that sector. In its decree concerning the simplification of planning which it issued within the framework of the rationalization drive, the Ministerial Council stated explicitly: 'It is necessary to put an end to the excessive centralization, bureaucracy and perfectionism which at present manifest themselves in the process of planning and of approving plans.'[3]

For a time it was occasionally maintained that rationalization had, in a fundamental sense, been successful. Thus, an article in *Közgazdasági Szemle*[4] stated: '... the tasks of individual planning agencies have been separated and defined. Excessive centralization in planning and in approving plans has been done away with.

In this way, individual planning agencies have achieved opportunities to display independent initiative.'[5]

---

[2] The decrees concerned with simplification in these various fields were collected together. These alone form a volume of 248 pages.
[3] *Collection of Decrees Concerning the Simplification of State Administration and the Administration of Enterprises*, p. 67.
[4] *Review of Economics.*
[5] Sándor Kovács, 'Of the measures taken to simplify our economic administration', *Közgazdasági Szemle*, Dec. 1955, p. 1494.

Such an attitude of satisfaction was, it seems to me, quite unwarranted. For the basic objectives of rationalization were not achieved in spite of the fact that it tied up vast energies. (It also created a good deal of disturbance in the State machine and in the machinery of economic administration.)

Let us list the changes which resulted from rationalization.

(*a*) The most tangible result was a slight fall in the numerical importance of salaried staffs. In enterprises attached to the Ministry of Light Industry this fell from 27–4 per 100 manual workers in 1954 to 24–8 in 1955. Reference back to Table XXXIV[6] suggests that this figure was still remarkably high.

(*b*) A few plan indices hitherto subject to approval by directorates had been dropped. This has, no doubt, eased the work of planning somewhat in particular fields.

In some cases this change was more apparent than real, as is illustrated by the following incident: the head of the planning department of a factory raised a point at a conference to the effect that the annual plan he had been issued with had not included target figures for his factory's spinning mill in terms of kilometres and for its weaving mill in terms of numbers of picks, in spite of the fact that these are the most suitable ways of measuring the work done by these parts of his factory. He was told by the representative of his industrial directorate, who was present at the conference, that he could have obtained these figures from them, since they had been calculated there. 'We did not', he added, 'give these figures to you in writing with the rest of the plan, because we did not want to run the risk of being charged, in the event of a check being made, with widening the field of approved plan index numbers.'

(*c*) A few of the usual reports ceased to be required after rationalization. The number of pages in plans, and the number of forms needing to be filled in, were somewhat reduced. This cuts out some administrative work, some typing, some copying of reports, &c. But this largely concerns reports and calculations which enterprises need for themselves in any case, so that the change often only amounts to no longer putting an extra sheet into one's typewriter. From the point of view of eliminating unnecessary excesses of centralization— which was the fundamental objective of rationalization—the crucial question is—*who has powers of decision* over plans, calculations, and reports?, and not how many copies of them are prepared. Rationalization generally failed to touch the crucial issue.

(*d*) An important change was made when it came to preparing annual plans for 1954–5; enterprises were then no longer under an obligation to 'plan back'

[6] Cf. p. 206 above.

their annual plans.[7] This is certainly an important easement for enterprises in present circumstances. It is also clear, however, that it does not represent any advance towards the ending of excessive centralization and towards the beginning of more independence for enterprises.

But all this is really largely beside the point. The present study is generally concerned with describing the position in 1955, i.e. after rationalization. No matter what questions we took up, they were found to show the influence of excessive centralization operating with full force. This entitles us to say that rationalization has failed to achieve what was expected from it, although some small and unimportant gains were made in certain matters of detail.

The cause of failure lay in the fact that rationalization amounted to no more than a treatment of symptoms. This despite the fact that references to the desirability of some measure of change in the economic mechanism itself did figure among the original intentions of the promoters of rationalization. Thus, the decree just quoted stated: 'It is necessary to develop methods which can serve as a basis of planning without involving the planners in a need to go into small details. (Examples of such methods are: the use of *incentives unrelated to plans*, the use of delivery contracts to promote decentralization of the determination of the composition of output in replacement of excessively detailed planning...)'[8] But this sort of thing never came to pass. An attempt was made to 'simplify' planning in itself in isolation from the entire mechanism of the economy. No wonder the results were meagre. The almost exclusive *dominance of instructions*, which is the essence of our economic mechanism, was left unaltered.

In the circumstances it is not surprising that the second of the trends I have distinguished—which involves attempts to deal with our problems by 'more refined' planning, i.e. by carrying centralization farther—soon reasserted itself after rationalization had been put through. The decree on simplifying planning, which I have already quoted several times, spoke in other terms: 'The simplification of planning which has been decreed is to be in effect for several years, and not just in 1955. The Central Planning Office and the Ministries are asked to secure that the new planning methods are kept in use. They must do everything in their power to keep the simplified system free of gradual bureaucratization.'[9] These intentions were not realized, as the examples which follow will show.

---

[7] I have attempted a detailed evaluation of this measure earlier in this book, pp. 4–5 above.

[8] *Collection of Decrees Concerning the Simplification of State Administration and the Administration of Enterprises*, p. 67.

[9] Loc. cit., p. 103.

Table XXXV Growth in the number of plan index numbers approved for enterprises in the leather trade

Section of plan	No. of approved indices	
	1955	1956
Production value	4	5
Quantum of production	46	47
Product-mix (proportion of first-, second-class articles, &c.)	14	14
Channels of trade	17	25
Technical indices	2	2
Utilization of basic materials	9	19
Labour plan	18	22
Plan of costs	7	5
Total	117	139

Source: Central Planning Office of the Leather and Shoe Trades' Directorate. The difference is not very large, but the trend is clear: the use of approved indices has risen again.

I have mentioned that one objective of rationalization was to secure a reduction of the use of approved plan index numbers. Let us now compare the number of plan indices approved for the quarterly operative plans of leather factories in 1955—which was the year following upon the rationalization measures—and in 1956.

The difference is not very large, but the trend is clear: the use of approved indices has risen again.

Methods of planning have also been becoming more complicated in a number of directorates and enterprises. More calculations and tabulations are being required.

For example, in 1956 the following changes were made, as compared with 1955, in the preparation of the annual production plan for commodities at the Cotton Trades' Directorate:

(a) In the previous year, comparable base-year data had only to be shown for one preceding year—this now became two years.

(b) In the previous year, comparable base-year data had only to be expressed in terms of quantities—now value data were also required.

(c) In the previous year, base-year data had only to be provided in respect of the aggregate production of particular products, irrespective of whether they were subsequently sold to other enterprises for further processing or not—now data on finished production value were also required.

(d) In 1956 data on daily production volume and a quarterly chain index of this statistic were both required. They were not required in the previous year.

(e) In the previous year, data on channels of trade had only to be presented in terms of quantities—now, value data had also to be shown.

As a result of all this, while a couple of summary sheets sufficed for the preparation of this plan in 1955, a separate form was needed for each important, specially designated product in 1956. On top of all this no collections of statistics were available in respect of some of the base-year data required because the supply of such statistics was suspended during the period of rationalization.

The chief planning officials of enterprises in the woollen industry have complained about a new system for planning the overhead costs of plants and enterprises. This had been introduced as from 1 August 1956. Nine new printed documents now have to be used. Of these only three have to be handed in to the directorate, but this requires filling up the other six as well. Some of these printed sheets are of enormous size. But the wage and salary element in overheads has always been 'well in hand' via the system of permitted outlays on these items; depreciation is a fixed sum; the cost of the most important materials is regulated. What remains after all these items of cost have been accounted for is unlikely to exceed 2–3 per cent, of costs. Essentially, all of this new paper work exists merely for planning this last amount. It is striking how, now that cost reductions have been placed in the limelight (having been previously much neglected), their planning has promptly been 'refined' and overcentralized.

I have stressed already that such matters as numbers of forms, of data collected, and of plan indices issued are of secondary significance from the point of view of eliminating excessive centralization. It is nevertheless an indication of the trend of things in this field that late in 1955 and early in 1956 we were again moving in the direction of more indices and more forms.

3. SOME ERRONEOUS VIEWS

During the interval between the rationalization period of the summer and autumn of 1954, and the beginning of 1956, no important measures were taken to simplify planning and economic administration and to get rid of excessive centralization. (If anything, as we have seen, a fortunately not very marked retreat occurred in this respect.)

However, debates about these topics continued among economic administrators and economists. This controversy was helpful in clarifying ideas.

Certain erroneous views were also put forward. At a time when new solutions to problems are sought, this is inevitable. In what follows I would like to discuss some proposals which I consider misguided. Some of the ideas I shall discuss have not hitherto appeared in print, but they are nevertheless worth dealing with as they are widely current among economic administrators.

(*a*) One view can be expressed in the slogan: 'Leave it to the enterprise!' The idea here is that if more independence were given to enterprises in any matter, that is bound to be beneficial even if no other changes are made in the forms of organization of the economy.

It will be clear from what I have written in this study that I am not by any means an opponent of greater autonomy in the conduct of the affairs of enterprises. I am nevertheless convinced that if the economic mechanism of excessive centralization is left substantially intact, then greater independence of enterprises in isolated spheres can entail risks and can do harm to the economy.

For example, the demand is often voiced that the restrictions inherent in the system of permitted outlays on wages and salaries be abolished altogether. In my opinion, if this demand were granted in isolation from other measures, this could lead to unjustifiable wage increases on a massive scale. For the proportion of wages in total costs is very low in most branches of light industry. Cost reduction attracts important premium payments, but, owing to the insensitivity of total costs to changes in wages, the latter may come to be considered as being of no consequence. Moreover, there is certainly strong pressure for wage increases in light industry from below, since in this field of industry wages have tended to lag behind others.

Wage increases might not make much difference to costs, particularly if parallel economies were made in using materials. But they could upset the balance between the wage bills of different industries and thus produce a disequilibrium between purchasing power and the volume of goods available. That is why wage increases are risky.

Take another example: it is often suggested that enterprises should be allowed to formulate their production programmes, in agreement with distributive enterprises, quite independently of higher authorities. But a number of people who advocate this would at the same time be quite happy to see a continuation of the system by which the indices of production value, of permitted outlays on wages and salaries, and of plans of cost reduction continue to be used as the bases of premium payments. Now, what would this lead to, say, in a setting of shortages with the distributive trades at the mercy of the factories? The latter would push the production of articles which 'bring in more forints' and would keep off articles requiring much labour and trouble. They might reduce their standards of quality and attempt to narrow the variety of goods they offer, &c.

One could multiply examples of this kind. It is necessary to recognize that greater independence for enterprises in isolated individual fields is no *panacea*.

Centralization is, even now, completely unnecessary in particular fields, and could be eliminated in such sectors without further ado. The central preparation of designs and models is an example.[10] There is no sense in denying enterprises the right to produce their own designs and models.

But the situation is not as simple as this when it comes to really important matters. Where these are concerned, the condition for an improvement being brought about by greater independence of enterprises is that some other force must replace the part previously played by instructions coming from the centre. This force may take one or more of several forms: financial interests, economic pressures exercised by customers, indirect weapons of central control (e.g. the credit system), &c. Real economic forces of some kind are required to channel the efforts of enterprises in desirable directions, without the employment of instructions from the centre. So long as no such real economic forces exist, giving up the issuing of instructions may produce anarchical phenomena and harm the economy.[11]

One cannot exchange a cog in an integrated, functioning machine for another one of quite a different type. The latter may be new, but it will obstruct the working of the machine nevertheless.

It is, therefore, necessary to accept the fact that the situation harbours contradictory elements within it. The more global and less detailed the plans approved for enterprises, i.e. the fewer instructions they contain, the greater the risk of enterprises doing things that are harmful. The more detailed plans are, so that there are many instructions, the more pronounced the disadvantages of excessive centralization will be. The solution cannot lie in choosing

---

[10] Cf. pp. 65–66 above.

[11] A widely held variant of this same false conception takes the form of the suggestion that excessive centralization can be eliminated by altering the plan index number and premium systems. Although I regard this as very important, even this is insufficient, taken by itself.

Let us recall the description I gave earlier of the 'model' of our present-day economic mechanism (cf. p. 194 above). I there showed that the system of operative direction of current production from the centre (which is what is meant by those who speak of altering the systems of plan index numbers and of premiums) is merely *one* of the 'levers' employed by the central economic authorities. If this is to play a different part, then consistency requires that consequential changes be made in the parts played by the other 'levers' too.

one or other extreme—the 'lesser evil'. Nor does it make sense to settle on some middle-of-the-road policy of compromise. A solution can only be found by taking a comprehensive view of both centralization and decentralization and by renouncing the idea of piecemeal tinkering with the economic mechanism in the course of efforts to change it.

The need for comprehensive and profound reforms has been repeatedly referred to in this study. I should, perhaps, make clear what I mean by this in case it is not clear already from what I have just been saying. It certainly does not mean that everything in our present-day economic mechanism must be jettisoned forthwith, so that something else of a diametrically opposite nature can be constructed and put in its place.

In principle it is possible to sketch out a system in which all economic choices, including even the distribution of consumer goods to individuals and people's choices of occupation, are governed by instructions from the centre. It is also possible to imagine a system in which the central authorities of the State refrain completely from all interference in economic life, everything being governed by the market mechanism. In practice, some mixture of these two is the inevitable rule. There has never been a period or type of economy in which either of the two 'pure' forms of economy has, in fact, existed. This is also true in regard to socialist economies based on public ownership of the means of production. The Hungarian economic mechanism of the present day also shows a mixture of these elements. The difference between the present mixture and the economic mechanism that I myself, and many others as well, regard as a better one, would lie, to a large extent, in the relative degrees of reliance they respectively place on instructions and administrative methods of direction, as against the use of market relationships. And yet, it is both legitimate and necessary to speak of far-reaching, even basic, changes in this connexion. For this use of words brings out the idea that it is not sufficient to make changes in individual parts of our methods of administering the economy in haphazard and isolated ways. The reforms we need are of a kind which will improve all the major methods and institutions of our economic mechanism in a systematic, parallel, and harmonious manner. In other words, the job of transforming the system of plan index numbers should be matched by an overhaul of the systems of incentives and of prices, as well as of the functioning of the monetary and credit systems, &c.

It is not necessary that all these changes should be brought about all at once in every sphere; this would probably create too much of an upheaval. It is possible to carry out the reforms which are needed in a number of stages. What is essential is that the changes brought about in various spheres should complement one another in an organic manner. They should constitute parts of a thoroughly thought out, centrally co-ordinated series of reforms based on a unified conception.

(b) It is maintained in some quarters that it is hopeless to elaborate a unified scheme of reforms for the entire national economy. It is stressed that every branch of industry has its own peculiarities, and it is inferred from this that it is necessary to fashion separate systems of planning and of economic administration for each.

There is much truth in this conception. One thing that has been wrong about our methods hitherto has been the way in which all branches of industry have been administered according to a single pattern. A great deal must evidently depend on the character of individual trades, and even of products.

(i)   The position will be different where one is dealing with the production of things of primary importance (for example, electric power production) and where it is a matter of turning out articles of less social importance (for example, neck-ties).

(ii) The position will also be different, according as one is dealing with highly concentrated branches of industry (e.g. foundries) or with decentralized industries (e.g. the bakery trade).

(iii) The position will be different where enterprises produce the same thing year in, year out (e.g. sulphuric acid) and where the product, or its mode of manufacture, are subject to constant change (e.g. fashionable footwear).

(iv) The position will be different where output consists of one, or at most two, products (e.g. in mines) and where products are numbered in thousands (e.g. in pharmaceutical factories).

(v)   The position will be different where products are to be distributed to a large number of different customers as compared to where there are only one or two outlets.

The question is, what are we to infer from the existence of such differences? A legitimate conclusion would be to expect that even if excessive centralization were to cease, there would be a greater need for State interference, direction, and control in the most important and highly concentrated industries (e.g. in electricity generation and foundries) than in others.

Another reasonable conclusion would be that trades which are, by their nature, most subject to change (e.g. fashion goods trades) should be granted most freedom of manœuvre.[12] Generally speaking it is necessary to put an end to the present-day practice of applying identical administrative methods to all industries.

What would be wrong would be to disturb the coherence of the economic set-up we have or may adopt. While the extent of central intervention in the direction of the economy may assume quantitatively different degrees, all industry must be organized in accordance with an *identical set of basic principles*, for otherwise the task of economic administration becomes quite unmanageable. The rational central pursuit of policies affecting all branches of industry (e.g. of wage, price, and monetary policies) becomes impossible without a coherent set of basic principles. It follows that the purusit, *à outrance*, of the line of thought we have been considering here would lead to anarchy, rather than to due attention being given to the peculiarities of individual industries.

(c) It has been suggested on a number of occasions that the replacement of the index of production value—which has hitherto been regarded as being of crucial importance—by some other plan index number would be capable of solving the basic problems of the economy.

A good example of this is the article by Sándor Balázsy in the journal *Többtermelés*.[13]

This article analysed several harmful features of our planning methods in a manner that was both bold and substantial. Several of the conclusions of the present study—which is based on light industrial experience—are in agreement with the results of the critical analysis of Balázsy, which mainly related to experience in the machinery industry. Yet I believe Balázsy's proposal was misguided.

The essence of his proposal was that 'net value added'[14] should replace total and finished production value, respectively, as the crucial plan index number attracting premium payments. The idea was that this index would be a good measure of the contribution made by each enterprise to the national income. It would also remove the incentives enterprises have in multiplying inter-firm dealings artificially and in promoting the manufacture of articles having high material content, since these things do not raise net value added, while they do raise total production value.

---

[12] Strangely enough, light industry is, at present, among the most tightly centralized industries of all!

[13] Sándor Balázsy, 'Let us improve our methods of planning', *Többtermelés*, Nov. 1954.

[14] Net value added = total production value in an enterprise minus the sum of the cost of materials and services bought from outside the enterprise and of depreciation.

It may be freely granted that indices of net value added could play a useful part in our industrial statistics when it comes to measuring the performances of enterprises. But Balázsy is after more than this—he wants to make it the crucial index with premium payments geared to it. As such, it would, besides having undoubted advantages, also have serious disadvantages.

The problem of profits comes in here. We have seen that, given our system of producers' prices, the profitability of various articles to an enterprise is not related to their relative importance or to the demand for them or to their quality or novelty, but is governed by a series of other factors which are not correlated with these except by accident. All this is not important in our present system, because managements have had practically no financial incentive to raise the profits of their enterprises. However, as soon as a switch is made to net value added, the importance of profits, and therefore of the factors that do determine them, will be very greatly enlarged.[15] It follows that the application of the index of net value added immediately raises the whole problem of what should be done about our system of producers' prices.

There is also another, more important objection to be raised. Even if pricing policy were changed, measurement by net value added would only solve one or two of the numerous problems outlined in this study.[16] A whole series of difficulties, unrelated to the gross character of our present index of production value, also exist. Their origin is traceable to our systems of planning, administration, financial incentives, and of prices, to the situation in regard to stocks, &c. Yet all these things would be left unaffected by Balázsy's proposal.

Other proposals also emerged in the course of the debate generated by Balázsy's article. One contributor to the discussion suggested that the index of adherence to plans, another that a more perfect index of costs be made into the most crucial index. Yet all these suffer from the disadvantages which, as I showed, affect the index of production value: they are not unambiguous; they have undesirable effects as well as effects of the kind intended by the authorities. Whichever of these indices is given pride of place, its incentive effect is liable to be one-sided, and it will, moreover, exert some harmful influences on the activity of enterprises as well.

[15] A single, greatly simplified example will suffice to make this clear. Suppose that the cost of an article to an enterprise is 100, of which purchased materials account for 80 and wages for 20. Suppose that profits on this article rise from 2 per cent, to 4 per cent. In present circumstances this will not provide a particularly strong inducement for enterprises to go in for making just this article. But under Balázsy's proposed system net value added would rise from 22 per cent, to 24 per cent., i.e. by almost 10 per cent., which will make it worth going in for manufacturing this article, if only in order to fulfil production plans.
[16] Its primary beneficial result would be that it would eliminate the tendency to go in or articles requiring a lavish use of materials.

(*d*) Some people are inclined to regard profits as the 'miracle-producing index', which is itself capable of solving our troubles. They envisage the provision of financial incentives to make profits in a manner analogous to the way we have hitherto encouraged attempts to increase total production value. They propose that, henceforth, 100 per cent, fulfilment of profits-plans be made the basis of premium payments, with additional premiums becoming payable in respect of higher profits. But they propose no changes in our economic mechanism in other respects, and are content to leave our systems of planning, of prices, of remunerating top managements, &c., more or less as they are today.

I regard this proposal, which has many supporters, as being of a hybrid nature; it seems to me to contain a mixture of reasonable and erroneous elements. There is no doubt that if profits were given a key position as an object of financial interest, this might have several advantages—but only if certain specific conditions are met at the same time! There are a number of such conditions, of which I will only indicate a few here.

First: we would require a *suitable system of prices* of a kind which helps to bring about equilibrium between the supply of and the demand for light industrial products. Prices would have to have a bearing both on the production techniques to be decided on in enterprises and on their choice of what commodities they are to include in their product-mixes.

Secondly: we would require to have a suitable balance between overall rates of production and consumption, and also, associated with this, the effective operation of the driving force implicit in *competition for custom among enterprises.*[17] It may be impossible to produce such a state of affairs in all trades and enterprises, but the more widespread such conditions were, the better it would be.

Thirdly: we would need a system of financial incentives which would reflect the performances of managements adequately, and would also induce them to pay attention to all aspects of good economic administration in a balanced manner.[18]

Fourthly—and this must certainly be added to the foregoing—the central authorities would need to make increased use of such levers of the economic mechanism as investment policy, financial and credit policy, the price system, &c. They would have to ensure that the greater independence of enterprises operating on the basis of a search for profitability was reconciled with the general requirements of planning; in particular, the central authorities would have

---

[17] Cf. pp. 176–91 above.
[18] Cf. Ch. II.

to keep in effective control of the main features of the general development of the economy.

Given the fulfilment of these conditions, profits would function as a superior form of a balanced, complex incentive system. For, in the circumstances here envisaged, profitability, and with it the shares in profits of both managements and the general body of workers in enterprises, would become dependent on all of the following:

(i) the quantity of production;
(ii) the quality of production;
(iii) costs of production;
(iv) observance of undertakings given by the enterprise (via interest charges and penalty clauses);
(v) sales (this is more or less lost sight of in our present plan index number system);
(vi) the degree to which the product-mix satisfies demand in a flexible manner.

Let us now turn to consider the consequences of not fulfilling the conditions I have just listed and of going ahead with what I have called a hybrid, incomplete type of reform instead.

There are some fields where this could be usefully done without incurring much risk. This will be the case where output is confined to a single product line, so that the problem of product-mixes does not arise at all. It may also be feasible where several products are turned out in fixed proportions determined by unalterable technical conditions. (For example, in a chemical factory only able to produce 3–4 specified products.)

In such cases, profits will be a good form of incentive even with our present price system.

But serious problems would arise in fields of industry where product-mixes are variable.

Let us take an example. Imagine that the managements of enterprises in textile factories are given an interest in raising the profits of their enterprises, while at the same time the central determination of production programmes is abolished, and enterprises are entrusted with settling their own product-mixes in agreement with the distributive trades.

This would instantly turn the question of the profits obtainable on individual articles into a highly interesting matter in the eyes of managements. Evidently, they would want to go in for the most profitable lines. But what would determine this? One determinant would be the suitability of particular enterprises for the production of specific goods. If this determinant prevailed, that would be excellent. Unfortunately, however, our present system of prices would cause several other factors to have an influence on the relative profitability of products. For example:

(i) There is the question of whether a product is a new one, or an established one. On new lines a profit of 2 per cent, is authorized. This was also done in respect of lines which have since become established. As a result of experience in producing them, established lines can, after a time, be produced at lower cost, so that profits on these will probably exceed the original 2 per cent. Hence, established articles are often more profitable than new ones. The result is that if financial incentives are related to profits, a tendency will be set up for enterprises to stick to their established products and to avoid new ones.

(ii) The price of any newly introduced article is much influenced by the character of the factory which first puts it on the market, because the approved price of such an article will be based on the cost calculations of the innovating factory. From the point of view of other enterprises subsequently embarking on the production of this article, it will be largely a matter of accident whether it is profitable for them to do so or not. For if the pioneering enterprise had been a low cost producer using up-to-date methods, then imitators of the new article are liable to find it unprofitable; while if the enterprise which first marketed the product happened to be a backward one, then other enterprises will find it easy to make large profits by making the product.

(iii) Producers' prices on established products are fixed with reference to the 'weighted costs of the industry'. The resulting price for particular products will therefore be high or low according as the bulk of it happens to be produced by backward or up-to-date factories. From the point of view of individual enterprises, whether individual products have 'good' or 'bad' prices appears as yet another accidental circumstance.

It would be possible to extend the list of such circumstances which have effects on profitability. It is clear that purely accidental factors play a large part in giving rise to variations in the profits obtainable on particular products. The fact that product X shows a profit of 10 per cent, over costs and product Y only 1 per cent., is in no way related to a greater social demand for X, because producers' prices are independent of supply and demand in our system.

It follows from all this that the result of attaching financial in centives to profits would cause managements to shift the composition of output towards

222 OVERCENTRALIZATION IN ECONOMIC ADMINISTRATION

more profitable articles even though there will frequently be no social gain at all in their producing just these articles rather than others.[19]

I must round off this train of thought by adding that much of what I have said here is best regarded as a provisional working hypothesis. Detailed study of the interconnexions of profits and of the price system is one of the subjects we intend to investigate in the course of further research work. At any rate, theoretical considerations suggest that given our present system of producers' prices, profits are frequently not a reliable measure of whether enterprises are working economically and effectively. They are particularly fallible in this respect where the composition of product-mixes and the range of available production techniques is widely variable. This should cause us to adopt a cautious attitude towards 'hybrid' proposals which reflect a desire to relate financial incentives increasingly to profitability in conjunction with a wish to retain our present system of producers' prices and, also, more generally, the entire economic mechanism we now have.

4. THE MOST RECENT MEASURES

Let us now leave polemics behind to take up the strands of chronological description once again.

As I have already said, no practical steps towards the dismantling of excessive centralization were taken between the end of the 'rationalization' period in late 1954 and the beginning of 1956. There was not even much public discussion of these matters because the 'cold' atmosphere which had again developed was unfavourable. Yet, even though these topics did not appear in the columns of newspapers or in public lecture rooms, they kept bobbing up in the private discussions and debates of economists and economic administrators.

The XXth Congress of the Communist Party of the Soviet Union ended this lull in the fight against excessive centralization. Several important references to

---

[19] The above can be further substantiated by reference to the results of the analysis presented earlier in this volume concerning the effects of the use of cost index numbers (cf. pp. 56–60). It was there shown that the incentives we currently provide with a view to reducing costs and raising factory productivity have harmful as well as beneficial results within the framework of our present economic mechanism, since they induce enterprises to lower quality, to restrict variety, and to avoid the production of new articles among other things. These harmful features of the index could only be removed if competition between enterprises and the operation of a refurbished price system forced factories to strive to improve quality and to develop new lines in a steady search for the favour of customers which, in turn, requires the flexible satisfaction of their demands.

these questions were made at the Congress itself. For example, A. I. Mikoyan said the following:

> The Central Committee has fought implacably against bureaucratic central-ism and for a full restoration of democratic centralism on Leninist lines;... [it has laboured] to increase the power of local soviets and enterprises, to draw the masses of the workers into far-reaching participation in the work of preparing and examining economic plans and to associate them more effectively with the process of finding solutions to questions relating to the direction of production; to reduce the size of the State administrative machine, and to simplify it...'[20]

In fact, the main influences behind the debates concerned with problems of economic administration at this time were not these direct references them-selves so much as those deeper social currents which were strengthened in the aftermath of the XXth Congress. By the summer of 1956 the development of a more courageous critical spirit and the growth of the fight against dogma-tism had produced a situation in which the topic of excessive centralization was constantly discussed in specialist periodicals and even in the daily press.

The fact that, at the time when this is being written, debates are being supplemented by practical measures is an important new development.[21]

One of these measures, namely, the organization of *economic experiments,* represents a new phenomenon in our economic life. Anew planning and incentive system was for the first time adopted experimentally in the Duna Shoe Factory on 1 April. The premiums of the top management were related primarily to profitability, this in turn being measured, not simply by profits, but by what is called 'gross accumulation'. (Profits plus turnover tax per 100 forints of cost.) The number of experimental enterprises was subsequently increased. It is reported that in September 1956 novel planning and incen-tive systems are in operation in the following light industrial enterprises, apart from the Duna Shoe Factory:

Magyar Selyemipari Vallalat.
Hazai Fésűsfonó.

---

[20] *The XXth Congress of the C.P.S.U.* (B), pp. 342–3, Szikra, 1956.
[21] Throughout this study I have tried to confine myself to the analysis of a period which we have already left behind, i.e. generally, the eighteen-month period of 1955 and the first half of 1956. Here, however, I take in quite recent events which are still unfolding themselves as I write, in Sept. 1956. I have done this very briefly for the sake of completeness and in order to be topical. Consequently, the remarks which follow cannot claim to represent a detailed analysis of the period to which they refer.

Magyar Posztógyár.
Magyar Gyapjufonó.
Ujpesti Gyapjúszövő.[22]

All these experiments are not identical; the index numbers which must be fulfilled differ in the various factories, and incentives are organized in varying ways. But it is a more or less general feature of the experiments that much emphasis is placed on profitability in them and that enterprises are given much more independence than hitherto.

The question of how far these experiments are useful is much debated. Some people assert that they are bound to be devoid of significance, owing to the fact that the experimental enterprises appear as alien, unassimilated excrescences on the body of the national economy, which itself continues to function in the old way. As someone put it at a debate: 'It is as if we wanted to change over to driving on the left, and made experimental arrangements for a few cars to drive on the left, while the rest continued driving on the right.' The analogy is undoubtedly witty, but it is exaggerated. It is of course true that these experiments cannot decide the issues which are at stake in the debate concerning the merits and drawbacks of alternative forms of economic organization. Nevertheless, they can undoubtedly yield a body of experience which it is useful and valuable to have. They also serve to 'break the ice' by helping to spread the idea that the methods of economic administration which we have employed hitherto are not the only possible ones and do not constitute a unique road to salvation.

Another new element in the situation is the large-scale work which has been going on in recent months in the ministries and other central organs of State administration in connexion with the *preparation of decrees concerning economic reforms*. A decree of the Ministerial Council relating to this was issued in June, which states: 'Excessive centralization, the survival of parallelism and of a highly bureaucratic style of work in many fields of administration at state and enterprise levels hampers the execution of the enormous tasks which face our people's democracy.' The decree goes on to lay down the following: 'The Ministerial Council orders the personnel in charge of all ministries and other national authorities, of executive bodies of local councils, government offices and institutions, and of enterprises, to elaborate and carry out in their own spheres practical measures designed both to simplify administration and to make it more effective.'[23]

---

[22] Experimental planning systems were also at this time in operation at nine additional enterprises controlled by other ministries.
[23] *Hungarian Gazette*, 3 June 1956.

A number of proposals were produced in the field of light industry as a result of this decree. The Ministry of Light Industry has drawn up proposals for reform which are designed to lead to a more rational organization of resource utilization and of other aspects of planning, to changes in the system of producers' prices, to a simplification of monetary and credit operations, and of the control of permitted outlays on wages and salaries by the banks, &c.

In the course of elaborating these proposals economic administrators have increasingly come to adopt the view that small, disjointed changes, carried out in isolation from one another, cannot yield adequate results. (This position has been consistently maintained in the present study.) Thus, the proposals put forward by the central planning division of the Ministry of Light Industry starts by stating the following, by way of introduction:

> The bureaucratic character of planning is not, for the most part, a spontaneous phenomenon. It is mainly a reflection of basic conditions created by the prevailing system of economic administration. The simplification of systems and methods of planning is, therefore, a function of the simplification of economic administration generally. Any basic changes in the former must await a simplification of the latter.

The decree of the Ministerial Council which I quoted earlier helps to focus the attention of the public on to these questions. But it has become clear that the problem cannot be solved by adhering to the principle that each of the authorities concerned should 'act within their own spheres'. More is required: we need a *unified system of comprehensive reforms* in the sense already adumbrated.[24]

We must not underrate the difficulties of such a task. The work of dismantling excessive centralization will not be brought to a full and successful completion without a great deal more theoretical work, controversy, and struggle.

I myself feel convinced that this work will eventually prove fruitful. The work required may be far from easy and it may be protracted. But it will succeed in the end because the need for what requires to be accomplished has been ripened by the passage of time and has been placed on our agenda irrevocably by the course of economic and social development. It will succeed because the working people have had enough of bureaucracy. The working class definitely demands a change for the better in our methods of economic administration.

---

[24] Cf. pp. 224–6.

NOTES ON THE BOOK'S PREVIOUS AND SUBSEQUENT HISTORY

CHRONOLOGY

June 1955: The author begins his researches in the General Department of the Hungarian Academy of Sciences' Institute of Economics. His director of studies is the head of the department, Tamás Nagy, and his research tutor Péter Erdös.

24 September 1956: There is a public debate at the Karl Marx University of Economics on the dissertation for candidate membership of the Academy of Sciences, which will serve as the basis for the book. Chairing the adjudicating committee is György Péter, the opponents are Mrs Tamás Gerö (Mária Augusztinovics) and Miklös Ajtay.

March 1957: The first edition is published. The editor is Margit Siklós.

June 1957: The author grants permission to Oxford University Press to publish an English edition of the book.

2 October 1957: István Friss, director of the Hungarian Academy of Sciences' Institute of Economics, sharply attacks the book in a lecture at the Political Academy of the Hungarian Socialist Workers' Party.

September 1958: János Kornai and András Nagy are dismissed from the Institute. The move has been preceded by several months of inquiries into the Institute at the instigation of the Central Committee and local district committee of the Hungarian Socialist Workers' Party. The investigation of the General Department is headed by László Háy and Endre Molnár.

22 October 1959: The English translation of the book appears under the title *Overcentralization in Economic Administration*, translated by *John Knapp* and published by Oxford University Press.

REVIEWS AND OTHER REFERENCES TO THE BOOK

'The study proves that in terms of their actual effectiveness, all-embracing central planning and control do not exist to this day... I feel the candidate's arguments that partial solutions or all powerful panaceas may do more harm than good in this matter are extremely important and useful.'

(Mrs Tamás Gerö (Mária Augusztinovics), in her opinion as opponent in the debate on the candidacy dissertation.)

Compiled by Közgazdasági és Jogi Könyvkiadó (Economic and Legal Publishing Co.), Budapest.

'János Kornai's book contributes something new in that it is the first to attempt to describe the organizational forms and leadership system of the national economy in all their relations and details... It discusses the phenomena with the kind of candour which people in firms use 'among themselves', when they are not being overheard by the representatives of the various superior control and supervisory organizations... The tone of the book is critical. It expressly places under the microscope the internal inconsistencies in the economic management methods and dissects them minutely, and it does so in a conscientious and temperate way... It sets out to be as objective as possible.'

(Gyögy Péter: 'Kornai János tanulmányáról' (On János Kornai's Study),
Magyarország (1 May 1957).)

'Kornai's book is a clinical survey of the overcentralization of economic administration... The discrediting of the fetishes, the precise economic and political analysis... these make Kornai's work valuable for readers in other countries as well.'

(J. W.: 'O nad mierniy centralizaciji na Wegrzech'
(On Overcentralization in Hungary), *Zycie Gospodarcze* (Warsaw) (26 May 1957).)

'The revisionist views appearing in economic studies were connected—even if not so directly as in other areas—with the ideological preparation for the counter-revolution, and served as a kind of economic foundation for them... The brunt of their criticism is directed at 'the system of planning instructions'. János Kornai describes as 'one-sided' and 'simplistic' Stalin's statement that the plans for the national economy should be taken as planning directives, not planning forecasts... The position [such economists] represent conflicts with the basic principles of the socialist planned economy and constitutes a surrender to the rules of market competition.'

(Géza Ripp: 'Revizionizmus "az új gazdasági mechanizmus" leple alatt'
(Revisionism under Cover of 'the New Economic Mechanism'),
Népszabadság (23 June 1957).)

'It is not true that economics in the strict sense have nothing to do with counter-revolution... Economists argued that our economic mechanism cannot be improved and that something quite new and different is required—the counter-revolution trumpeted out to the world that socialism has not worked... The lesson is not to be indulgent even with the germ of revisionism... A summary of the main message of János Kornai's dissertation is that our planning system, the system of material incentives and the system of controlling the national economy cannot be darned and patched, if we want to be rid of the faults in it; a radically new and different economic mechanism has to be created instead...'

(Endre Molnár: 'Revizionista nézetek a szocialista állam gazdasági szerepéről'
(Revisionist Views on the Economic Role of the Socialist State),
Társadalmi Szemle, 2 (1957).)

'Kornai's dissertation fitted perfectly into the political and ideological campaign that prepared intellectually for the counter-revolution, which rejected, under the pretext of battling against the faulty economic policy, all that characterized the socialist economy... This concept, which rejects the whole mechanism of economic activity, occupied a very prominent place in among the views which implicitly or openly attacked our people's democratic system. Komai, by proclaiming the successes of "the ever stronger... pressure from below", mobilizing against the "regressive forces", and agitating against the untalented economic leaders without professional expertise, whose sole virtue is political reliability etc., blended perfectly into the chorus of the Petőfi Circle. Even in January 1957, Kornai, terming the counter-revolution not a counter-revolution but "events with importance for decades", proudly declared of himself, as opposed to those who had changed their position on political and economic issues more than once in the space of a few months (and there is something in that, by the way), that his notion remained the same in January 1957 as it had been in October 1956.'

(Emil Gulyás: "Az árutermelés, értéktörvény és pénz a szocializmusban" (Commodity Production, the Law of Value, and Money under Socialism), duplicated teaching text for the Party Academy, 1957/8 academic year.)

'It is a fascinating piece of work; essentially well-meaning and sympathetic towards the basic features of the tortuous socio-economic system which led to the explosion of last October, but at the same time— unintentionally—a damning indictment of it... His intent is description on a practical plane. However, the shadows of many problems of pure theory, of profit – versus output-maximization, "entrepreneurial" expectations, forecasting, games and bribery, welfare economics, and so on stalk the whole book. As the description gathers momentum, analysis creeps into it, and the reader is privileged to witness the process of the author stumbling across the basic principles of non-Marxian economics, following them up some of the way, stopping short of the ultimate logical implications, and leaning over backwards to regain his *bien-pensant* balance. Considering the paucity of the tools which he allows himself to use, the analysis is quite remarkably sound in most places.'

(A. E. Jasay, 'Overcentralization in Economic Administration', *Economic Journal* (Dec. 1957).)

'Mr Kornai's study.... is an outstanding contribution. . . The analysis is refreshingly frank, realistic, and free from dogma. . . Certainly if more realistic studies of the kind undertaken by Mr Kornai were available we should all understand more clearly how these economies actually work...'

(*Ely Devons*, 'A Study in Central Planning. Evidence from the Inside', *Guardian* (Manchester) (22 Oct. 1959).)

'Mr K.'s criticisms of the economy as it was up to 1956 are extraordinarily cogent... Mr K. paints a masterly picture of the abuses which were produced by excessive centralization.'

(R.N.W.O.: 'Iron Curtain Economy', Financial Times, (28 Dec. 1959).)

'This is an important book... The study was begun at the Institute of Economics of the Hungarian Academy of Sciences during the spring of 1955... Despite the fact that the book was produced under these auspices, there is little effort to discuss administrative problems in terms of Marxist ideology. The approach is basically a fact-finding one... The book is of interest to the specialist on the USSR because, so far as I know, it is the only such book in English written "from the inside" about any of the Soviet-type economies... But the issue of "solutions" is, in a sense, carping. The function of the book, and one which it fulfilled admirably, was one of analysis of a going system. The reform of it is another matter.'

(David Granick, 'Overcentralization in Economic Administration', *Soviet Studies* (Apr. 1960).)

'The great merit of Mr Kornai's book is that it shows how the behaviour of the various persons involved is a natural consequence of the system itself, and cannot be altered by merely piecemeal reforms... It is true that... he does not attempt to deal with all aspects of planning. However, the fact remains that this excellent book, well translated, is essential reading for anyone interested in Soviet-style economics.'

'Bureaucrats at large', Times Literary Supplement (15 Apr. 1960).)

'Economists do not often have justification for feeling special pride in their profession; but János Kornai provides one such occasion... This dissertation could only have been written by an economist, and it must have required moral and intellectual courage to present an objective critique of a part of the economy so plainly at variance with doctrinaire communist beliefs... This summary does less than justice to the even-tempered, reasonable argument, and careful sifting of evidence which pervades the book. This is no shrill diatribe, but a scholarly examination of the performance of Hungarian light industry.'

(Harry Townsend, 'Overcentralization in Economic Administration',
Crossbow (spring 1960).)

'This is definitely an important book—candid in tone, rich in insights, abundant in valid analyses... Kornai's book is an outstanding essay in the field of centralized planning and deserves to be carefully studied by all students interested in these problems.'

(Nicolas Spulber, 'Overcentralization in Economic Administration',
American Economic Review (Sept, 1960).)

'Hungarian economists have acquired a great reputation from Moscow to California, via Oxford, Cambridge, Manchester, and New York. It seems that in their mother country the seed of a good school is still vigorous... The author's analysis of the market-to-plan relations are very interesting... The law of centralized planning is underproduction and underconsumption in the relative sense: There are shortages of raw-materials and semi-finished products relative to planned capacity, and shortages of consumer goods relative to effective demand... Centralization creates only an illusion of rapid progress... Kornai... warns that the reform of the system has to be both consistent and bold.'

(Rudolf Bicanic: 'Centralism and Planning: The Hungarian Experience',
Kyklos (Oct. 1960).)

'Mr Kornai has put us all in his debt by providing a logically argued and coherent picture, admirably rendered into English by Mr Knapp, of what might be called the microeconomics of industry under centralized planning, and his work is so far unique. Nowhere else in the Communist world has such a study appeared... while centralization is often self-defeating, or breeds inflexibility and bureaucracy, decentralization would not in itself improve matters...'

(Alec Nove, 'Overcentralization in Economic Administration',
Economica (Nov. 1960).)

'To a Western student of politics János Kornai's excellent analysis gives great encouragement. Just as totalitarian societies have been unable to control the minds of men they have even failed in the much easier task of controlling the economy. In each case they have come up against the idiosyncrasies of men and each time they have been defeated.'

(H. Hanak, 'Overcentralization in Economic Administration',
Political Studies (Oct. 1960).)

'In this intellectual context of search for concepts to understand patterns of institutional regularity and thus form the basis for genuine cross-systemic comparisons, the work of János Kornai occupies exemplary status. Kornai's doctoral dissertation... was completed in the summer of 1956 under the title Over centralization in Economic Administration and published in 1957... A model of rigorous empirical research, Kornai's work set the standard for a generation of young economists trained in the late 1960's and 1970's. Kornai's subsequent books, Anti-Equilibrium, Rush Versus Harmonic Growth, and most important,

The Economics of Shortage, provided the theoretical breakthrough that made the analysis of such phenomena as investment cycles, the second economy, and plan bargaining.'
(David Stark and Victor Nee, 'Toward an Institutional Analysis of State Socialism', in Remarking the Economic Institutions of Socialism. China and Eastern Europe, D. Stark and V. Nee, eds. (Stanford, Calif.: Stanford University Press, 1989).)

Index

Tables and figures are indicated by an italic *t*, and *f* following the page number. Notes are indicated by an n. and the note number following the page number.